# The Lake English Classics

*REVISED EDITION WITH HELPS TO STUDY*

# SELECTED POEMS

BY

## ROBERT BURNS

AND

# ESSAY ON BURNS

BY

## THOMAS CARLYLE

EDITED FOR SCHOOL USE

BY

## GEORGE L. MARSH

THE UNIVERSITY OF CHICAGO

## SCOTT, FORESMAN AND COMPANY

CHICAGO                    NEW YORK

6813

ROBERT O. LAW COMPANY

EDITION BOOK MANUFACTURERS

CHICAGO, U. S. A.

# PREFACE

The purpose of this volume is to present adequate material for appreciation of the best poems of Burns, and for an understanding of Carlyle's estimate of Burns. Carlyle's famous essay, starting ostensibly as a book review and passing into a general discussion of the works and personality of Burns, naturally assumes a certain familiarity with the poet on the part of his readers. The primary business, then, of the Introduction (pages 9-27) is to supply students who have not this assumed familiarity, with the proper background for understanding and appreciating the poems here selected and Carlyle's essay as comment on both the poems and the poet.

The first consideration in choosing poems for the volume was to include as many as possible of those mentioned by Carlyle; but a number of important ones which he happened not to discuss have been added in order to make the collection thoroughly representative. The customary division into "Poems" and "Songs" is retained, but within each of these main classes the arrangement is approximately chronological. When exact dates are not known, related poems are placed together.

The text of the selections from Burns, while not differing materially from so-called "standard" texts, has really been made anew in details for this volume, by comparison of the editions issued during Burns's life and various facsimiles of manuscripts in Burns's hand. The text of the Carlyle essay is that which the author approved for his collected works, differing in some particulars from the essay as it originally appeared in the *Edinburgh Review* (1828).

Scottish words are defined in footnotes, and the number of these is made as small as possible on the assumption that study of the section of the Introduction on the dialect (pages 24-27) will enable the reader to recognize most words which differ from ordinary English in spelling only. In addition to this definition of Scottish words at the foot of the page, matter calling for more extended annotation is treated in notes near the end of the volume (pages 305-326), and passages so annotated are indicated by an *. An effort has been made to identify all passages quoted by Carlyle, but a few have eluded search.

The volume is completed by an appendix containing helps for teachers and by a comprehensive index that includes the Scottish words defined on the pages of the text, as well as the principal topics presented in the introduction, the text of both poems and essay, and notes.

# CONTENTS

PAGE

# INTRODUCTION

## ROBERT BURNS

### HISTORICAL BACKGROUND

The life of Burns, short though it was, covered a most interesting period in history. He was born a little more than a year before George III ascended the throne of England. In the year of his birth the British captured Quebec, and French rule in Canada virtually ended. During his boyhood the arbitrary policies of the British King—German in blood and ideals—so roused the colonies on the western shore of the Atlantic that in 1775 the American Revolution began, and in 1776 (when Burns was a plowboy of seventeen) the Declaration of Independence stirred the world. Cornwallis surrendered at Yorktown in 1781; peace between the United States and Great Britain was concluded in 1783; and in 1789—after some rather chaotic years under the Articles of Confederation—the American Constitution went into effect and Washington's presidency began. In this same year the spirit of liberty that was in the air—a spirit often and forcefully expressed by Burns—prompted an uprising in France which affected the whole of Europe. During the summer of 1789, when Burns, after the first success of his poems, had gone "back to the land" as farmer and exciseman, the mob in Paris destroyed the Bastille. King Louis XVI was virtually deposed at once, though allowed to live till January, 1793. In the meantime the other old monarchies of Europe formed a coalition to repress the republican movement. In

spite of much outspoken sympathy in Great Britain
with the early aims of the French revolutionists, the
government of England joined the coalition; and the
excesses of the Reign of Terror in Paris (June 2, 1793,
to July 27, 1794) alienated even many Englishmen
who had at first sympathized with the French uprising.
During the last year of Burns's life Napoleon Bonaparte
was just emerging as the most significant figure of the
time.

In literature the period was less important than in
history, yet a great movement was taking place. When
Burns was born, the "classical" tradition of Dryden and
Pope was still predominant in literature. Poets wrote
according to strict rules; they dealt mainly with external
details of life and manners in the higher social circles;
they were interested in the general more than in the
specific and the individual; they seemed to care little for
the beauty and grandeur of nature, for the remote and
romantic in time and place, for the lives of humble folk,
for the "rights of man." During the life of Burns,
however, the "classic" tradition, though vigorously supported by the great Doctor Johnson, who lived till 1784,
gradually yielded ascendancy to the "romantic movement" in which Burns played so vital a part. The year
after Burns was born (1760), Macpherson's Ossian
roused the greatest enthusiasm for supposed ancient
Celtic poetry—for the remote and romantic in time and
place. Percy's *Reliques* (1765), the first great collection of English and Scottish ballads, sprang from and
stimulated an interest in the kind of verses that originate more or less spontaneously among common folk.
Professional poets, such as Goldsmith and Crabbe, took
up this interest in the humble; Goldsmith in his *Deserted
Village* (1770), Crabbe in his more realistic *Village*
(1783). And in Cowper's *Task* (1785), published one
year before Burns's Kilmarnock volume, we find a truly

"romantic" love of nature, realistic portrayal of rustic scenes, sympathetic interest in the lives of those of lowly station, strong emphasis on liberty and the rights of the individual. It takes but a slight acquaintance with Burns's work to realize that all these characteristics of "romanticism" are *his* characteristics; that he is the most important product of the new movement before it reached full stature in the works of Wordsworth, Coleridge, Scott, Byron, Shelley, and Keats.

## BURNS'S LIFE

Robert Burns was born January 25, 1759, in a crude little clay cottage thatched with straw and containing but two rooms, a little more than a mile south of the town of Ayr and only a short distance from the Alloway Kirk and the "auld brig o' Doon" which he made famous in "Tam o' Shanter." His father was William Burnes (so he spelled the name), a gardener in the employ of the provost of Ayr, Mr. Ferguson of Doonholm; and lessee, besides, of seven acres on which the "auld clay biggin" stood. William Burnes was from Kincardineshire, on the east coast north of Edinburgh, of a family which the poet said had suffered reverses, along with its hereditary lords, in the cause of the Stuart Pretender of 1745. William Burnes was well educated for his time and station and of a fine, strong, sturdy character, though his eldest son (Robert) once mentioned an irascible temper as one of the reasons for his lack of worldly success. The father in "The Cotter's Saturday Night" is essentially a sincere portrait of the poet's own father. The mother was Agnes Brown, daughter of a Carrick farmer, of a more lively temperament than her very Scottish husband, and dowered with glowing black eyes which, by one of the pleasing tricks of heredity, she passed on to her eldest son.

In the straw-roofed cottage which is still a shrine
for visitors to Ayr, the future poet's earliest years were
spent; but when he was seven years old his father took
a lease of a farm of seventy acres at Mount Oliphant,
only three or four miles up the River Doon from Ayr.
Here the family lived for eleven years, till 1777. Provost
Ferguson was at first the owner and landlord, but on his
death the farm passed into the hands of a cruel factor (or
agent, as we should say) whom Burns later satirized in
"The Twa Dogs."

Robert Burns's education began before the family left
the "auld clay biggin" at Ayr, when his father and some
neighbors arranged to have a youth of eighteen, named
John Murdoch, teach their children and "board around"
among the patrons. Murdoch left an interesting record
of his famous pupil, from which it seems that the lad
received a really good foundation for effective use of
language. He read everything he could get hold of—and
in those days printed matter was mainly good literature.
The result was that while only a boy Robert Burns was
"absolutely a critic in substantives, verbs, and parti-
cles" and "remarkable for the fluency and correctness
of his expression." Though he never acquired a complete school education, he heard good language at home,
and all his meager training tended to give him power of
speech. After a few years with Murdoch, Robert and
Gilbert Burns (his next younger brother) studied mainly
at home under their father's direction, with only occasional brief terms of schooling (usually for some special
subject such as penmanship or the like) when one or
the other could be spared from the work of the farm.

By the time he was fifteen Burns was his father's
chief helper on the "poorest land in Ayrshire." His
life in these years he later described as combining "the
cheerless gloom of a hermit with the unceasing toil of a
galley-slave." Though he was naturally strong, a leader

in feats of strength throughout his life, there can be little doubt that he was permanently injured by the hardships of his boyhood. And the injury was not purely physical. Through lack of the harmless, normal pleasures of boyhood, he was the more inclined toward excesses when opportunity came. More than one of the puzzling facts about Robert Burns's later life may have its roots in those years of harder work than a growing boy should be subjected to.

Hardships or no hardships, however, a born poet will sing. Burns has told how he wrote his earliest poem, at the age of fifteen, in praise of a "bonnie, sweet sonsie lass," his partner in some of the work of the harvest— "Handsome Nell." It was fitting and prophetic that one who indited sweet songs to almost every girl or woman he ever met should have made this sort of beginning. For a number of years, however, "Handsome Nell" had no companions of whom we know certainly, and in the meantime the Burns family succeeded in escaping from the "factor's snash" at Mount Oliphant, by removing to a larger farm, Lochlea (or Lochlie), one hundred and thirty acres, in Tarbolton parish, about ten miles north of their former home, and near the River Ayr, as Mount Oliphant was near Doon.

Lochlea also was difficult land to farm successfully, and the last years of William Burnes on this place were clouded by financial difficulties and a serious quarrel and lawsuit with the landlord. In 1784 the elder Burnes died, and Robert and Gilbert, by putting in claims for wages from the estate, managed to secure enough money to stock another farm, two or three miles away—Mossgiel, in Mauchline parish, whither they removed the whole family. In the last few years at Lochlea the poet had done some writing, most notably the poems about "Mailie," the immortal ewe; but it was not till the residence at Mossgiel that his real poetic outburst came.

There, within two or three years, between tasks on the farm, he wrote the great bulk of his best poetry.

During this time almost everything that happened in his life was "grist for his mill." Religious controversies raged between "Auld Lichts" (strict Calvinists) and "New Lichts" (the liberal party). The clever young farmer at Mossgiel, having friends among the New Lichts and being temperamentally a liberal, wrote racy lampoons against "Holy Willie" or "Daddy Auld." In plowing he turned up a field-mouse's nest or destroyed a daisy; in church he noticed a louse on a fine lady's bonnet—material for poetry! If he wished to write a letter to a friend, or to the author of a poem that took his fancy, verse was as ready a medium as prose. A "cotter's Saturday night," the customs of Hallowe'en, a semi-disreputable church picnic, a drunken carousal in a tavern—of such unlovely stuff the "plowman poet" made masterpieces.

But poetry and plowing were not Burns's only activities at Mossgiel. During his residence there occurred his two most important love affairs—affairs which demand attention because one of them affected the whole remaining course of his life, and both were the inspiration of beautiful poems.

The first and more important was with Jean Armour, who became Mrs. Burns. She was evidently a pretty and lively girl, daughter of a stone mason at Mauchline; and the "First Epistle to Davie" indicates sincere affection for her on Burns's part rather early in his residence in the same parish with her. Probably in February or March, 1786, he gave her a written acknowledgment which, under Scottish common law, made her legally his wife. But her father, not fancying Burns for a son-in-law, induced her to destroy this paper and refused to let her have anything to do with him. Burns by this time was planning to publish his poems, and in despair over his general prospects in Scotland (the trouble with the Armours included) he expected to emigrate to Jamaica with the proceeds of his book. This was the situation when John Wilson, printer of Kilmarnock, published *Poems, Chiefly in the Scottish Dialect,* by Robert Burns, late in July, 1786.

Meanwhile, apparently during the despondency that resulted from the action of the Armours, occurred the episode with Mary Campbell—"Highland Mary." Authorities on Burns disagree hopelessly as to this matter, but at any rate a romantic story that grew up should be known in order that the poems about Highland Mary may be understood. This story is that the lovers plighted their troth on the banks of the Ayr, exchanging Bibles, and Mary went to her Highland home to prepare for marriage with Robert, but died soon of a malignant fever without his seeing her again. From the fervency of the poems about her, and the deep feeling he was said to have shown when composing "To Mary in Heaven," grew a theory that Mary Campbell was "the only woman he ever really loved." This is most unfair to Jean Armour, however, and while she was still living as Mrs. Burns, the poet himself and his first biographers represented Highland Mary as an early sweetheart. Nevertheless, the evidence is indisputable that 1786 was the year of the episode with her, and perhaps the best explanation is that he took up with her "on the rebound" from the Armour trouble.

After the success of the Kilmarnock volume and the poet's welcome in Edinburgh, he became reconciled with the Armours, and in 1788 he and Jean were formally and regularly married. She was a woman of little education or intellectuality, and probably not an inspiring companion for her brilliant husband; but she was evidently amiable and patient, a faithful wife and a good mother. She survived her husband and kept his name for nearly forty years after his early death, and was honored by his brother Gilbert and his early biographers.

The Kilmarnock edition succeeded far beyond anyone's expectation. It made the "Scottish bard" the most prominent figure in contemporary literature. There was immediately a call for more copies of the poems and for a visit to Edinburgh by the poet. Carlyle deals extensively with this visit, which began November 28, 1786. From this date until the summer of 1788, Burns lived mainly in the Scottish capital, taking incidentally a number of trips on horseback to see historic places, and occasionally visiting his old haunts in Ayrshire. He associated in Edinburgh with both literary society and the convivial "Crochallan Fencibles." He had a singular love affair with the lady whom he addressed as "Clarinda" in a series of bombastic letters signed "Sylvander," and who inspired one of his greatest songs—"Had we never loved sae kindly." He gained enough money from the Edinburgh edition to be generous to his mother and his brother Gilbert, and he made a number of useful friends; but on the whole he lost more than he.gained. Only occasionally did he produce poetry at all comparable with that of the rich years at Mossgiel (especially 1785-6) ; and his lack of a steadfast aim in life, which Carlyle so emphasizes, is much more obvious after the period in Edinburgh.

During that time, with the assistance of some of the new-made friends, Burns procured an appointment in the Excise—an "internal revenue" position, as we should say—but he did not undertake the actual work of a gauger until the summer of 1789. Meanwhile he returned to the "plowtail," taking a farm at Ellisland, on the River Nith in Dumfriesshire, to the southeast of his former haunts. Here in 1788 he and Jean settled in their first home together. The income from the farm was so scanty, however, that the next year he undertook

to supplement it by performing the duties of an exciseman. As gauger he had to ride over a wide district and
could give little attention to affairs at home, with the
result that the previously inadequate income from the
farm dwindled still more, while the rental increased.
In 1791 the poet ceased his striving to be a farmer and
became only an exciseman, living in a little house in
Dumfries, the most important city in the extreme south
of Scotland.

Various matters as to Burns's life in Dumfries have
been in controversy. He did not rise in the Excise as
rapidly as he hoped; he had some trouble, or feared
trouble at least, on account of charges that he sympathized more with the French Revolutionists than a loyal
Briton of those days was expected to do, especially if he
was a public officer, even in a small way. His habits in
Dumfries have been much criticized and much defended
from criticism. That they were materially worse, or
better, than in Mossgiel or Edinburgh, has not been
conclusively demonstrated. The poet of "Scotch Drink"
undoubtedly drank; he was no hypocrite, and more than
once he testified to the harm that "hard drinking" had
done him. But neither was he a drunkard. He was diligent in his exciseship and made a good record, as he could
not have done if he had been a drunkard. He produced
little important poetry except songs during the Dumfries period; but it is easy to believe that his occupation
gave him small opportunity for sustained composition,
and the interest he displayed in the collections of Scottish song made by Johnson and Thomson was lively and
fruitful. Perhaps an examination of his letters to Thomson and of the songs he wrote from 1791 to 1796
furnishes the best answer to the severest critics. Nevertheless his later years were disappointing, and his life
was on the whole the tragedy that Carlyle represents it
to have been. He had a continual struggle for a bare

living, and he died at the age of thirty-seven (July 21, 1796), leaving his family almost in want, though a few years later the profits of Currie's edition of the poet's works put them in comfortable circumstances.

## BURNS'S WORKS

For appreciative criticism of the poems of Burns, and for analysis of his merits and defects and of the causes for his worldly failure, it is still impossible to do much better than to read and study Carlyle's brilliant essay. Research has added some facts that were unknown when the essay was written in 1828 and has proved Carlyle's primary authority, Lockhart, to have been wrong in some particulars. Disagreements as to specific critical judgments there will always be. Yet on the whole few critical essays nearly a hundred years old require so little qualification as this one of Carlyle on Burns.

The chief merits of Burns's poetry are truly, as Carlyle says, his sincerity; his power to make any subject—however commonplace it may seem—interesting and important because of the poetic feeling with which he invests it; his "clearness of sight" and vividness and force of expression; his "genuine all-embracing Love" for man and nature; his success in finding "a tone and words for every mood of man's heart." He was tender; he was humorous; yet he could express the most withering scorn of pretension and hypocrisy and "inhumanity to man." These merits are so amplified and illustrated in Carlyle's essay that only summary is needed here.

Matthew Arnold, it is true, denied Burns a place among the highest poets because a world of "Scotch drink, Scotch religion, and Scotch manners" is "not a beautiful world"; but to most readers Burns reveals beauty in much of that world—or, when beauty does not exist, makes such racy revelation of essential truth that the criticism seems a bit supercilious and almost pointless. Arnold's total estimate is about as flattering as Carlyle's. While he says Burns "comes short of the high seriousness of the great classics," he comments on this poet's "large, free, shrewd, benignant, truly poetic" view of the world; on his "fiery, reckless energy," his "overwhelming sense of the pathos of things," his "bounding swiftness," his "infinite archness and wit" (in such poems as "Duncan Grey" and "Tam Glen") ; and in conclusion Arnold says that Burns was "a poet with thorough truth of substance and an answering truth of style"—just below the greatest poets of all the ages.

Being no democrat, Carlyle fails to indicate adequately the democrat and the rebel in Burns. The poet, however, sympathized with the American Revolution and with the French Revolution. The most noted song of his last year but one—"A man's a man for a' that"—has been called "the Marseillaise of Humanity." He believed fervently in individual freedom to do what the individual conscience approved as right, in religious tolerance, in the leveling of artificial distinctions of class, in genuine brotherhood. Indeed, had Burns been less a democrat and less a rebel, no doubt his life would have been less tragic than Carlyle found it; the "noblemen and gentlemen" to whom he dedicated his poems might have done more for him had they been less fearful of his "Spirit fierce and bold."

One of Carlyle's statements, though in a way true, may give a wrong impression. He says Burns's "poems are, with scarcely any exception, mere occasional effusions." Suppose they are—are not the best short poems, those of real inspiration, usually "occasional effusions," prompted by some incident or some thought that stirs the poet to utterance which is by no means imperfect because perhaps largely impromptu? Burns had the true artist's feeling about his work—viewed it critically and tried to polish it; but the best of it was struck off

at white heat, spontaneous, truly inspirational; and his
really labored poems in literary English are mostly conventional and commonplace. For this reason Carlyle's
notion that if Burns had received a complete education
and had devoted himself single-heartedly to being a poet
on accepted models he would have risen to greater heights
seems more than doubtful. A Burns who studied to
secure the "high seriousness" Arnold demanded for the
greatest poetry would not be the "amazing peasant of
genius" who wrote of Holy Willie and Poosie Nansie
and Tam o' Shanter.

Burns had models, however. His mind was saturated
with Scottish popular poetry, of which there was an
abundance of good quality; and he acknowledged particular indebtedness to the two best Scotch poets who preceded him in the eighteenth century—Allan Ramsay and
Robert Fergusson. Ramsay died (at the age of seventy-
one) during the year before Burns was born. His most
famous work is *The Gentle Shepherd,* a pastoral drama
in dialect; but his influence on Burns appears mainly
in the latter's verse epistles, in the form and spirit of
"The Holy Fair," and in various songs. Fergusson had
a very brief and unfortunate career, dying at the age
of only twenty-four during the year when Burns says
he wrote his first song (1774). Fergusson's "Farmer's
Ingle" directly suggested "The Cotter's Saturday Night,"
and other poems of his provided hints for his great
successor. Burns, however, was over-generous in ac-
knowledging debt, especially to Fergusson and Ramsay,
for he far surpassed their poems even when his themes
were more or less imitative.

The traditional division of Burns's work is into two
main classes, poems and songs, and each class may be
subdivided in various ways. The earliest poems here
printed express sympathy with animals, a sympathy
highly characteristic of Burns throughout his life; see

the "Mailie" poems (1781-2), "To a Mouse" (1785), "The Auld Farmer to His Auld Mare" (1786), "The Wounded Hare" (1789). "The Twa Dogs," though it shows a love of dogs, is primarily a verse tale and a social satire. As a verse tale in the same metrical form, "Tam o' Shanter" superficially resembles "The Twa Dogs"; but its true relations are with the group of poems that realistically portray Scottish rural life—especially "The Holy Fair," "Halloween," "The Jolly Beggars," and "The Cotter's Saturday Night." A very important theme for Burns was the narrowness of strict Calvinism, on which he expressed his views with startling irony in "Holy Willie's Prayer," with humorous fancy in the "Address to the Deil," with serious scorn in the "Address to the Unco Guid." With these poems directed against hypocrisy in religion belong also the "Epistle to McMath" and "The Holy Fair." Notably characteristic of Burns are the verse epistles to his friends—to "Davie," to Lapraik, to Simpson, to James Smith, to Mrs. Scott, to Dr. Blacklock (and others scarcely less interesting that are not in this book). These poems are intimate personal revelations: they tell us how Burns became a poet, how he viewed his art, what he thought about various topics that occupied his mind. Intimately personal, too, are the lyrics that reflect his troubles of 1786, when he planned to emigrate to Jamaica. There is a touch of despondent feeling in the last stanza of "To a Mouse," and "To a Mountain Daisy" and "A Bard's Epitaph" are supreme expressions of that feeling.

A few of the selected poems remain unclassified above. "Man Was Made to Mourn" is an early expression—almost pure English and conventional—of a pessimistic mood. "To a Louse" is essentially a bit of social satire. The "Epistle to a Young Friend" is neatly expressed worldly advice. "A Winter Night," beginning in dialect as a sincere expression of sympathy with the poor, wanders off into grandiloquent English on a theme from *King Lear*. The "Address to a Haggis" contributes a bit to Burns's presentation of the Scottish peasant as he lived—and ate and drank. The "Address to Beëlzebub" is political satire—withering irony against those who would curb man's freedom. The "Petition of Bruar Water" displays the same kind of sympathy for abused nature that "To a Mouse" or "The Wounded Hare" displays for abused animals. The "Elegy on Henderson" is a rich reflection of the poet's love and knowledge of nature.

Passing now to the songs, it must be remembered that these were mostly written after Burns's contemporary reputation had been made by the publication of the bulk of his longer poems. The vast majority of his songs doubtless owe their very existence to his agreement to help, first James Johnson, then George Thomson, in their efforts to perpetuate Scottish tunes. Burns's work for the song collections of these men usually began with his hearing and learning an air to which he endeavored to fit appropriate words. Often the old words associated with the melody gave him his theme; sometimes he kept a considerable portion of an old song, or made a clever patchwork from several sources. *Always he was fitting words to a known tune*—and this is a very important consideration in regard to the songs.

Quite naturally a majority of those here selected, as well as of the total number Burns wrote, are in some way love songs. The general approval of "the sex" which he expressed so happily in one of his earliest songs—"Green Grow the Rashes"—was sincere. "When I want to be more than ordinary in song," he once wrote to Thomson, "I have a glorious recipe . . . . I put myself on a regimen of admiring a fine woman; and in proportion to the adorability of her charms, in proportion you are delighted with my verses." Of course it does not follow that Burns was seriously "in love" whenever he wrote in the fervent terms of that emotion; he had the true lyric poet's power to make a passing fancy—a burst of admiration—seem real. And he also had some of the dramatic poet's power to give expression to feelings natural to other persons; as in his songs that purport to be sung by women—songs as varied in mood as "John Anderson, My Jo," "Tam Glen," "The Banks o' Doon," and "Whistle an' I'll Come to Ye." The truth is that Burns in his songs is the "complete lover," with felicitous expression for every mood from the worldly wisdom which cannily seeks "A Lass wi' a Tocher," to the rapt enthusiasm of "To Mary in Heaven" or "Ae Fond Kiss."

Of the selections that are not love songs one is intimately personal—the "Farewell" written when Burns expected to leave Scotland; one is another sort of "Farewell"—that of McPherson from the gallows; one is the world's most famous song of friendship, "Auld Lang Syne"; two are rollicking drinking songs; two are Jacobite songs alluding pensively to the failure of "Charlie" in 1745; one is that wonderful "war-ode" (as Carlyle calls it), "Scots wha hae"; and one gives immortal expression to the idea of universal brotherhood. These are not quite all the songs in this volume, but the range of feeling is evident. One may not agree with Carlyle that Burns's songs were his best work. Perfect as many of them are, they may seem too slight to weigh down the scales against his most important poems of greater length. Yet they rank with the best songs in English—and that is praise enough.

### SCOTTISH DIALECT IN BURNS

The Scottish of Burns is not a distinct language, but a dialect of English—the only English dialect, however, with an important independent literary tradition. As

long ago as the time of Chaucer there was a famous
Scottish poet, John Barbour, who wrote in his northern
dialect of the deeds of Robert Bruce. During the century
and a half after Chaucer's death the best poets among
his imitators were Scots and wrote in Scottish—notably
Henryson, Dunbar (the greatest of Burns's predecessors
in the Lowland vernacular), Gavin Douglas, and Sir
David Lyndesay (who appears in Scott's *Marmion* as
"Lion King at Arms"). Then for a time the northern
dialect was preserved mainly in ballads and other popular
poetry; but in the early part of Burns's own century
Allan Ramsay began the restoration of Scottish to a position of literary importance which it has since maintained,
largely because of Burns.

The peculiarity of the dialect in Burns's poems consists partly in the use of words totally strange to ordinary English—words which the reader simply must learn
by use of a glossary. Herein lies most of the difficulty
of such poems as "Halloween" or "The Auld Farmer to
His Auld Mare." Many words, however, vary only
slightly from ordinary English, so that a summary of
differences in spelling and pronunciation as found in
Burns will greatly reduce the need of glosses.

### Vowel Changes

1. Scottish ă often represents an English ŏ (or the *o* in such
   words as *work*).

   > Examples: aff (off), aft (oft), drap (drop), gat (got),
   > lang (long), saft (soft), sang (song), strang
   > (strong), wark (work), warld (world),
   > wrang (wrong), etc.

2. A longer *a* (as in *father*) may represent ō (or, in sound, o͞o).
   Examples: na (no), twa (two), wha (who), etc.

3. *A*, *ae*, or *ai* (pronounced, according to Burns, like "French *e*
   masculine"—which is nearly modern English ā) very
   often represents ō.

   > Examples of ā: ane (one), bane (bone), hale (whole),

hame (home), lane (lone), rape (rope), stane (stone).

Examples of *ae:* ae (Middle English *o*, one), claes (clothes), fae (foe), frae (fro, from), gae (go), mae (mo, more), nae (no), sae (so), wae (woe).

Examples of *ai:* aits (oats), baith (both), claith (cloth), laith (loath), mair (more), maist (most), sair (sore).

4. *Au* sometimes represents *ai*.

Examples: saunt (saint), straught (straight). The same sound also occurs in awa' (away), daur (dare).

5. *Au* may represent *ō*.

Examples: auld (old), bauld (bold), cauld (cold), fauld (fold), gaun (going), tauld (told), waur (worse).

6. *Aw* (usually so spelled, pronounced like *au*) often represents *ow*.

Examples: awe (owe), blaw (blow), craw (crow), law (low), maw (mow), saw (sow), shaw (show), snaw (snow).

7. Short *e* sometimes represents *ŏ*.

Example: het (hot).

8. *Ee, ei, ie* (pronounced like *ee* in *bee*) often correspond to *ȳ* (or some other English spelling of the same sound).

Examples: flee, flie (fly), hie (high), slee (sly). It is important to remember that words like *die*, *lie*, etc., are pronounced *dee*, *lee*, etc.

9. *Eu* frequently represents *ōō*.

Examples: beuk (book), heuk (hook), leuk (look), neuk (nook), sheuk (shook), teuk (took).

10. Short *i* may represent *ŏ* (usually in words in which the sound is that of *ŭ*).

Examples: ither (other), anither (another), tither (t'other), dizzen (dozen), mither (mother), sin (son).

11. Short *i* may represent *u* (or some other spelling of the sound).

Examples: bill (bull), fit (foot), jimp (jump), nit (nut), pit (put), rin (run), simmer (summer).

12. *U* or *ui* (pronounced like French *u* or German *ü*) often represents *oo*. Burns, however, often wrote *oo* even when he expected the French *u* pronunciation.

Examples: bluid (blood), guid, gude (good), luve (love), muir or moor, puir or poor, sune or soon.

### Consonant Changes

1. Final *d*. The ending *ed*, pronounced *it* or *et*, was also often so spelled.

Examples: negleckit (neglected), reestit (rested), whiskit (whisked).

2. Final *g*. The ending *ing* (pronounced much like the older Scottish participle ending *and*—with the *d* silent) is often written *in*.

Examples: breakin (breaking), rantin (ranting), speakin (speaking).

3. *L*, and especially final *ll*, is often dropped, with the following important results:

*A'* (sometimes written without the apostrophe) represents final *all*.

Examples: a' (all), ba' (ball), ca' (call), befa' (befall), ha' (hall), sma' (small).

*Au* represents English *al*.

Examples: caudron (caldron), faut (fault), maut (malt), saut (salt), scaud (scald). Haud (for hold —old form, hald) really belongs here also.

*Ou* represents *ull*.

Examples: fou (full), pou (pull), pou'd (pulled).

*Ow* represents *ol* or *oll*.

Examples: cowt (colt), gowd (gold), howe (hollow), knowe (knoll), pow (poll, meaning head), rowe (roll), stown (stolen).

4. *V* within a word or at the end may be dropped; sometimes the omission is indicated by an apostrophe, sometimes not.

Examples: aboon (above-n), deil (devil), e'en (even), ga'e (gave), gie (give), hae (have), hairst (harvest), lea'e (leave), lee-lang (live-long), lo'e (love), sair (serve), shool (shovel), siller (silver), twal' (twelve). Sel' (self) really belongs to this class also.

*Pronunciation*

Most of the essential points have been given in the notes of vowel and consonant changes, but a few additions may be helpful.

1. *Ch* and *gh* are strong gutturals in Scottish (like German *ch*). Even when Burns wrote such words as *light, right, brought, sought,* with the ordinary English spelling, he expected them to be pronounced *licht, richt, brocht, socht,* etc. And *rough,* for example, is *roch* (similar to *loch = lake*).

2. *H* is strongly aspirated except in English words in which it is silent (such as *honor*).

3. *Ng* within a word is pure nasal without any of the hard *g* sound. Thus *langer* (longer) is pronounced as in German, without the *g* sound that appears in *anger* or in *longer*.

4. *Ou* is pronounced like English *ōō*.

5. *R* is always rolled, sometimes to the extent of adding a syllable. Thus Burns treats *fire* and *mire* as metrically two syllables each.

## BURNS'S RIMES

An observant student will very soon notice that many of Burns's rimes are inexact. On the first page of the poems in this volume we find *thegither* and *tether, ended* and *mendit.* In many cases like the latter, the inexactness of the rime disappears with the proper Scottish pronunciation (*ended = endit*) ; but Burns made a good deal of deliberate use of assonance in place of rime, and in general Scottish poetry is less sensitive to difference of vowel than is English poetry. When we find such combinations as *clatter, water, whitter, better; wrench, inch, glunch, punch; woods, buds, whids, croods,* we must not hastily pronounce these bad or careless rimes, but must recognize them as poetic liberties that the Scotch regarded as legitimate.

## THOMAS CARLYLE

### LIFE

Within the territory that Burns traversed as exciseman, about fifteen miles east of Dumfries, is the little town of Ecclefechan, where, during the last winter of Burn's life, Thomas Carlyle was born—December 4, 1795. Carlyle's father, James Carlyle, told his son of once seeing Burns standing in "Rob Scott's smithy" at Ecclefechan—"a man with boots on, like a well-dressed farmer." This bit of a link in the lives of the poet and one of his best critics points to a reason for the understanding and sympathy of Carlyle, for he was of the land of Burns and knew the conditions that Burns faced.

James Carlyle was a stone mason (as was Burns's father-in-law, James Armour)—a man of little formal education but—said his son—"of perhaps the very largest natural endowment of any it has been my lot to converse with"; of a "bold, glowing style" in talk, extremely humorous, "emphatic . . . beyond all men," "of rigid, even scrupulous veracity," very active and industrious— all these being qualities transmitted to his son. He was a religious man, of the New Licht sect which Burns had so fervently supported. Carlyle's mother, Margaret Aitken, was "a woman of . . . the fairest descent—that of the pious, the just and wise"; of milder temperament than her fiery husband. "No man of my day, or hardly any man," said Carlyle, "can have had better parents."

Living in a town, in a moderately prosperous though always frugal household, Thomas Carlyle—unlike Burns —received the best education that could be procured for him. He was unable to remember a time when he could not read. At the age of ten he was taken by his father, on foot, to the academy in the town of Annan, a few miles south of Ecclefechan, near Solway Firth. The autumn before he was fourteen he entered the University of Edinburgh, tramping all the way to the capital over some of the most historic ground in Scotland.

At this time (1809) the University of Edinburgh is said to have resembled a bear-garden, "where the youth of the land, drawn from every rank of the population, were let loose to browse as they listed."* There were no entrance examinations; there was very little systematic instruction, and what there was Carlyle afterwards pronounced bad; on the whole, he extravagantly declared, "out of England and Spain, ours was the worst of all hitherto discovered universities." But he read widely in the library, thus laying a foundation for his work as historian, biographer, and critic.

When his family made sacrifices to keep him in the University, it was with the plan that he should enter the ministry, as the "bright boy" in any pious Scottish family was then expected to do. Accordingly, on leaving the University in 1814, without a degree, he was enrolled as a non-resident student in divinity, with the obligation to make a report on his work every year. His chief occupation for several years, however, was teaching: first in the school at Annan which he himself had attended; then at Kirkcaldy, a coast town about twenty miles north of Edinburgh; finally at Edinburgh, where, after definitely giving up plans for the ministry in 1818, he took private pupils when he could get them, studied law intermittently, read English and foreign literature incessantly, and made a small start as a writer by contributing some articles to an encyclopedia.

For several years his situation at Edinburgh was very hard—his income small and uncertain, his means of sustenance chiefly oat-cakes sent from home, his health impaired by dyspepsia (to which he continued subject

*J. G. Robertson in *Cambridge History of English Literature*, Vol. XIII.

all his life), his mind unsettled as to the work he could and should do. He disliked teaching, preaching, and law, and the way into successful authorship seemed very slow. In one of the most famous portions of his *Sartor Resartus,* which is a sort of spiritual autobiography, Carlyle deals with his own mental state during this period. "The Everlasting No had said: 'Behold, thou art fatherless, outcast, and the Universe is mine (the Devil's).'" In other words, at least in his darkest hours, he sank to loss of faith in God and man; he had no confidence in his ability to accomplish anything useful. But at a fortunate hour of "Spiritual New-Birth" the "Everlasting Yea" became dominant in his life, asserting the rule of God in the world, the freedom of the individual, and his duty to "Produce! Produce! Were it but the pitifullest infinitesimal fraction of a Product, produce it, in God's name." From this time Carlyle no longer vacillated, but studied indefatigably and produced books which had more spiritual influence on his generation than those of any other man.

Not long before his acceptance of the "Everlasting Yea," Carlyle had met Miss Jane Baillie Welsh, the beautiful and brilliant young woman who some years later (in 1826) became his wife. She too was of Lowland Scotch blood; but whereas Carlyle was of peasant stock, she was the daughter of a noted and successful surgeon and had been used to the best society. Nevertheless she had such faith in the ability of the struggling young writer, and such affection for the "warm, true heart" beneath his rough exterior, that she rejected suitors more promising from a worldy point of view, made over to her mother all interest in the comfortable estate left by her father, and faced the world with Thomas Carlyle. First they lived in a tiny house at the edge of Edinburgh, but city life did not allow such quiet as Carlyle thought he needed for his work. Accord-

ingly in the spring of 1828 they removed to Craigenputtock, a moorland farm belonging to the Welshes,
some fifteen or twenty miles northwest of Dumfries—
"the dreariest spot in all the British dominions." Here
for six years they lived almost in solitude, while by the
most persistent and toilsome labor Carlyle slowly made
his way to such recognition that they could afford to
give up so isolated and frugal a life. "At this Devil's
Den, Craigenputtock," says a memorandum by Carlyle, he
finished his *Essay on Burns,* September 16, 1828. Here
he wrote *Sartor Resartus* and did much of the reading
from which his *French Revolution* was to result.

In 1834 the Carlyles moved to London, where books
for research could be more readily obtained; and at
number 24, Cheyne Row, Chelsea, near the Thames and
not very far above the Houses of Parliament and Westminster Abbey, in a plain brick house that is now a
Carlyle museum and a shrine for tourists, they henceforth made their home. Here in a secluded study, protected as well as might be from intrusions, Carlyle
pursued his researches and painfully wrote his books;
while Mrs. Carlyle, socially one of the most charming of
women, conducted a salon in her drawing room to which
the cleverest people of the day were delighted to come.
After thirty-two years of this sort of life, Mrs. Carlyle
died suddenly in 1866, in her sixty-fifth year, while her
distinguished husband was absent in Scotland on the
greatest worldly triumph of his career—his induction
into the lord rectorship of the University of Edinburgh,
to which he had been elected over Disraeli, Gladstone's
great rival in politics. For fifteen years longer Carlyle
lived in the Chelsea home, the broken, grieving old man
of Whistler's famous portrait, bitterly remorseful because he felt that in his absorption in his work he had
neglected her whom he loved best of all human beings.
He died in 1881, at the age of eighty-five, and was buried,

according to his own request, in the churchyard at Ecclefechan.

## CARLYLE'S WORKS AND INFLUENCE

After the unsigned and uncollected contributions to Brewster's *Edinburgh Encyclopedia* (mentioned on page 29), Carlyle's first writings appeared in magazines, and a majority of these early articles were on the great idealistic authors of the German romantic movement— Goethe, Schiller, Richter, and others. These men Carlyle knew better than any other British writer of his time knew them, and much of their influence in Great Britain was due to him. His earliest important magazine article was on Goethe's *Faust,* in the *New Edinburgh Review* for 1822. His first published book of a literary character* was a translation of Goethe's novel, *Wilhelm Meister's Apprenticeship* (1824). His first original work to be issued as a book was a *Life of Schiller* (1825 —it had appeared in the *London Magazine* in 1823-4). His first contribution to the *Edinburgh Review,* the most influential magazine of the time, was an essay on Jean Paul Richter (1827). These are only "first things" in a list which also includes a volume of translations called *German Romance* and magazine essays on "The State of German Literature," on Heine, on "German Playwrights," on Novalis, on the *Nibelungen Lied,* and on various topics relating to Carlyle's prime favorites— Richter, Schiller, and Goethe. Not the least valuable product of this period of German influence on Carlyle was his correspondence with Goethe, then an old man.

Out of this period, also, the chief immediate result of the strenuous years at Craigenputtock, came Carlyle's most characteristic and significant book, in which he expressed the main theories of life and work that pervade

*Somewhat earlier he had published a translation of Legendre's *Elements of Geometry and Trigonometry.*

all his writing. *Sartor Resartus* (the "Tailor Retailored") pretends to be an English edition of a collection of notes made by a fictitious German, Diogenes Teufelsdröckh, professor of "things in general" in the University of "Don't-know-where." Part of these notes are biographical, and in dealing ostensibly with Teufelsdröckh's life Carlyle is commenting—sometimes with humorous or grotesque exaggeration, but with much essential truth— on his own childhood and youth, his education, and his struggles to reach the "Everlasting Yea." In the main, however, the book is an expression of Carlyle's philosophy of life. The "clothes philosophy" by which he accounts for his odd title is, in substance, "that man and society are only vestures—transient wrappings of the one reality, God." This, the germ idea of the book, Carlyle found in Swift's *Tale of a Tub*, but he elaborated it ingeniously and powerfully, making it thoroughly his own. With great vigor he attacked the shams and pretenses and wrongs of the world—outworn social distinctions, useless customs, mechanical education, war, insincere religion—and preached earnestly his gospel of diligent, sincere work at whatever one finds he can do best.

The style of *Sartor Resartus* is very singular. Because he pretended to be translating from the German, Carlyle imitated the German custom of capitalizing nouns, he rendered German idioms literally into English, he often followed a German rather than an English sentence order, he coined strange compound words. Furthermore, under the special influence of Richter, the book is an odd combination of grotesque or grim satiric humor, fiery eloquence, and tender pathos. Its figurative quality is particularly remarkable; the most imaginative poetry contains no more striking metaphors than *Sartor Resartus*. Carlyle's mastery of English in this book and in all his work is exceptional. He took liberties with words and with the English sentence, but he made both

words and sentences do what he wished; he was—said
Richard Garnett, one of his biographers—"one of the
very few in whose hands language is wholly flexible and
fusible."

*Sartor Resartus* appeared serially in *Fraser's Magazine*
in 1833-4, but no publisher had the courage to make a
book of it till Emerson was sponsor for an edition at
Boston in 1836. A London edition finally appeared in
1838, after the publication of *The French Revolution*
(1837) had roused public interest in the author.

While *The French Revolution* is not exactly a history
in the ordinary sense of the word, it is the first and on
the whole the best exemplification of one of Carlyle's
"pet ideas"—that history should be chiefly a record of
the lives and character and work of great men, told for
the effect of its political or moral lessons on the historian's own generation. A reader needs to know well
the main events of the French Revolution in order to
understand and appreciate Carlyle's discussion; but the
book is a wonderful series of flashlights of persons and
scenes, and interprets the spirit of the revolutionary
movement with the utmost vividness and power. It is a
work of creative imagination rather than an orthodox
and conventional history.

Carlyle's theory of history was popularly explained a
little later in the series of lectures (delivered 1840, published 1841), *On Heroes, Hero-Worship, and the Heroic
in History,* and was continuously in his mind during the
preparation of the two most laborious and extensive
tasks of his life. These were an edition of *Oliver Cromwell's Letters and Speeches,* with extensive "elucidations"
by Carlyle (1845-6), and the enormous *History of Fried-
rich II of Prussia, called Frederick the Great,* the six
volumes of which appeared at intervals from 1858 to
1865.

During "breathing spells" in his larger labors on the

French Revolution, on Cromwell, on Frederick the Great, Carlyle collected his *Critical and Miscellaneous Essays* from the reviews and published them in four volumes in 1839; wrote several important volumes of political discussion—*Chartism,* 1839; *Past and Present* 1843; *Latter-Day Pamphlets,* 1850; and prepared a *Life of John Sterling* (1851) which lovers of regularity and critics of eccentricity or violence sometimes call his "most perfect" work. After the completion of *Frederick the Great,* closely followed as it was by the death of his wife, he was an old man and did no more important writing except his *Reminiscences.*

In the foregoing statement of Carlyle's theory of history, and of the main ideas of *Sartor Resartus,* an almost complete epitome of his message has been given. Because he believed in "heroes," in government by the best men, he distrusted democracy, and in his works on contemporary political questions he declaimed vigorously against extension of the franchise and other liberal measures. He heaped abuse upon the developing science of political economy because he considered that it put a "profit and loss" basis for human relations in place of principles of religion and morality. In all his books, at every opportunity, he preached his doctrine of earnest and sincere work as man's primary duty, and his faith in the "mystery and power of life as the garment of God." With infinite variety he thundered forth "an intense moral indignation against whatever is weak or false or mechanical; an intense moral enthusiasm for whatever is sincere and heroically helpful."*

Carlyle's value as a writer worth reading in the twentieth century depends not so much on his views on practical questions as upon his inspirational power. In his originality and vigor he is still tonic; he makes one think, and think hard. Whatever be one's attitude

*Moody and Lovett's *History of English Literature.*

toward his anti-democratic opinions or other specific doctrines, one must recognize that few writers of English have said more memorable things in a more striking way. Many of his counsels, too, are as valuable for the world of 1920 as they were for the world of 1830 or 1840 or 1850. Scorn of shams and pretenses and insincerities is as pertinent as it ever was; men still forget too often the divine or spiritual element that pervades all things; and there has never been a time in the world's history when Carlyle's "gospel of work" was more needed.

## THE ESSAY ON BURNS

In the preceding discussion of Carlyle no specific attention has been given to his merits as a critic. The *Essay on Burns,* the third of his contributions to the *Edinburgh Review,* is valuable as criticism of literature and as criticism of life. Beginning as a review of a biography of Burns by Lockhart (the son-in-law and biographer-to-be of Sir Walter Scott), it proceeds in the fashion of the reviews of the time to attempt a complete and final estimate of the subject. As criticism of literature it is especially valuable for setting up principles on which to base critical judgments. Carlyle does not say arbitrarily, "I like this. I don't like that." He examines Burns's poems to see what qualities they have; and according to their sincerity, truth, vividness—all their observed characteristics—he expects us to be interested in them. Most of the best English literary criticism since the publication of this essay has made like efforts to discover and display the qualities of the work reviewed.

But it is as a critic of life that Carlyle did his best work; always he was interested primarily in personalities. As the explanation of his theory of history has shown, the biography of great men was to him one of the most important kinds of writing, if not the most important, and the principles which in his opinion should govern the writing of biography receive in this very essay (page 237) a fundamental statement. For the kind of estimate of Burns that he believed all great men should receive, Carlyle was remarkably well equipped. He could approach his subject with the sympathy born of experience of the sort of life Burns had to lead, while at the same time his broad reading and stern moral principles prevented either a narrowly prejudiced or an unduly generous apologetic view. We may not agree wholly with his estimate, but disagreement on any point must be based on evidence and careful consideration.

The *Essay on Burns* is not "easy reading." Carlyle never "wrote down" to his audience. If they did not understand the words he used or the allusions he made— well, the loss was theirs; it was their task to equip themselves to understand. Nevertheless, this essay is simpler and more normal in structure and style than most of Carlyle's work written after he had developed the "Carlylese" of *Sartor Resartus;* while at the same time it displays much of his characteristic eloquence. In it is expressed or implied the essence of Carlyle's great message to his generation, and it has long been regarded one of the most sympathetic and at the same time discriminating of critical essays in the English language.

# A SELECTED BIBLIOGRAPHY

## BURNS

EDITIONS

Burns made three collections of his poems, all having the title—
*Poems, Chiefly in the Scottish Dialect*.
The first was the Kilmarnock edition of 1786. In the second,
the Edinburgh edition of 1787, twenty-two additional poems
were included. After various reprints of this edition, a new one
with twenty more additions was issued in two volumes in 1793,
and reprinted in 1794. (Poems on the following pages appeared in all these editions unless otherwise noted.)

Meanwhile numerous songs by Burns had been appearing in—
*The Scots Musical Museum*
edited by James Johnson, of which Volume I was published in
1787, II in 1788, III in 1790, IV in 1792, V in 1796. The last
volume, VI, was not issued till 1803. In Johnson's entire collection there were 184 songs written or collected by Burns.

The other important song collection with which Burns was
concerned was—
*A Select Collection of Original Scottish Airs for the Voice*
edited by George Thomson. Part I was published in 1793, II in
1798, Parts III and IV in 1799. These four parts made two
volumes of fifty songs each, and three additional volumes appeared in 1801, 1805, and 1818. Thomson printed about
seventy songs by Burns, a number of which Johnson also had
printed.

In 1800 the first approximately complete edition of Burns's
*Works* was published—Dr. Currie's edition in four volumes, with
an account of Burns's life to which Carlyle several times refers
The Currie edition was often reprinted, and to the eighth edition
(1820) Gilbert Burns contributed many notes.

Other editions have been very numerous, and for a good many
years additions to the poems or letters were frequently made.
A few of the most important editions (important mainly because
of additions to the poet's works) are as follows:

    *Reliques of Robert Burns*, Cromek, 1808. (Not an edition
        of the then known works, but miscellaneous additional
        poems and letters.)

*Poetical Works*, Aldine edition by Sir H. Nicolas, 1830, revised 1839; revised again by G. A. Aitken, 3 vols., 1893.

*Works*, edited by Allan Cunningham, 8 vols., 1834, and often reprinted.

*Works*, edited by the Ettrick Shepherd (Hogg) and Motherwell, 5 vols., 1836.

*Works*, edited by A. Whitelaw, 2 vols., 1843-4.

*Life and Works*, Robert Chambers, 1851, 4 vols. An important revision and partial rewriting of this edition was issued by W. Wallace in 1896.

*Poetical Works*, George Gilfillan, 1864, etc. *The National Burns*, 2 vols., illustrated, 1879, etc., is the best form of Gilfillan's edition.

*Poetical Works*, 2 vols., 1865; *Complete Works*, Globe edition, 1868, both by Alexander Smith and often reprinted (the latter, one of the best editions in one volume).

*Life and Works*, P. H. Waddell, 1867.

*Complete Works*, W. Scott Douglas, 6 vols., 1877-79; reissued in 1891.

*The Poetry of Burns*, Centenary edition, Henley and Henderson, 4 vols., 1896. (Henley's introductory essay, the text, and the most important notes of this edition have been reprinted in the Cambridge edition, one of the best in one volume.)

*The Songs of Burns*, J. C. Dick, 1903.

BIOGRAPHY AND CRITICISM

Biographies of Burns and essays on him are very numerous. In addition to the early biographies mentioned by Carlyle, and biographical and critical material in the editions mentioned above, note the following very rigidly selective list:

A. Angellier, *Robert Burns, sa Vie et ses Oeuvres;* Paris, 1893 (an important French study).

Matthew Arnold, *Essays in Criticism*, second series (also in Ward's *English Poets*).

J. S. Blackie, *Life of Burns*, in Great Writers series, 1888.

Thomas Carlyle, *Heroes and Hero-Worship* (The Hero as a Man of Letters).

W. A. Craigie, *Primer of Burns*, 1896.

T. F. Henderson, *Robert Burns*, Little Biographies, 1904.

Francis Jeffrey, review of Cromek's *Reliques*, in *Edinburgh Review*, 1809.

W. A. Neilson, *Burns—How to Know Him*, 1917.

Sir Walter Scott, review of Cromek's *Reliques* in *Quarterly Review*, 1809.

J. C. Shairp, *Burns*, in English Men of Letters series, 1879.

Sir Leslie Stephen, article on Burns in *Dictionary of National Biography*.

R. L. Stevenson, essay in *Familiar Studies of Men and Books*, 1882.

See also poems on Burns by Lowell, Whittier, Wordsworth, Campbell, Holmes, Longfellow; and Wordsworth's *Letter to a Friend of Burns*, 1816.

## CARLYLE

Carlyle's most important works have been mentioned on pages 32-35. It is not important to consider editions. Particularly interesting material as to Carlyle is found in his—

*Reminiscences*, edited by Froude, 1881

and his *Correspondence*—

With Emerson, edited by C. E. Norton, 1883;

With Goethe, edited by C. E. Norton, 1887;

With Mrs. Carlyle, edited by Froude, 1883, and additional material edited by Alexander Carlyle, 1903, 1904, 1909.

Some of the most important sources of information on or criticism of Carlyle are the following:

Matthew Arnold, *Discourses in America*.

John Burroughs, *Fresh Fields; Indoor Studies*.

R. W. Emerson, *English Traits; Lectures and Biographical Sketches*.

J. A. Froude, *Thomas Carlyle*, 4 vols., 1882-4; *My Relations with Carlyle*, 1903 (written in 1886).

Richard Garnett, *Life of Carlyle*, Great Writers series.

J. R. Lowell, essay in *My Study Windows* (vol. II of collected essays).

John Morley, *Critical Miscellanies*.

John Nichol, *Thomas Carlyle*, English Men of Letters series.

Bliss Perry, *Carlyle—How to Know Him*.

Sir Leslie Stephen, article in *Dictionary of National Biography*.

# POEMS

## THE DEATH AND DYING WORDS
## OF POOR MAILIE

### THE AUTHOR'S ONLY PET YOWE[1]

#### AN UNCO[2] MOURNFU' TALE

[This poem and the "Elegy" that follows are among Burns's earliest compositions, dating from 1782 or a little earlier. Gilbert Burns made the following interesting explanation of the circumstances that prompted the poems: Robert "had, partly by way of frolic, bought a ewe and two lambs from a neighbor, and she was tethered in a field adjoining the house at Lochlea. He and I were going out with our teams, and our two younger brothers to drive for us, at mid-day, when Hugh Wilson, a curious-looking, awkward boy, clad in plaiding, came to us with much anxiety in his face, with the information that the ewe had entangled herself in the tether, and was lying in the ditch. Robert was much tickled with Hughoc's appearance and postures on the occasion. Poor Mailie was set to rights, and when we returned from the plow in the evening he repeated to me 'Death and Dying Words' pretty much in the way they now stand."

"Mailie" is the same as "Mollie"—a nickname for Mary.]

As Mailie, an' her lambs thegither,[3]
Was ae[4] day nibbling on the tether,
Upon her cloot[5] she coost[6] a hitch,
An' owre[7] she warsl'd[8] in the ditch;
5  There, groaning, dying, she did lie,
When Hughoc he cam doytin[9] by.

Wi' glowrin een[10] and lifted han's
Poor Hughoc like a statue stan's;
He saw her days were near-hand ended,
10  But, wae's my heart! he could na mend it!
He gapèd wide, but naething spak;
At length poor Mailie silence brak.

1. **Yowe.** Ewe.
2. **Unco.** Very.
3. **Thegither.** Together.
4. **Ae.** One.
5. **Cloot.** Hoof.
6. **Coost.** Past tense of *cast.*
7. **Owre.** Over.
8. **Warsl'd.** Wrestled.
9. **Doytin.** Doddering.
10. **Glowrin een.** Staring eyes.

41

"O thou, whase lamentable face
Appears to mourn my woefu' case!
15  My dying words attentive hear,
An' bear them to my Master dear.


"Tell him, if e'er again he keep
As muckle gear[11] as buy a sheep,
O, bid him never tie them mair
20  Wi' wicked strings o' hemp or hair!
But ca'[12] them out to park or hill,
An' let them wander at their will;
So may his flock increase an' grow
To scores o' lambs an' packs o' woo'![13]


25  "Tell him, he was a Master kin',
An' ay was guid to me an' mine;
An' now my dying charge I gie[14] him,
My helpless lambs, I trust them wi' him.


"O, bid him save their harmless lives
30  Frae dogs an' tods[15] an' butchers' knives!
But gie them guid cow-milk their fill
Till they be fit to fend[16] themsel;
An' tent[17] them duly, e'en an' morn,
Wi' teats[18] o' hay an' ripps[19] o' corn.


35  "An' may they never learn the gaets[20]
Of ither vile, wanrestfu'[21] pets!
To slink thro' slaps,[22] an' reave[23] an' steal,
At stacks o' pease, or stocks o' kail.[24]

11. **Muckle gear.**  Much money.
12. **Ca'.**  Call, drive.
13. **Woo'.**  Wool.
14. **Gie.**  Give.
15. **Tods.**  Foxes.
16. **Fend.**  Look after.
17. **Tent.**  Tend.
18. **Teats.**  Small quantities.
19. **Ripps.**  Handfuls.
20. **Gaets.**  Ways.
21. **Wanrestfu'.**  Restless.
22. **Slaps.**  Holes in fences.
23. **Reave.**  Rob.
24. **Kail.**  Colewort (a plant somewhat like cabbage).

So may they, like their great forbears,
40   For monie a year come thro' the sheers;
So wives will gie them bits o' bread,
An' bairns greet[25] for them when they're dead.

"My poor toop-lamb,[26] my son an' heir,
O, bid him breed him up wi' care!
45   An' if he live to be a beast,
To pit[27] some havins[28] in his breast!
An' warn him, what I winna name,
To stay content wi' yowes[29] at hame;
An' no to rin[30] an' wear his cloots[31]
50   Like ither menseless,[32] graceless brutes.

"An' niest,[33] my yowie, silly thing,
Gude[34] keep thee frae a tether string!
O, may thou ne'er forgather up
Wi' onie blastit, moorland toop;
55   But ay keep mind to moop an' mell,[35]
Wi' sheep o' credit like thysel!

"And now, my bairns, wi' my last breath,
I lea'e my blessin wi' you baith;
An' when you think upo' your mither,
60   Mind to be kind to ane anither.

"Now, honest Hughoc, dinna fail
To tell my master a' my tale;
An' bid him burn this cursed tether,
An' for thy pains thou'se[36] get my blather.[37]

65       This said, poor Mailie turn'd her head,
An' clos'd her een[38] amang the dead!

| | |
|---|---|
| 25. **Bairns greet.** Children weep. | 32. **Menseless.** Unmannerly. |
| 26. **Toop-lamb.** A young ram. | 33. **Niest.** Next. |
| 27. **Pit.** Put. | 34. **Gude.** God. |
| 28. **Havins.** Good manners. | 35. **Moop an' mell.** Nibble and meddle. |
| 29. **Yowes.** Ewes. | 36. **Thou'se.** Thou shalt. |
| 30. **Rin.** Run. | 37. **Blather.** Bladder. |
| 31. **Cloots.** Hoofs. | 38. **Een.** Eyes |

## POOR MAILIE'S ELEGY*

### I

Lament in rhyme, lament in prose,
Wi' saut[1] tears trickling down your nose;
Our Bardie's fate is at a close,
        Past a' remead;[2]
The last, sad cape-stane[3] of his woes;
        Poor Mailie's dead!

### II

It's no the loss o' warl's gear,[4]
That could sae bitter draw the tear,
Or mak our Bardie, dowie,[5] wear
        The mourning weed:
He's lost a friend an' neebor dear
        In Mailie dead.

### III

Thro' a' the toun she trotted by him;
A lang half-mile she could descry him;
Wi' kindly bleat, when she did spy him,
        She ran wi' speed;
A friend mair faithfu' ne'er cam nigh him
        Than Mailie dead.

### IV

I wat[6] she was a sheep o' sense,
An' could behave hersel wi' mense;[7]
I'll say't, she never brak a fence,
        Thro' thievish greed.
Our Bardie, lanely, keeps the spence[8]
        Sin'[9] Mailie's dead.

1. **Saut.** Salt.
2. **A' remead.** All remedy.
3. **Cape-stane.** Cope-stone.
4. **Warl's gear.** Worldly goods.
5. **Dowie.** Mournful.
6. **Wat.** Know.
7. **Mense.** Good manners.
8. **Spence.** Parlor.
9. **Sin'.** Since.

V

Or, if he wanders up the howe,[10]
Her living image in her yowe[11]
Comes bleating till[12] him, owre the knowe,[13]
   For bits o' bread;
An' down the briny pearls rowe[14]
   For Mailie dead.

VI

She was nae get[15] o' moorlan tips,[16]
Wi' tawted ket,[17] an' hairy hips;
For her forbears were brought in ships
   Frae yont[18] the Tweed :*
A bonier fleesh[19] ne'er cross'd the clips[20]
   Than Mailie's dead.

VII

Wae worth[21] the man wha first did shape
That vile, wanchancie[22] thing—a rape![23]
It maks guid fellows girn[24] an' gape
   Wi' chokin dread;
An' Robin's bonnet wave wi' crape
   For Mailie dead.

VIII

O a' ye bards on bonie Doon!*
An' wha on Ayr* your chanters[25] tune!
Come, join the melancholious croon[26]
   O' Robin's reed!
His heart will never get aboon![27]
   His Mailie's dead!

10. **Howe.** Hollow.
11. **Yowe.** Ewe.
12. **Till.** To.
13. **Knowe.** Knoll.
14. **Rowe.** Roll.
15. **Nae get.** No issue.
16. **Tips.** Rams.
17. **Tawted ket.** Matted fleece.
18. **Frae yont.** From beyond.
19. **Fleesh.** Fleece.
20. **Clips.** Sheep-shears.
21. **Wae worth.** Woe befall.
22. **Wanchancie.** Unlucky.
23. **Rape.** Rope.
24. **Girn.** Grin, twist the face
25. **Chanters.** Bagpipes.
26. **Croon.** Moan.
27. **Get aboon.** Get above, rejoice.

## MAN WAS MADE TO MOURN—A DIRGE

[This was Burns's earliest pure English poem of any consequence, and is generally believed to date from the latter part of 1784. Gilbert Burns made the following note on it: "Several of the poems were produced for the purpose of bringing forward some favorite sentiment of the author. He used to remark to me that he could not well conceive a more mortifying picture of human life than a man seeking work. In casting about in his mind how this sentiment might be brought forward, the elegy 'Man Was Made to Mourn' was composed." In 1788 Burns wrote to Mrs. Dunlop of a grand-uncle of his who had gone blind and whose "most voluptuous enjoyment was to sit down and cry, while my mother would sing the simple old song of 'The Life and Age of Man'"—a song of which the refrain was, "Man was made to moan."]

I

When chill November's surly blast
　　Made fields and forests bare,
One ev'ning, as I wander'd forth
　　Along the banks of Ayr,
I spy'd a man, whose agèd step
　　Seem'd weary, worn with care;
His face was furrow'd o'er with years,
　　And hoary was his hair.

II

"Young stranger, whither wand'rest thou?"
　　Began the rev'rend sage;
"Does thirst of wealth thy step constrain,
　　Or youthful pleasure's rage?
Or haply, prest with cares and woes,
　　Too soon thou hast began
To wander forth, with me to mourn
　　The miseries of man.

III

"The sun that overhangs yon moors,
　　Out-spreading far and wide,
Where hundreds labor to support
　　A haughty lordling's pride;

I've seen yon weary winter-sun
  Twice forty times return;
And ev'ry time has added proofs,
  That man was made to mourn.


IV

"O man! while in thy early years,
  How prodigal of time!
Mis-spending all thy precious hours,
  Thy glorious, youthful prime!
Alternate follies take the sway;
  Licentious passions burn;
Which tenfold force gives Nature's law,
  That man was made to mourn.


V

"Look not alone on youthful prime,
  Or manhood's active might;
Man then is useful to his kind,
  Supported is his right:
But see him on the edge of life,
  With cares and sorrows worn;
Then Age and Want—O! ill-match'd pair!
  Show man was made to mourn.


VI

"A few seem favorites of Fate,
  In Pleasure's lap carest;
Yet, think not all the rich and great
  Are likewise truly blest.
But oh! what crowds in ev'ry land,
  All wretched and forlorn,
Thro' weary life this lesson learn,
  That man was made to mourn.

### VII

"Many and sharp the num'rous ills
    Inwoven with our frame!
More pointed still we make ourselves
    Regret, remorse, and shame!
And man, whose heav'n-erected face
    The smiles of love adorn—
Man's inhumanity to man
    Makes countless thousands mourn!

### VIII

"See yonder poor, o'erlabor'd wight,
    So abject, mean, and vile,
Who begs a brother of the earth
    To give him leave to toil;
And see his lordly fellow-worm
    The poor petition spurn,
Unmindful, though a weeping wife
    And helpless offspring mourn.

### IX

"If I'm design'd yon lordling's slave,
    By Nature's law design'd,
Why was an independent wish
    E'er planted in my mind?
If not, why am I subject to
    His cruelty, or scorn?
Or why has man the will and pow'r
    To make his fellow mourn?

### X

"Yet, let not this too much, my son,
    Disturb thy youthful breast:
This partial view of human-kind
    Is surely not the last!

The poor, oppressèd, honest man
  Had never, sure, been born,
Had there not been some recompense
  To comfort those that mourn!


### XI

"O Death! the poor man's dearest friend,
  The kindest and the best!
Welcome the hour my agèd limbs
  Are laid with thee at rest!
The great, the wealthy fear thy blow,
  From pomp and pleasure torn;
But, oh! a blest relief for those
  That weary-laden mourn!"


## EPISTLE TO DAVIE, A BROTHER POET*

### January

[The "January" at the head of this poem was doubtless
January, 1785, when presumably the poem was finished. Gilbert Burns, however, declared, "It was, I think, in the summer
of 1784 when in the intervals of harder labor Robert and I
were weeding in the garden, that he repeated to me the principal parts of this 'Epistle.'"

"Davie" was David Sillar, a member of the Tarbolton
Bachelors' Club (in which Burns was prominent), and author
of a volume of poems printed at Kilmarnock in 1789. He was a
teacher at Tarbolton and ultimately became a magistrate of
the town. One of the manuscripts of this poem in Burns's
handwriting is headed, "An Epistle to Davie, a Brother Poet,
Lover, Ploughman, and Fiddler."]


### I

While winds frae aff Ben-Lomond* blaw,
And bar the doors wi' driving snaw,
  And hing¹ us owre the ingle,²
I set me down to pass the time,
And spin a verse or twa o' rhyme,
  In hamely, westlin³ jingle.

1. **Hing.** Hang.                    3. **Westlin.** Western.
2. **Ingle.** Fire.

While frosty winds blaw in the drift,
  Ben to the chimla lug,[4]
I grudge a wee the great-folk's gift
  That live sae bien[5] an' snug:
    I tent[6] less, and want less
      Their roomy fire-side;
    But hanker and canker,
      To see their cursèd pride.

## II

It's hardly in a body's pow'r
To keep, at times, frae being sour,
  To see how things are shar'd;
How best o' chiels[7] are whyles[8] in want,
While coofs[9] on countless thousands rant,[10]
  And ken na[11] how to wair't;[12]
But Davie, lad, ne'er fash[13] your head,
  Tho' we hae little gear;[14]
We're fit to win our daily bread
  As lang's we're hale and fier:[15]
    "Mair spier na,[16] nor fear na,"*
    Auld age ne'er mind a feg;[17]
      The last o't, the warst o't,
        Is only but to beg.

## III

To lie in kilns and barns at e'en,
When banes[18] are craz'd and bluid is thin,
  Is, doubtless, great distress!
Yet then content could make us blest;
Ev'n then, sometimes, we'd snatch a taste
  Of truest happiness.

4. **Ben to the chimla lug.** In the chimney corner.
5. **Bien.** Comfortable.
6. **Tent.** Heed.
7. **Chiels.** Fellows.
8. **Whyles.** Sometimes.
9. **Coofs.** Fools.
10. **Rant.** Sport noisily.
11. **Ken na.** Know not.
12. **Wair't.** Spend it.
13. **Fash.** Trouble.
14. **Gear.** Property.
15. **Fier.** Sound.
16. **Mair spier na.** More ask not.
17. **Feg.** Fig.
18. **Banes.** Bones.

The honest heart that's free frae a'
 Intended fraud or guile,
However Fortune kick the ba',[19]
 Has aye some cause to smile;
  An' mind still, you'll find still
  A comfort this nae sma';[20]
 Nae mair then we'll care then,
  Nae farther can we fa'.


## IV

What tho', like commoners of air,
We wander out, we know not where,
 But [21] either house or hal'?
Yet Nature's charms, the hills and woods,
The sweeping vales, and foaming floods,
 Are free alike to all.
In days when daisies deck the ground,
 And blackbirds whistle clear,
With honest joy our hearts will bound,
 To see the coming year;
  On braes[22] when we please, then,
  We'll sit an' sowth[23] a tune;
  Syne[24] rhyme till't[25] we'll time till't,
  And sing't when we hae done.


## V

It's no in titles nor in rank;
It's no in wealth like Lon'on bank,
 To purchase peace and rest;
It's no in makin muckle mair;[26]
It's no in books, it's no in lear,[27]
 To make us truly blest:

19. **Ba'.** Ball.
20. **Nae sma'.** Not small.
21. **But.** Without.
22. **Braes.** Hillsides.
23. **Sowth.** Hum.
24. **Syne.** Then.
25. **Till't.** To it.
26. **Muckle mair.** Much more.
27. **Lear.** Learning.

If happiness hae not her seat
    And center in the breast,
We may be wise, or rich, or great,
    But never can be blest;
        Nae treasures nor pleasures
            Could make us happy lang;
        The heart ay's the part ay
            That makes us right or wrang.

### VI

Think ye, that sic[28] as you and I,
Wha drudge an' drive thro' wet and dry
    Wi' never-ceasing toil;
Think ye, are we less blest than they,
Wha scarcely tent[29] us in their way,
    As hardly worth their while?
Alas! how aft, in haughty mood,
    God's creatures they oppress!
Or else, neglecting a' that's guid,
    They riot in excess!
        Baith careless and fearless
            Of either Heaven or Hell;
        Esteeming and deeming
            It's a' an idle tale!

### VII

Then let us cheerfu' acquiesce,
Nor make our scanty pleasures less
    By pining at our state;
And, even should misfortunes come,
I, here wha sit, hae met wi' some,
    An's[30] thankfu' for them yet.
They gie the wit of age to youth;
    They let us ken oursel;[31]
They make us see the naked truth,
    The real guid and ill.

28. **Sic.**  Such.
29. **Tent.**  Heed.

30. **An's.**  And am.
31. **Ken oursel.**  Know ourselves.

Tho' losses and crosses
  Be lessons right severe,
There's wit there, ye'll get there,
  Ye'll find nae other where.

## VIII

But tent[32] me, Davie, ace o' hearts!
(To say aught less wad wrang the cartes,[33]
  And flatt'ry I destest)
This life has joys for you and I,
And joys that riches ne'er could buy,
  And joys the very best.
There's a' the pleasures o' the heart,
  The lover an' the frien';
Ye hae your Meg, your dearest part,
  And I my darling Jean!*
    It warms me, it charms me,
      To mention but her name;
    It heats me, it beets[34] me,
      An' sets me a' on flame!

## IX

O all ye Pow'rs who rule above!
O Thou whose very self art love!
  Thou know'st my words sincere!
The life-blood streaming thro' my heart,
Or my more dear immortal part,
  Is not more fondly dear!
When heart-corroding care and grief
  Deprive my soul of rest,
Her dear idea brings relief
  And solace to my breast.
    Thou Being, All-seeing,
      O hear my fervent pray'r!
    Still take her, and make her
      Thy most peculiar care!

32. Tent.  Mark.                    34. **Beets.**  Kindles.
33. Cartes.  Cards.

### X

All hail, ye tender feelings dear!
The smile of love, the friendly tear,
　　The sympathetic glow!
Long since, this world's* thorny ways
Had number'd out my weary days,
　　Had it not been for you!
Fate still has blest me with a friend
　　In ev'ry care and ill;
And oft a more endearing band,
　　A tie more tender still.
　　It lightens, it brightens
　　　　The tenebrific scene,
　　　To meet with, and greet with
　　　　My Davie, or my Jean.

### XI

O, how that name inspires my style!
The words come skelpin,[35] rank an' file,
　　Amaist[36] before I ken!
The ready measure rins as fine
As Phœbus and the famous Nine*
　　Were glowrin[37] owre my pen.
My spaviet[38] Pegasus will limp
　　Till ance[39] he's fairly het;[40]
And then he'll hilch, and stilt, and jimp,[41]
　　And rin an unco fit;[42]
　　But lest then the beast then
　　　　Should rue this hasty ride,
　　　I'll light now, and dight[43] now
　　　　His sweaty, wizen'd hide.

35. **Skelpin.** Hastening.
36. **Amaist.** Almost.
37. **Glowrin.** Staring.
38. **Spaviet.** Spavined.
39. **Ance.** Once.
40. **Het.** Hot.
41. **Hilch, and stilt, and jimp.** Hobble and limp and jump.
42. **Unco fit.** Surprising spurt.
43. **Dight.** Wipe.

## SECOND EPISTLE TO DAVIE

### A BROTHER POET

[This was written considerably later than the first "Epistle
to Davie"—apparently in 1786, after Burns had decided to
publish his poems (see the fourth stanza)—but is placed here,
out of chronological order, to keep the related poems together.
This "Second Epistle" was prefixed to an edition of "Davie's"
poems in 1789, but was not printed with Burns's poems during
his lifetime.]

I

Auld Neebor,
   I'm three times doubly o'er your debtor
For your auld-farrant,[1] frien'ly letter;
Tho' I maun say't, I doubt ye flatter,
       Ye speak sae fair;
For my puir, silly, rhymin clatter
      Some less maun sair.[2]

II

Hale be your heart, hale be your fiddle,
Lang may your elbuck jink an' diddle,[3]
To cheer you thro' the weary widdle[4]
      O' war'ly[5] cares,
Till bairns' bairns* kindly cuddle
      Your auld grey hairs.

III

But Davie, lad, I'm red[6] ye're glaikit;[7]
I'm tauld the muse ye hae negleckit;
An' gif[8] it's sae, ye sud[9] be licket
      Until ye fyke;[10]
Sic han's as you sud ne'er be faiket,[11]
      Be hain't[12] wha like.

1. **Auld-farrant.** Sagacious.
2. **Maun sair.** Must serve.
3. **Elbuck jink an' diddle.** Elbow move quickly.
4. **Widdle.** Struggle.
5. **War'ly.** Worldly.
6. **Red.** Afraid.
7. **Glaikit.** Foolish.
8. **Gif.** If.
9. **Sud.** Should.
10. **Fyke.** Fidget.
11. **Faiket.** Let off, excused.
12. **Hain't wha like.** Spared who likes.

### IV

For me, I'm on Parnassus' brink,*
Rivin[13] the words to gar them clink;[14]
Whyles[15] daez't[16] wi' love, whyles daez't wi' drink,
      Wi' jads[17] or Masons;
An' whyles, but ay owre[18] late, I think
      Braw[19] sober lessons.

### V

Of a' the thoughtless sons o' man,
Commen' me to the bardie clan;
Except it be some idle plan
      O' rhymin clink[20]—
The devil-haet[21] that I sud ban![22]—
      They never think.

### VI

Nae thought, nae view, nae scheme o' livin,
Nae cares to gie us joy or grievin,
But just the pouchie[23] put the nieve[24] in,
      An' while ought's there,
Then, hiltie-skiltie,[25] we gae scrievin,[26]
      An' fash[27] nae mair.

### VII

Leeze[28] me on rhyme! It's ay a treasure,
My chief, amaist[29] my only pleasure;
At hame, a-fiel', at wark or leisure,
      The Muse, poor hizzie![30]
Tho' rough an' raploch[31] be her measure,
      She's seldom lazy.

13. **Rivin.** Rending.
14. **Gar them clink.** Make them rime.
15. **Whyles.** Sometimes.
16. **Daez't.** Dazed.
17. **Jads.** Jades.
18. **Owre.** Too.
19. **Braw.** Fine.
20. **Clink.** Jingle.
21. **Devil-haet.** The devil have it.
22. **Ban.** Curse.
23. **Pouchie.** Pocket.
24. **Nieve.** Fist.
25. **Hiltie-skiltie.** Helter-skelter.
26. **Gae scrievin.** Go gliding.
27. **Fash.** Trouble.
28. **Leeze me on.** How well I love (literally, dear to me is).
29. **Amaist.** Almost.
30. **Hizzie.** Girl.
31. **Raploch.** Homespun.

### VIII

Haud[32] to the Muse, my dainty Davie:
The warl' may play you monie a' shavie,[33]
But for the Muse, she'll never leave ye,
      Tho e'er sae puir,
Na, even tho' limpin wi' the spavie[34]
      Frae door to door.


# EPISTLE TO J. LAPRAIK

### AN OLD SCOTTISH BARD.—APRIL 1, 1785

[John Lapraik was a little over thirty years older than Burns. His song which Burns mentions so flatteringly in stanza iii was entitled, "When I Upon Thy Bosom Lean." Fasten-een (stanza ii) was the evening before Lent. A "rockin" was a festivity in which there was spinning upon the "rock" or distaff. Lapraik's poems were printed at Kilmarnock in 1788. Burns was over-generous in his comments on Lapraik, to whom he wrote two other poetical epistles.]

### I

While briers an' woodbines budding green,
An' paitricks scraichin[1] loud at e'en,
And morning poussie whiddin[2] seen,
      Inspire my Muse,
This freedom, in an unknown frien',
      I pray excuse.

### II

On Fasten-een we had a rockin,
To ca' the crack[3] and weave our stockin;
And there was muckle[4] fun and jokin,
      Ye need na doubt;
At length we had a hearty yokin[5]
      At sang about.[6]

32. **Haud.** Hold.
33. **Shavie.** Trick.
34. **Spavie.** Spavin.

1. **Paitricks scraichin.** Partridges screeching.

2. **Poussie whiddin.** Hare scudding.
3. **Ca' the crack.** Tell stories.
4. **Muckle.** Much.
5. **Yokin.** Set to.
6. **Sang about.** Singing in turn

### III

There was ae[7] sang, amang the rest,
Aboon[8] them a' it pleas'd me best,
That some kind husband had addrest
        To some sweet wife;
It thirl'd[9] the heart-strings thro' the breast,
        A' to the life.


### IV

I've scarce heard ought described sae weel,
What gen'rous, manly bosoms feel;
Thought I, "Can this be Pope, or Steele,*
        Or Beattie's* wark?"
They tald me 'twas an odd kind chiel[10]
        About Muirkirk.*


### V

It pat me fidgin-fain[11] to hear't,
And sae about him there I spier't;[12]
Then a' that kent[13] him round declar'd
        He had ingíne;[14]
That nane excell'd it, few cam near't,
        It was sae fine:


### VI

That, set him to a pint of ale,
An' either douce[15] or merry tale,
Or rhymes an' sangs he'd made himsel,
        Or witty catches,
'Tween Inverness* and Tiviotdale,*
        He had few matches.

| | |
|---|---|
| 7. **Ae.** One. | 12. **Spier't.** Asked. |
| 8. **Aboon.** Above. | 13. **Kent.** Knew. |
| 9. **Thirl'd.** Thrilled. | 14. **Ingíne.** Genius. |
| 10. **Chiel.** Fellow. | 15. **Douce.** Serious. |
| 11. **Pat me fidgin-fain.** Made me fidget with eagerness. | |

### VII

Then up I gat, an' swoor an aith,[16]
Tho' I should pawn my pleugh an' graith,[17]
Or die a cadger pownie's[18] death,
   At some dyke-back,
A pint an' gill I'd gie them baith,[19]
   To hear your crack.[20]

### VIII

But, first an' foremost, I should tell,
Amaist as soon as I could spell,
I to the crambo-jingle[21] fell;
   Tho' rude an' rough,
Yet crooning to a body's sel
   Does weel eneugh.

### IX

I am nae poet, in a sense,
But just a rhymer, like, by chance,
An' hae to learning nae pretence;
   Yet, what the matter?
Whene'er my Muse does on me glance,
   I jingle at her.

### X

Your critic-folk may cock their nose,
And say, "How can you e'er propose,
You wha ken hardly verse frae prose,
   To mak a sang?"
But, by your leaves, my learned foes,
   Ye're maybe wrang.

16. **Swoor an aith.** Swore an oath.
17. **Pleugh an' graith.** Plow and tools.
18. **Cadger pownie.** Carrier pony.
19. **Gie them baith.** Give them both.
20. **Crack.** Talk.
21. **Crambo-jingle.** Riming.

### XI

What's a' your jargon o' your schools,
Your Latin names for horns an' stools?
If honest Nature made you fools,
                What sairs[22] your grammars?
Ye'd better taen up spades and shools,[23]
                Or knappin-hammers.[24]

### XII

A set o' dull, conceited hashes[25]
Confuse their brains in college-classes!
They gang in stirks,[26] and come out asses,
                Plain truth to speak;
An' syne[27] they think to climb Parnassus*
                By dint o' Greek!

### XIII

Gie me ae[28] spark o' Nature's fire,
That's a' the learning I desire;
Then tho' I drudge thro' dub[29] an' mire
                At pleugh or cart,
My Muse, tho' hamely in attire,
                May touch the heart.

### XIV

O for a spunk[30] o' Allan's* glee,
Or Fergusson's, the bauld an' slee,[31]
Or bright Lapraik's, my friend to be,
                If I can hit it!
That would be lear[32] eneugh for me,
                If I could get it.

22. **Sairs.** Serve.
23. **Shools.** Shovels.
24. **Knappin-hammers.** Hammers for breaking stone.
25. **Hashes.** Dunderheads.
26. **Stirks.** Calves more than a year old.
27. **Syne.** Then.
28. **Ae.** One.
29. **Dub.** Puddle.
30. **Spunk.** Spark.
31. **Bauld an' slee.** Bold and sly.
32. **Lear.** Learning.

### XV

Now, sir, if ye hae friends enow,
Tho' real friends I b'lieve are few,
Yet, if your catalogue be fow,[33]
   I'se no[34] insist;
But, gif[35] ye want ae friend that's true,
   I'm on your list.


### XVI

I winna blaw about mysel,
As ill I like my fauts to tell;
But friends, an' folks that wish me well,
   They sometimes roose[36] me;
Tho' I maun own, as monie still
   As far abuse me.


### XVII

There's ae wee faut they whyles[37] lay to me,
I like the lasses—Gude forgie[38] me!
For monie a plack[39] they wheedle frae me
   At dance or fair;
Maybe some ither thing they gie me,
   They weel can spare.


### XVIII

But Mauchline Race or Mauchline Fair,
I should be proud to meet you there;
We'se gie[40] ae night's discharge to care,
   If we forgather,
An' hae a swap o' rhymin-ware
   Wi' ane anither.

33. **Fow.** Full.
34. **I'se no.** I shall not.
35. **Gif.** If.
36. **Roose.** Praise.

37. **Whyles.** Sometimes.
38. **Gude forgie.** God forgive.
39. **Plack.** A small coin.
40. **We'se gie.** We shall give.

### XIX

The four-gill chap,[41] we'se gar[42] him clatter,
An' kirsen[43] him wi' reekin[44] water;
Syne we'll sit down an' tak our whitter,[45]
    To cheer our heart;
An' faith, we'se be acquainted better
    Before we part.

### XX

Awa, ye selfish, warly [46] race,
Wha think that havins,[47] sense, an' grace,
Ev'n love an' friendship, should give place
    To catch-the-plack![48]
I dinna like to see your face,
    Nor hear your crack.[49]

### XXI

But ye whom social pleasure charms,
Whose hearts the tide of kindness warms,
Who hold your being on the terms,
    "Each aid the others,"
Come to my bowl, come to my arms,
    My friends, my brothers!

### XXII

But, to conclude my lang epistle,
As my auld pen's worn to the grissle,
Two lines frae you wad gar me fissle,[50]
    Who am most fervent,
While I can either sing or whissle,
    Your friend and servant.

41. **Chap.** A quart measure, made of brass.
42. **Gar.** Make.
43. **Kirsen.** Christen.
44. **Reekin.** Steaming.
45. **Whitter.** A hearty draught.
46. **Warly.** Worldly.
47. **Havins.** Good behavior.
48. **Catch-the-plack.** Catch the penny (a game).
49. **Crack.** Talk.
50. **Gar me fissle.** Make me tingle with delight.

# EPISTLE TO WILLIAM SIMPSON

## SCHOOLMASTER, OCHILTREE.—MAY, 1785

[This correspondent of Burns was a few months the poet's senior; he was the son of a farmer in the parish of Ochiltree, not far east of Ayr; after being educated at the University of Glasgow he became schoolmaster at Ochiltree in 1780.

This epistle, like some of the other personal epistles in this volume and like "The Vision," which is not included here, is interesting as an expression of Burns's ambition to be primarily a patriotic poet—a "Scottish bard"—and of the way in which the natural scenes in which he lived inspired him to composition.]

### I

I gat your letter, winsome Willie;
Wi' gratefu' heart I thank you brawlie;[1]
Tho' I maun say't, I wad be silly
    And unco[2] vain,
Should I believe, my coaxin billie,[3]
    Your flatterin strain.

### II

But I'se[4] believe ye kindly meant it:
I sud be laith[5] to think ye hinted
Ironic satire, sidelins sklented[6]
    On my poor Musie;
Tho' in sic phraisin[7] terms ye've penn'd it,
    I scarce excuse ye.

### III

My senses wad be in a creel,[8]
Should I but dare a hope to speel,[9]
Wi' Allan, or wi' Gilbertfield,*
    The braes[10] o' fame;
Or Fergusson, the writer-chiel,[11]
    A deathless name.

1. **Brawlie.** Heartily.
2. **Unco.** Very.
3. **Billie.** Fellow, brother.
4. **I'se.** I shall.
5. **Sud be laith.** Should be loath.
6. **Sidelins sklented.** Sidewise squinted.
7. **Phraisin.** Flattering.
8. **Creel.** An osier basket (the line means, "I should be perplexed).
9. **Speel.** Climb.
10. **Braes.** Hillsides.
11. **Writer-chiel.** Lawyer chap.

### IV

(O Fergusson! thy glorious parts
Ill suited law's dry, musty arts!
My curse upon your whunstane[12] hearts,
   Ye E'nbrugh gentry!*
The tythe o' what ye waste at cartes
   Wad stow'd his pantry!)

### V

Yet when a tale comes i' my head,
Or lassies gie my heart a screed[13]—
As whiles they're like to be my dead,
   (O sad disease!)
I kittle[14] up my rustic reed;
   It gies me ease.

### VI

Auld Coila[15] now may fidge fu' fain,[16]
She's gotten poets o' her ain;
Chiels wha their chanters winna hain,[17]
   But tune their lays,
Till echoes a' resound again
   Her weel-sung praise.

### VII

Nae poet thought her worth his while
To set her name in measur'd style;
She lay like some unken'd-of isle
   Beside New Holland,*
Or whare wild-meeting oceans boil
   Besouth[18] Magellan.

12. **Whunstane.** Whinstone—a kind of hard stone.
13. **Screed.** Rip or rent.
14. **Kittle.** Tickle.
15. **Coila.** Kyle, the portion of Ayrshire in which Burns lived.
16. **Fidge fu' fain.** Wriggle with eagerness.
17. **Chanters winna hain.** Bagpipes will not spare.
18. **Besouth.** To the south of.

## VIII

Ramsay an' famous Fergusson
Gied Forth an' Tay a lift aboon;[19]
Yarrow an' Tweed, to monie a tune,
      Owre Scotland rings;
While Irwin, Lugar, Ayr, an' Doon*
      Naebody sings.

## IX

Th' Illissus,* Tiber, Thames, an' Seine,
Glide sweet in monie a tunefu' line:
But, Willie, set your fit[20] to mine,
      An' cock your crest;
We'll gar[21] our streams an' burnies[22] shine
      Up wi' the best.

## X

We'll sing auld Coila's plains an' fells,
Her moors red-brown wi' heather bells,
Her banks an' braes, her dens an' dells,
      Whare glorious Wallace
Aft bure the gree,[23] as story tells,
      Frae Southron billies.[24]

## XI

At Wallace' name, what Scottish blood
But boils up in a spring-tide flood!
Oft have our fearless fathers strode
      By Wallace' side,
Still pressing onward, red-wat-shod,[25]
      Or glorious died!

19. **Aboon.** Above.
20. **Fit.** Foot.
21. **Gar.** Make, cause.
22. **Burnies.** Brooklets.
23. **Bure the gree.** Bore off the prize, won the victory.
24. **Southron billies.** Southern fellows, the English.
25. **Red-wat-shod.** Red-wet-shod, wading in blood.

### XII

O sweet are Coila's haughs[2] an woods,
When lintwhites[27] chant amang the buds,
And jinkin[28] hares, in amorous whids,[29]
      Their loves enjoy;
While thro' the braes the cushat croods[30]
      With wailfu' cry!

### XIII

Ev'n winter bleak has charms to me,
When winds rave thro' the naked tree;
Or frosts on hills of Ochiltree
      Are hoary gray;
Or blinding drifts wild-furious flee,
      Dark'ning the day!

### XIV

O Nature! a' thy shews and forms
To feeling, pensive hearts hae charms!
Whether the summer kindly warms,
      Wi' life an' light;
Or winter howls, in gusty storms,
      The lang, dark night!

### XV

The Muse, nae poet ever fand her,
Till by himsel he learn'd to wander,
Adown some trottin burn's meander,[34]
      An' no think lang:
O sweet to stray, an' pensive ponder
      A heart-felt sang!

26. **Haughs.** Valleys.
27. **Lintwhites.** Linnets.
28. **Jinkin.** Frisking.
29. **Whids.** Gambols.

30. **Cushat croods.** Wood pigeon coos.
31. **Burn's meander.** Brook's winding.

### XVI

The warly[32] race may drudge an' drive,
Hog-shouther, jundie,[33] stretch, an' strive;
Let me fair Nature's face descrive,[34]
      And I, wi' pleasure,
Shall let the busy, gumbling hive
      Bum[35] owre their treasure.

### XVII

Fareweel, my rhyme-composing brither!
We've been owre lang unken'd to ither:
Now let us lay our heads thegither,
      In love fraternal:
May Envy wallop[36] in a tether,
      Black fiend, infernal!

### XVIII

While Highlandmen hate tolls an' taxes;
While moorlan' herds like guid, fat braxies;[37]
While terra firma, on her axis,
      Diurnal turns;
Count on a friend, in faith an' practice,
      In Robert Burns.

32. **Warly.** Worldly.
33. **Hog-shouther, jundie.** Jostle with the shoulder.
34. **Descrive.** Describe.
35. **Bum.** Hum.
36. **Wallop.** Move quickly but clumsily.
37. **Braxies.** Sheep that have died of the disease called braxie.

## HOLY WILLIE'S PRAYER

"And send the godly in a pet to pray."—POPE.

[Written early in 1785; not included by Burns in any
authorized edition during his life, but evidently widely known.
"Holy Willie" was William Fisher, an elder in the parish
church at Mauchline. He was a zealous assistant of the
pastor, the Rev. Mr. Auld, in watching the morals of the
parishioners, in spite of the fact that his own conduct was at
least questionable. Those to whom the poem seems irreverent
should remember that the poet is merely parodying the com-
placent utterances of a self-righteous hypocrite of the intolerant
"Auld Licht" party. Burns unquestionably "had a grudge"
against "Holy Willie," perhaps on his own account, certainly
on behalf of his friend Gavin Hamilton; but here, as in the
"Address to the Unco Guid," (page 156) he is primarily expressing matchless satire against self-righteous hypocrisy
masquerading under the cloak of religion.

Gau'n Hamilton (stanza xi) was a writer (that is, attor-
ney) in Mauchline, friend and patron of Burns. Not long
before this poem was written, Hamilton had been charged,
probably by "Holy Willie," with various violations of the
strict church discipline, and a church feud had arisen in which
Burns took ardent part on the "New Licht," or liberal side.
Robert Aiken (stanza xiv) was Hamilton's counsel in the
trial before the Presbytery of Ayr (stanza xiii), which decided in favor of Hamilton. Burns once said that Aiken had
"read" him (the poet) "into fame."]

I

O Thou, that in the Heavens does dwell,
Wha, as it pleases best Thysel,
Sends ane to Heaven an' ten to Hell,
            A' for Thy glory,
And no for onie guid or ill
            They've done before Thee!

II

I bless and praise Thy matchless might,
When thousands Thou hast left in night,
That I am here before Thy sight,
            For gifts an' grace,
A burning and a shining light
            To a' this place.

### III

What was I, or my generation,
That I should get sic[1] exaltation?
I, wha deserv'd most just damnation
   For broken laws,
Sax[2] thousand years ere my creation,
   Thro' Adam's cause?


### IV

When from my mither's womb I fell,
Thou might hae plung'd me deep in hell,
To gnash my gooms[3] and weep and wail
   In burning lakes,
Where damnèd devils roar and yell,
   Chain'd to their stakes.


### V

Yet I am here, a chosen sample,
To show Thy grace is great and ample;
I'm here, a pillar o' Thy temple,
   Strong as a rock,
A guide, a buckler, and example
   To a' Thy flock.


### VI

But yet, O Lord! confess I must,
At times I'm fash'd[4] wi' fleshly lust;
An' sometimes, too, in warldly trust,
   Vile self gets in;
But Thou remembers we are dust,
   Defil'd wi' sin.


\* \* \* \* \* \* \*

| | |
|---|---|
| 1. Sic.   Such. | 3. Gooms.   Gums. |
| 2. Sax.   Six. | 4. Fash'd.   Troubled. |

### IX

Maybe Thou lets this fleshly thorn
Buffet Thy servant e'en and morn,
Lest he owre⁵ proud and high should turn,
        That he's sae gifted;
If sae, Thy han' maun⁶ e'en be borne
        Until Thou lift it.


### X

Lord, bless Thy chosen in this place,
For here Thou hast a chosen race;
But God confound their stubborn face,
        An' blast their name,
Wha bring Thy elders to disgrace
        An' public shame.


### XI

Lord, mind Gau'n Hamilton's deserts!
He drinks, an' swears, an' plays at cartes,
Yet has sae mony takin arts
        Wi' great and sma',
Frae God's ain priest the people's hearts
        He steals awa.


### XII

And when we chasten'd him therefor,
Thou kens how he bred sic a splore,⁷
And set the warld in a roar
        O' laughin at us—
Curse Thou his basket and his store,
        Kail⁸ an' potatoes!

---

5. **Owre.**  Over, too.
6. **Maun.**  Must.
7. **Bred sic a splore.**  Raised such a
row.

8. **Kail.**  Cabbage in general or,
more specifically, colewort.

### XIII

Lord, hear my earnest cry and pray'r
Against that Presbyt'ry of Ayr!
Thy strong right hand, Lord, mak it bare
      Upo' their heads!
Lord, visit them, an' dinna[9] spare,
        For their misdeeds!

### XIV

O Lord, my God, that glib-tongu'd Aiken!
My vera heart and flesh are quakin,
To think how we stood sweatin, shakin,
      An' filled wi' dread,
While he, wi' hinging lip an' snakin,[10]
        Held up his head.

### XV

Lord, in Thy day o' vengeance try him!
Lord, visit them wha did employ him!
And pass not in Thy mercy by them,
      Nor hear their pray'r;
But for Thy people's sake destroy them,
      An' dinna spare!

### XVI

But, Lord, remember me and mine
Wi' mercies temporal and divine,
That I for grace an' gear[11] may shine,
      Excell'd by nane;
And a' the glory shall be Thine—
      Amen, Amen!

9. **Dinna.** Do not.
10. **Snakin.** Sneering.
11. **Gear.** Wealth.

# EPISTLE TO THE REV. JOHN McMATH

INCLOSING A COPY OF "HOLY WILLIE'S PRAYER," WHICH
HE HAD REQUESTED.  SEPT. 17, 1785.

[The Reverend Mr. McMath was a young "New Licht"
minister with whom Burns had some acquaintance. This
poem alludes to the prosecution of Gavin Hamilton ("Gaw'n,"
stanza v) which is also mentioned in "Holy Willie's Prayer,"
and is a defense of the part Burns himself took in the controversy. On the whole it is one of the best expressions of
the poet's contempt for hypocrisy and intolerance, while at
the same time it—taken with many passages in his letters—
demonstrates a sincere reverence for religion of a kindly and
charitable sort. Burns never included this epistle in his collected works; it was first printed long after his death in
Cromek's *Reliques of Robert Burns*, 1808.]

I

While at the stook¹ the shearers² cow'r
To shun the bitter blaudin³ show'r,
Or in gulravage rinnin scowr;⁴
      To pass the time,
To you I dedicate the hour
      In idle rhyme.

II

My musie, tir'd wi' mony a sonnet
On gown, an' ban',⁵ an' douse⁶ black bonnet,
Is grown right eerie⁷ now she's done it,
      Lest they should blame her,
An' rouse their holy thunder on it
      And anathém⁸ her.

III

I own 'twas rash, an' rather hardy,
That I, a simple country bardie,

1. **Stook.** Shock.
2. **Shearers.** Reapers.
3. **Blaudin.** Driving.
4. **Gulravage rinnin scowr.** Horse-play run swiftly
5. **Ban'.** Band (of a clergyman—a portion of the regular ministerial attire).
6. **Douse.** Sedate.
7. **Eerie.** Frightened.
8. **Anathém.** Curse.

Should meddle wi' a pack sae sturdy,
　　Wha, if they ken[9] me,
Can easy, wi' a single wordie,
　　　　Louse[10] hell upon me.

### IV

But I gae[11] mad at their grimaces,
Their sighin, cantin, grace-proud faces,
Their three-mile prayers, an' hauf-mile graces,
　　　　Their raxin[12] conscience,
Whase greed, revenge, an' pride disgraces
　　　　Waur nor[13] their nonsense.

### V

There's Gaw'n, misca'd[14] waur than a beast,
Wha has mair honor in his breast
Than mony scores as guid's[15] the priest
　　　　Wha sae abus'd him:
And may a bard no crack his jest
　　　　What way[16] they've used him?

### VI

See him, the poor man's friend in need,
The gentleman in word an' deed—
An' shall his fame an' honor bleed
　　　　By worthless skellums,[17]
An' not a muse erect her head
　　　　To cowe the blellums?[18]

### VII

O Pope, had I thy satire's darts
To gie[19] the rascals their deserts,
I'd rip their rotten, hollow hearts,
　　　　An' tell aloud
Their jugglin, hocus-pocus arts
　　　　To cheat the crowd.

9. **Ken.**　Know.
10. **Louse.**　Loose.
11. **Gae.**　Go.
12. **Raxin.**　Elastic.
13. **Waur nor.**　Worse than.
14. **Misca'd.**　Miscalled, abused.
15. **Guid's.**　Good as.
16. **What way.**　On the way.
17. **Skellums.**　Good-for-nothings.
18. **Blellums.**　Blusterers.
19. **Gie.**　Give.

### VIII

God knows, I'm no the thing I should be,
Nor am I even the thing I could be,
But twenty times I rather would be
   An atheist clean,
Then under gospel colors hid be,
   Just for a screen.

### IX

An honest man may like a glass,
An honest man may like a lass,
But mean revenge, an' malice fause[20]
   He'll still disdain,
An' then cry zeal for gospel laws,
   Like some we ken.

### X

They take religion in their mouth;
They talk o' mercy, grace, an' truth,
For what?—to gie their malice skouth[21]
   On some puir wight,
An' hunt him down, owre[22] right and ruth,
   To ruin streight.

### XI

All hail, Religion, maid divine!
Pardon a muse sae mean as mine,
Who in her rough imperfect line
   Thus daurs[23] to name thee;
To stigmatise false friends of thine
   Can ne'er defame thee.

### XII

Tho' blotch't and foul wi' mony a stain,
An' far unworthy of thy train,

20. **Fause.** False.
21. **Skouth.** Vent.
22. **Owre.** Against.
23. **Daurs.** Dares.

With trembling voice I tune my strain
      To join with those
Who boldly dare thy cause maintain
      In spite of foes:


### XIII

In spite o' crowds, in spite o' mobs,
In spite o' undermining jobs,
In spite o' dark banditti stabs
      At worth an' merit,
By scoundrels, even wi' holy robes,
      But hellish spirit.


### XIV

O Ayr! my dear, my native ground,
Within thy presbyterial bound
A candid liberal band is found
      Of public teachers,
As men, as Christians too, renown'd,
      An' manly preachers.


### XV

Sir, in that circle you are nam'd;
Sir, in that circle you are fam'd;
An' some, by whom your doctrine's blam'd
      (Which gies you honor),
Even, sir, by them your heart's esteem'd,
      An' winning manner.


### XVI

Pardon this freedom I have ta'en,
An' if impertinent I've been,
Impute it not, good sir, in ane
      Whase heart ne'er wrang'd ye,
But to his utmost would befriend
      Ought that belang'd ye.

## THE HOLY FAIR*

A robe of seeming truth and trust
    Hid crafty observation;
And secret hung, with poison'd crust,
    The dirk of defamation:
A mask that like the gorget show'd,
    Dye-varying on the pigeon;
And for a mantle large and broad,
    He wrapt him in *Religion*.
                HYPOCRISY A-LA-MODE.

[Dated "Autumn 1785" in the manuscript in Burns's own hand at Kilmarnock. This is probably the most important of Burns's satires of abuses in the name of religion. "Holy fair," says Burns's own note, "is a common phrase in the west of Scotland for a sacramental occasion." The event was evidently a sort of religious picnic. Of the preachers mentioned in this poem all but one (Smith) were of the "Auld Licht" party. Peebles (stanza xvi) published an attack on Burns after the latter's death, under the title *Burnomania*. The comments on Smith (stanzas xiv, xv) are intended to be complimentary, the meaning being that he is too sensible and reasonable to please such a crowd.]

I

Upon a simmer¹ Sunday morn,
    When Nature's face is fair,
I walkèd forth to view the corn,
    An' snuff the caller² air.
The rising sun, owre Galston* muirs,
    Wi' glorious light was glintin;
The hares were hirplin³ down the furs,⁴
    The lav'rocks⁵ they were chantin
        Fu' sweet that day.

II

As lightsomely I glowr'd⁶ abroad,
    To see a scene sae gay,
Three hizzies,⁷ early at the road,
    Cam skelpin⁸ up the way.

---

1. **Simmer.** Summer.
2. **Caller.** Fresh.
3. **Hirplin.** Limping.
4. **Furs.** Furrows.

5. **Lav'rocks.** Larks.
6. **Glowr'd.** Stared.
7. **Hizzies.** Hussies, young women.
8. **Skelpin.** Hurrying.

Twa had manteeles o' dolefu' black,
　　But ane wi' lyart[9] lining;
The third, that gaed[10] a wee a-back,
　　Was in the fashion shining
　　　　　Fu' gay that day.

### III

The twa appear'd like sisters twin,
　　In feature, form, an' claes;[11]
Their visage wither'd, lang an' thin,
　　An' sour as ony slaes:[12]
The third cam up, hap-stap-an'-lowp,[13]
　　As light as ony lambie,
An' wi' a curchie[14] low did stoop,
　　As soon as e'er she saw me,
　　　　　Fu' kind that day.

### IV

Wi' bonnet aff, quoth I, "Sweet lass,
　　I think ye seem to ken[15] me;
I'm sure I've seen that bonie face,
　　But yet I canna name ye."
Quo' she, an' laughin as she spak,
　　An' taks me by the han's,
"Ye, for my sake, hae gi'en the feck[16]
　　Of a' the Ten Comman's
　　　　　A screed[17] some day.

### V

"My name is Fun—your cronie dear,
　　The nearest friend ye hae;
An' this is Superstition here,
　　An' that's Hypocrisy.

9. **Lyart.** Gray.
10. **Gaed.** Went.
11. **Claes.** Clothes.
12. **Slaes.** Sloes.
13. **Hap-stap-an'-lowp.** Hop, step, and jump.
14. **Curchie.** Curtsey.
15. **Ken.** Know.
16. **Feck.** Greater part.
17. **Screed.** Rip.

I'm gaun[18] to Mauchline holy fair,
    To spend an hour in daffin:[19]
Gin[20] ye'll go there, yon runkl'd[21] pair,
    We will get famous laughin
        At them this day."

### VI

Quoth I, "With a' my heart I'll do't;
    I'll get my Sunday's sark[22] on,
An' meet you on the holy spot;
    Faith, we'se hae[23] fine remarkin!"
Then I gaed[24] hame at crowdie-[25]time,
    An' soon I made me ready;
For roads were clad, frae side to side,
    Wi' monie a wearie body,
        In droves that day.

### VII

Here farmers gash,[26] in ridin graith,[27]
    Gaed hoddin[28] by their cotters;
There swankies[29] young, in braw braid-claith,[30]
    Are springing owre the gutters.
The lasses, skelpin barefit,[31] thrang,[32]
    In silks an' scarlets glitter;
Wi' sweet-milk cheese, in monie a whang,[33]
    An' farls,[34] bak'd wi' butter,
        Fu' crump[35] that day.

### VIII

When by the plate we set our nose,
    Weel heapèd up wi' ha'pence,

18. **Gaun.** Going.
19. **Daffin.** Fun.
20. **Gin.** If.
21. **Runkl'd.** Wrinkled.
22. **Sark.** Shirt.
23. **We'se hae.** We shall have.
24. **Gaed.** Went.
25. **Crowdie.** Porridge.
26. **Gash.** Wise.
27. **Graith.** Array.
28. **Hoddin.** Jolting.
29. **Swankies.** Strapping fellows.
30. **Braw braid-claith.** Fine broadcloth.
31. **Skelpin barefit.** Hurrying barefoot.
32. **Thrang.** Crowded.
33. **Whang.** A large slice.
34. **Farls.** Thin oat-cakes.
35. **Fu' crump.** Full crisp.

A greedy glowr[36] black-bonnet* throws,
  An' we maun draw our tippence.[37]
Then in we go to see the show:
  On ev'ry side they're gath'rin;
Some carryin dails,[38] some chairs an' stools,
  An' some are busy bleth'rin[39]
        Right loud that day.


\* \* \* \* \* \* \*


X

Here some are thinkin on their sins,
  An' some upo' their claes;[40]
Ane curses feet that fyl'd[41] his shins,
  Anither sighs an' prays:
On this hand sits a chosen swatch,[42]
  Wi' screw'd-up, grace-proud faces;
On that a set o' chaps, at watch,
  Thrang[43] winkin on the lasses
        To chairs that day.


\* \* \* \* \* \* \*


XII

Now a' the congregation o'er
  Is silent expectation;
For Moodie speels[44] the holy door,
  Wi' tidings o' damnation.
Should Hornie,[45] as in ancient days,
  'Mang sons o' God present him,*
The vera sight o' Moodie's face
  To 's ain het hame[46] had sent him
        Wi' fright that day.

---

36. **Glowr.** Stare.
37. **Tippence.** Two-pence.
38. **Dails.** Deals, planks.
39. **Bleth'rin.** Talking nonsense.
40. **Claes.** Clothes.
41. **Fyl'd.** Defiled, dirtied.

42. **Swatch.** Sample.
43. **Thrang.** Busy.
44. **Speels.** Climbs.
45. **Hornie.** The devil.
46. **To 's ain het hame.** To his own hot home.

### XIII

Hear how he clears the points o' Faith
    Wi' rattlin an' thumpin!
Now meekly calm, now wild in wrath,
    He's stampin, an' he's jumpin!
His lengthen'd chin, his turned-up snout,
    His eldritch[47] squeel an' gestures,
O how they fire the heart devout,
    Like cantharidian plaisters[48]
            On sic[49] a day!

### XIV

But hark! the tent has chang'd its voice;
    There's peace an' rest nae langer;
For a' the real judges rise,
    They canna sit for anger.
Smith opens out his cauld harangues,
    On practice and on morals;
An' aff the godly pour in thrangs,
    To gie[50] the jars an' barrels
            A lift that day.

### XV

What signifies his barren shine,
    Of moral pow'rs an' reason?
His English style, an' gesture fine,
    Are a' clean out o' season.
Like Socrates or Antonine,*
    Or some auld pagan heathen,
The moral man he does define,
    But ne'er a word o' faith in
            That's right that day.

---

47. **Eldritch.** Unearthly.
48. **Cantharidian plaisters.** Blister-
    ing plasters.
49. **Sic.** Such.
50. **Gie.** Give.

### XVI

In guid time comes an antidote
 Against sic poison'd nostrum;
For Peebles, frae the water-fit,[51]
 Ascends the holy rostrum:
See, up he's got the word o' God,
 An' meek an' mim[52] has view'd it,
While Common-sense has taen[53] the road,
 An' aff, an' up the Cowgate*
  Fast, fast that day.

### XVII

Wee Miller niest[54] the guard relieves,
 An' orthodoxy raibles,[55]
Tho' in his heart he weel believes
 An' thinks it auld wives' fables:
But faith! the birkie[56] wants a manse,
 So cannilie he hums[57] them;
Altho' his carnal wit an' sense
 Like hafflins-wise[58] o'ercomes him
  At times that day.

### XVIII

Now butt an' ben[59] the change-house[60] fills,
 Wi' yill-caup[61] commentators;
Here's crying out for bakes an' gills,[62]
 An' there the pint-stowp[63] clatters;
While thick an' thrang, an' loud an' lang,
 Wi' logic and wi' Scripture,
They raise a din, that in the end
 Is like to breed a rupture
  O' wrath that day.

51. **Water-fit.** Water-foot, river's mouth.
52. **Mim.** Prim.
53. **Taen.** Taken.
54. **Niest.** Next.
55. **Raibles.** Gabbles.
56. **Birkie.** Conceited fellow.
57. **Cannilie he hums.** Prudently he tricks.
58. **Like hafflins-wise.** Almost half.
59. **Butt an' ben.** In rear and front.
60. **Change-house.** Tavern.
61. **Yill-caup.** Ale-cup.
62. **Bakes an' gills.** Biscuits and glasses of whiskey.
63. **Pint-stowp.** A two-quart measure (a Scottish pint equaled two English quarts).

### XIX

Leeze me on drink![64] it gies us mair
　Than either school or college;
It kindles wit, it waukens lear,[65]
　It pangs us fou[66] o' knowledge.
Be't whisky-gill or penny wheep,[67]
　Or ony stronger potion,
It never fails, on drinkin deep,
　To kittle[68] up our notion,
　　　　　By night or day.

### XX

The lads an' lasses, blythely bent
　To mind baith saul an' body,
Sit round the table, weel content,
　An' steer[69] about the toddy.
On this ane's dress, an' that ane's leuk,
　They're makin observations;
While some are cozie i' the neuk,[70]
　An' formin assignations
　　　　　To meet some day.

### XXI

But now the Lord's ain trumpet touts,
　Till a' the hills are rairin,[71]
And echoes back return the shouts;
　Black Russell is na spairin:
His piercin words, like Highlan' swords,
　Divide the joints an' marrow;
His talk o' Hell, whare devils dwell,
　Our vera "sauls does harrow"*
　　　　　Wi' fright that day!

---

64. **Leeze me on drink.** Dear to me
　　is drink.
65. **Waukens lear.** Wakens learning.
66. **Pangs us fou.** Crams us full.
67. **Penny wheep.** Small beer.
68. **Kittle.** Tickle.
69. **Steer.** Stir.
70. **Neuk.** Corner.
71. **Rairin.** Roaring.

### XXII

A vast, unbottom'd, boundless pit,
    Fill'd fou o' lowin brunstane,[72]
Wha's ragin flame, an' scorchin heat,
    Wad melt the hardest whun-stane![73]
The half asleep start up wi' fear,
    An' think they hear it roarin;
When presently it does appear,
    'Twas but some neebor snorin
        Asleep that day.

### XXIII

'Twad be owre lang a tale to tell,
    How monie stories past;
An' how they crouded to the yill,[74]
    When they were a' dismist;
How drink gaed round, in cogs and caups,[75]
    Amang the furms[76] an' benches;
An' cheese an' bread, frae women's laps,
    Was dealt about in lunches,[77]
        An' dawds[78] that day.

### XXIV

In comes a gawsie, gash[79] guidwife,
    An' sits down by the fire,
Syne[80] draws her kebbuck[81] an' her knife;
    The lasses they are shyer.
The auld guidmen, about the grace,
    Frae side to side they bother,
Till some ane by his bonnet lays,
    An' gies them't,[82] like a tether,
        Fu' lang that day.*

72. **Lowin brunstane.** Burning brimstone.
73. **Whun-stane.** Granite.
74. **Yill.** Ale.
75. **Cogs and caups.** Wooden drinking vessels.
76. **Furms.** Wooden forms.
77. **Lunches.** Full portions.
78. **Dawds.** Lumps.
79. **Gawsie, gash.** Buxom, sage.
80. **Syne.** Then.
81. **Kebbuck.** Cheese.
82. **Gies them't.** Gives it to them.

## XXV

Waesucks![83] for him that gets nae lass,
    Or lasses that hae naething!
Sma' need has he to say a grace,
    Or melvie[84] his braw claithing!
O wives, be mindfu', ance yoursel,
    How bonie lads ye wanted;
An' dinna for a kebbuck-heel[85]
    Let lasses be affronted
        On sic a day!

## XXVI

Now Clinkumbell,[86] wi' rattlin tow,[87]
    Begins to jow an' croon;[88]
Some swagger hame the best they dow,[89]
    Some wait the afternoon.
At slaps[90] the billies[91] halt a blink,[92]
    Till lasses strip their shoon:[93]
Wi' faith an' hope, an' love an' drink,
    They're a' in famous tune
        For crack[94] that day.

## XXVII

How monie hearts this day converts
    O' sinners and o' lasses!
Their hearts o' stane, gin[95] night, are gane
    As saft as ony flesh is.
There's some are fou o' love divine;
    There's some are fou o' brandy;
An' monie jobs that day begin,
    May end in houghmagandie[96]
        Some ither day.

83. **Waesucks!** Alas!
84. **Melvie.** Soil.
85. **Kebbuck-heel.**    Remnant of cheese.
86. **Clinkumbell.** The bell-ringer.
87. **Tow.** Rope.
88. **Jow an' croon.** Swing and ring (the bell).
89. **Dow.** Can.
90. **Slaps.** Openings in fences.
91. **Billies.** Young fellows.
92. **Blink.** Moment.
93. **Shoon.** Shoes.
94. **Crack.** Talk.
95. **Gin.** By.
96. **Houghmagandie.** Disgrace.

# HALLOWEEN

"Yes! let the rich deride, the proud disdain,
The simple pleasures of the lowly train;
To me more dear, congenial to my heart,
One native charm, than all the gloss of art."—GOLDSMITH.

[Written in the autumn of 1785. The stanzaic form is like
that of "The Holy Fair" (see page 307). Burns wrote a set of
notes explaining the customs portrayed, which will be found,
as far as needed, on pages 308-310.]

### I

Upon that night, when fairies light
   On Cassilis Downans* dance,
Or owre the lays,[1] in splendid blaze,
   On sprightly coursers prance;
Or for Colean the rout is taen,
   Beneath the moon's pale beams;
There, up the Cove,* to stray an' rove,
   Amang the rocks an' streams
      To sport that night.

### II

Amang the bonie, winding banks,
   Where Doon rins, wimplin,[2] clear,
Where Bruce ance rul'd the martial ranks,
   An' shook his Carrick spear,*
Some merry, friendly, countra folks
   Together did convene,
To burn their nits,[3] an' pou their stocks,[4]
   An' haud[5] their Halloween
      Fu' blythe that night.

### III

The lasses feat,[6] an' cleanly neat,
   Mair braw[7] than when they're fine;
Their faces blythe fu' sweetly kythe[8]
   Hearts leal,[9] an' warm, an' kin':

1. **Lays.** Pastures.
2. **Wimplin.** Winding.
3. **Nits.** Nuts.
4. **Pou their stocks.** Pull their stalks.
5. **Haud.** Hold, keep.
6. **Feat.** Trim.
7. **Mair braw.** More handsome.
8. **Kythe.** Show.
9. **Leal.** Loyal.

The lads sae trig,[10] wi' wooer-babs[11]
    Weel-knotted on their garten,[12]
Some unco blate,[13] an' some wi' gabs[14]
Gar[15] lasses' hearts gang startin
            Whyles[16] fast at night.

### IV

Then, first an' foremost, thro' the kail,[17]
    Their stocks maun[18] a' be sought ance:*
They steek their een,[19] an' grape an' wale[20]
    For muckle anes,[21] an' straught[22] anes.
Poor hav'rel[23] Will fell aff the drift,[24]
    An' wandered thro' the bow-kail,[25]
An' pou't,[26] for want o' better shift,[27]
    A runt,[28] was like a sow-tail,
            Sae bow't[29] that night.

### V

Then, straught or crooked, yird[30] or nane,
    They roar an' cry a' throu'ther;[31]
The vera wee-things, toddlin, rin,[32]
    Wi' stocks out-owre their shouther;[33]
An' gif[34] the custock's[35] sweet or sour,
    Wi' joctelegs[36] they taste them;
Syne[37] coziely, aboon[38] the door,
    Wi' cannie[39] care, they've plac'd them
            To lie that night.

\* \* \* \* \* \* \*

10. **Trig.** Neat.
11. **Wooer-babs.** Love-krots.
12. **Garten.** Garter.
13. **Unco blate.** Very shy.
14. **Gabs.** Chatter.
15. **Gar.** Make.
16. **Whyles.** Sometimes.
17. **Kail.** Colewort.
18. **Maun.** Must.
19. **Steek their een.** Close their eyes.
20. **Grape an' wale.** Grope and choose.
21. **Muckle anes.** Big ones.
22. **Straught.** Straight.
23. **Hav'rel.** Foolish.
24. **Fell aff the drift.** Lost the way.
25. **Bow-kail.** Cabbage.
26. **Pou't.** Pulled.
27. **Shift.** Choice.
28. **Runt.** Stalk.
29. **Bow't.** Bent.
30. **Yird.** With earth attached to the root.
31. **A' throu'ther.** All in confusion.
32. **Rin.** Run.
33. **Shouther.** Shoulder.
34. **Gif.** If.
35. **Custock.** Stalk.
36. **Joctelegs.** Clasp-knives.
37. **Syne.** Then.
38. **Aboon.** Above.
39. **Cannie.** Prudent.

## VII

The auld guidwife's weel-hoordet nits[40]
 Are round an' round divided,*
An' monie lads' an' lasses' fates
 Are there that night decided:
Some kindle, couthie,[41] side by side,
 An' burn thegither trimly;
Some start awa wi' saucy pride,
 An' jump out-owre the chimlie[42]
  Fu' high that night.

## VIII

Jean slips in twa wi' tentie e'e;[43]
 Wha 'twas, she wadna tell;
But this is *Jock*, an' this is *me*,
 She says in to hersel:
He bleez'd[44] owre her, an' she owre him,
 As they wad never mair part,
Till fuff! he started up the lum,[45]
 An' Jean had e'en a sair[46] heart
  To see't that night.

## IX

Poor Willie, wi' his bow-kail runt,[47]
 Was brunt[48] wi' primsie[49] Mallie;
An' Mary, nae doubt, took the drunt,[50]
 To be compar'd to Willie:
Mall's nit lap[51] out, wi' pridefu' fling,
 An' her ain fit,[52] it brunt it;
While Willie lap, and swoor by jing,
 'Twas just the way he wanted
  To be that night.

40. **Weel-hoordet nits.** Well-hoarded nuts.
41. **Couthie.** Comfortably.
42. **Out-owre the chimlie.** Out of the chimney.
43. **Tentie e'e.** Heedful eye.
44. **Bleez'd.** Blazed.
45. **Lum.** Chimney.
46. **Sair.** Sore.
47. **Bow-kail runt.** Cabbage stalk.
48. **Brunt.** Burned.
49. **Primsie.** Prim.
50. **Drunt.** A fit of sullenness.
51. **Lap.** Leaped.
52. **Fit.** Foot.

X

Nell had the fause-house* in her min',
  She pits[53] hersel an' Rob in;
In loving bleeze they sweetly join,
  Till white in ase[54] they're sobbin:
Nell's heart was dancin at the view;
  She whisper'd Rob to leuk[55] for't:
Rob, stownlins, prie'd[56] her bonie mou,[57]
  Fu' cozie in the neuk[58] for't,
        Unseen that night.


XI

But Merran sat behint their backs,
  Her thoughts on Andrew Bell;
She lea'es[59] them gashin at their cracks,[60]
  An' slips out by hersel:
She thro' the yard the nearest taks,
  An' to the kiln she goes then,
An' darklins[61] grapit[62] for the bauks,[63]
  And in the blue-clue throws then,*
        Right fear't that night.


XII

An' ay she win't,[64] an' ay she swat[65]—
  I wat[66] she made nae jaukin;[67]
Till something held within the pat,[68]
  Guid Lord! but she was quakin![69]
But whether 'twas the Deil himsel,
  Or whether 'twas a bauk-en',[70]

---

53. **Pits.** Puts.
54. **Ase.** Ashes.
55. **Leuk.** Look.
56. **Stownlins, prie'd.** By stealth tasted.
57. **Mou.** Mouth.
58. **Neuk.** Corner.
59. **Lea'es.** Leaves.
60. **Gashin at their cracks.** Gabbling at their chat.
61. **Darklins.** In the dark.
62. **Grapit.** Groped.
63. **Bauks.** Beams.
64. **Win't.** Wound.
65. **Swat.** Sweated.
66. **Wat.** Know.
67. **Jaukin.** Trifling.
68. **Pat.** Kiln-pot.
69. **Quakin.** Quaking.
70. **Bauk-en'.** Beam-end.

Or whether it was Andrew Bell,
  She did na wait on talkin
    To spier[71] that night.


### XIII

Wee Jenny to her graunie[72] says,
  "Will ye go wi' me, graunie?
I'll eat the apple at the glass,*
  I gat frae uncle Johnie."
She fuff't[73] her pipe wi' sic a lunt,[74]
  In wrath she was sae vap'rin,
She notic't na an aizle brunt[75]
  Her braw new worset[76] apron
    Out thro' that night.


### XIV

"Ye little skelpie-limmer's face![77]
  I daur[78] you try sic sportin,
As seek the foul thief[79] ony place,
  For him to spae[80] your fortune:
Nae doubt but ye may get a sight!
  Great cause ye hae to fear it;
For monie a ane has gotten a fright,
  An' liv'd an' di'd deleeret,[81]
    On sic a night.


### XV

"Ae hairst[82] afore the Sherra-moor,[83]
  I mind't as weel's yestreen,[84]
I was a gilpey[85] then, I'm sure
  I was na past fyfteen:

71. **Spier.** Ask.
72. **Graunie.** Grandmother.
73. **Fuff't.** Puffed.
74. **Sic a lunt.** Such a smoke.
75. **Aizle brunt.** Cinder burnt.
76. **Worset.** Worsted.
77. **Skelpie-limmer's face.** "A technical term in female scolding" (R. B.)—you little hussy!
78. **Daur.** Dare.
79. **Foul thief.** The devil.
80. **Spae.** Foretell.
81. **Deleeret.** Delirious.
82. **Ae hairst.** One harvest.
83. **Sherra-moor.** A battle of the Jacobite rebellion of 1715.
84. **Yestreen.** Last night.
85. **Gilpey.** Young girl.

The simmer had been cauld an' wat,
    An' stuff was unco[86] green;
An' ay a rantin kirn[87] we gat,
    An' just on Halloween
        It fell that night.

### XVI

"Our stibble-rig[88] was Rab M'Graen,
    A clever, sturdy fallow;
      *   *   *   *   *   *   *

He gat hemp-seed,* I mind it weel,
    An' he made unco light o't;
But monie a day was by himsel,[89]
    He was sae sairly frighted
        That vera night."

### XVII

Then up gat fechtin[90] Jamie Fleck,
    An' he swoor by his conscience,
That he could saw[91] hemp-seed a peck;
    For it was a' but nonsense:
The auld guidman raught[92] down the pock,[93]
    An' out a handfu' gied him;
Syne[94] bad him slip frae 'mang the folk,
    Sometime when nae ane see'd him,
        An' try't that night.

### XVIII

He marches thro' amang the stacks,
    Tho' he was something sturtin;[95]
The graip[96] he for a harrow taks,
    An' haurls[97] at his curpin;[98]

---

86. **Unco.** Very.
87. **Rantin kirn.** Rollicking harvest-home.
88. **Stibble-rig.** Chief harvester.
89. **By himsel.** Beside himself.
90. **Fechtin.** Fighting.
91. **Saw.** Sow.

92. **Raught.** Reached.
93. **Pock.** Bag.
94. **Syne.** Then.
95. **Sturtin.** Frightened.
96. **Graip.** Dung-fork.
97. **Haurls.** Trails.
98. **Curpin.** Back (crupper).

And ev'ry now an' then, he says,
 "Hemp-seed, I saw thee,
An' her that is to be my lass,
 Come after me, an' draw thee
  As fast this night."

## XIX

He whistl'd up Lord Lenox' March,
 To keep his courage cheery;
Altho' his hair began to arch,
 He was sae fley'd an' eerie;[99]
Till presently he hears a squeak,
 An' then a grane an' gruntle;[100]
He by his shouther[101] gae a keek,[102]
 An' tumbl'd wi' a wintle[103]
  Out-owre that night.

## XX

He roar'd a horrid murder-shout,
 In dreadfu' desperation!
An' young an' auld come rinnin out,
 An' hear the sad narration:
He swoor 'twas hilchin[104] Jean M'Craw,
 Or crouchie[105] Merran Humphie,
Till stop! she trotted thro' them a';
 An' wha was it but Grumphie[106]
  Asteer[107] that night?

## XXI

Meg fain wad to the barn gaen,[108]
 To winn[109] three wechts[110] o' naething;*
But for to meet the Deil her lane,[111]
 She pat[112] but little faith in:

99. **Fley'd an' eerie.** Scared and awe-struck.
100. **Grane an' gruntle.** Groan and grunt.
101. **Shouther.** Shoulder.
102. **Gae a keek.** Gave a peep.
103. **Wintle.** Roll.
104. **Hilchin.** Halting.
105. **Crouchie.** Hunchbacked.
106. **Grumphie.** The sow.
107. **Asteer.** Astir.
108. **Gaen.** Have gone.
109. **Winn.** Winnow.
110. **Wechts.** Sieve-fulls.
111. **Her lane.** Alone.
112. **Pat.** Put.

She gies the herd[113] a pickle[114] nits,
　　An' twa red-cheekit apples,
To watch, while for the barn she sets,[115]
　　In hopes to see Tam Kipples
　　　　That vera night.

### XXII

She turns the key wi' cannie thraw,[116]
　　An' owre the threshold ventures;
But first on Sawnie gies a ca',[117]
　　Syne[118] bauldly in she enters:
A ratton[119] rattl'd up the wa',
　　An' she cry'd, Lord preserve her!
An' ran thro' midden-hole[120] an a',
　　An' pray'd wi' zeal an' fervor,
　　　　Fu' fast that night.

### XXIII

They hoy't[121] out Will, wi' sair advice;
　　They hecht[122] him some fine braw ane;
It chanc'd the stack he faddom't[123] thrice*
　　Was timmer-propt for thrawin:[124]
He taks a swirlie,[125] auld moss-oak
　　For some black grousome carlin;[126]
An' loot a winze,[127] an' drew a stroke,
　　Till skin in blypes[128] cam haurlin[129]
　　　　Aff's nieves[130] that night.

### XXIV

A wanton widow Leezie was,
　　As cantie[131] as a kittlin;[132]

113. **Herd.** Herd-boy.
114. **Pickle.** A few.
115. **Sets.** Sets off.
116. **Cannie thraw.** Careful twist.
117. **Gies a ca'.** Gives a call.
118. **Syne.** Then.
119. **Ratton.** Rat.
120. **Midden-hole.** Dung-hill gutter.
121. **Hoy't.** Urged.
122. **Hecht.** Promised.
123. **Faddom't.** Fathomed, measured.
124. **Timmer-propt for thrawin.** Timber-propped to prevent its leaning over.
125. **Swirlie.** Twisted.
126. **Carlin.** Old woman.
127. **Loot a winze.** Uttered a curse.
128. **Blypes.** Shreds.
129. **Haurlin.** Peeling.
130. **Aff's nieves.** Off his fists.
131. **Cantie.** Lively.
132. **Kittlin.** Kitten.

But och! that night, amang the shaws,[133]
    She gat a fearfu' settlin!
She thro' the whins,[134] an' by the cairn,
    An' owre the hill gaed scrievin;[135]
Whare three lairds' lands met at a burn,*
    To dip her left sark[136] sleeve in,
        Was bent that night.


XXV

Whyles[137] owre a linn[138] the burnie[139] plays,
    As thro' the glen it wimpl't;[140]
Whyles round a rocky scaur[141] it strays,
    Whyles in a wiel[142] it dimpl't;
Whyles glitter'd to the nightly rays,
    Wi' bickerin, dancin dazzle;
Whyles cookit[143] underneath the braes[144]
    Below the spreading hazle,
        Unseen that night.


XXVI

Amang the brachens[145] on the brae,
    Between her an' the moon,
The Deil, or else an outler quey,[146]
    Gat up an' gae a croon:[147]
Poor Leezie's heart maist lap the hool;[148]
    Near lav'rock-[149] height she jumpit,
But mist a fit,[150] an' in the pool
    Out-owre the lugs[151] she plumpit,
        Wi' a plunge that night.

133. **Shaws.** Woods.
134. **Whins.** Furze.
135. **Gaed scrievin.** Went hurrying.
136. **Sark.** Shirt.
137. **Whyles.** Sometimes.
138. **Linn.** Waterfall.
139. **Burnie.** Brooklet.
140. **Wimpl't.** Wound.
141. **Scaur.** Cliff.
142. **Wiel.** Whirlpool.
143. **Cookit.** Hid.
144. **Braes.** Hillsides.
145. **Brachens.** Ferns.
146. **Outler quey.** Unhoused heifer.
147. **Croon.** Moan, low.
148. **Lap the hool.** Leaped out of its covering.
149. **Lav'rock.** Lark.
150. **Fit.** Foot.
151. **Lugs.** Ears.

### XXVII

In order, on the clean hearth-stane,
　The luggies[152] three are ranged,*
And ev'ry time great care is taen
　To see them duly changed:
Auld uncle John, wha wedlock's joys
　Sin' Mar's-year[153] did desire,
Because he gat the toom[154] dish thrice,
　He heav'd them on the fire,
　　　　In wrath that night.

### XXVIII

Wi' merry sangs, an' friendly cracks,
　I wat they did na weary;
And unco[155] tales, an' funnie jokes—
　Their sports were cheap an' cheery:
Till butter'd sow'ns,* wi' fragrant lunt,[156]
　Set a' their gabs a-steerin;[157]
Syne,[158] wi' a social glass o' strunt,[159]
　They parted aff careerin
　　　　Fu' blythe that night.


## TO A MOUSE

ON TURNING HER UP IN HER NEST WITH THE PLOUGH,
NOVEMBER, 1785

[Gilbert Burns testified that these verses were composed
"while the author was holding the plough." Long years after,
a laborer who had worked for Burns declared that he remembered the "turning up" of the mouse and had started
after it to kill it, till reproved by Burns.]

### I

Wee, sleekit,[1] cowrin, tim'rous beastie,
O, what a panic's in thy breastie!

152. **Luggies.** Wooden dishes.
153. **Mar's-year.** The rebellion of 1715.
154. **Toom.** Empty.
155. **Unco.** Strange.
156. **Lunt.** Steam.
157. **Gabs a-steerin.** Tongues wagging.
158. **Syne.** Then.
159. **Strunt.** Liquor.
1. **Sleekit.** Sleek.

Thou need na start awa sae hasty,
　　　　Wi' bickering brattle![2]
I wad be laith[3] to rin an' chase thee,
　　　　Wi' murd'ring pattle![4]


II

I'm truly sorry man's dominion
Has broken Nature's social union,
An' justifies that ill opinion
　　　　Which makes thee startle
At me, thy poor, earth-born companion,
　　　　An' fellow-mortal!


III

I doubt na, whyles,[5] but thou may thieve;
What then? poor beastie, thou maun[6] live!
A daimen-icker in a thrave[7]
　　　　'S a sma' request;
I'll get a blessin wi' the lave,[8]
　　　　An' never miss't!


IV

Thy wee-bit housie, too, in ruin!
It's silly wa's[9] the win's are strewin!
An' naething, now, to big[10] a new ane,
　　　　O' foggage[11] green!
An' bleak December's winds ensuin,
　　　　Baith snell[12] an' keen!


2. **Bickering brattle.** Hurrying scamper.
3. **Laith.** Loath.
4. **Pattle.** Plow-staff.
5. **Whyles.** Sometimes.
6. **Maun.** Must.
7. **Daimen-icker in a thrave.** An occasional ear of grain in 24 sheaves.
8. **Lave.** Rest, remainder.
9. **Silly wa's.** Frail walls.
10. **Big.** Build.
11. **Foggage.** Rank grass.
12. **Baith snell.** Both bitter.

V

Thou saw the fields laid bare an' waste,
An' weary winter comin fast,
An' cozie here, beneath the blast,
    Thou thought to dwell,
Till crash! the cruel coulter[13] past
    Out thro' thy cell.


VI

That wee-bit heap o' leaves an' stibble[14]
Has cost thee monie a weary nibble!
Now thou's turn'd out, for a' thy trouble,
    But[15] house or hald,[16]
To thole[17] the winter's sleety dribble,[18]
    An' cranreuch[19] cauld!


VII

But, Mousie, thou art no thy lane,[20]
In proving foresight may be vain:
The best-laid schemes o' mice an' men
    Gang aft agley,[21]
An' lea'e[22] us nought but grief an' pain,
    For promis'd joy.


VIII

Still thou art blest, compar'd wi' me!
The present only toucheth thee:
But och! I backward cast my e'e[23]
    On prospects drear!
An' forward, tho' I canna see,
    I guess an' fear!

13. **Coulter.** Plowshare.
14. **Stibble.** Stubble.
15. **But.** Without.
16. **Hald.** Holding, possessions.
17. **Thole.** Endure.
18. **Dribble.** Drizzle.
19. **Cranreuch.** Hoar-frost.
20. **No thy lane.** Not alone.
21. **Gang aft agley.** Go often amiss.
22. **Lea'e.** Leave.
23. **E'e.** Eye.

## THE JOLLY BEGGARS—A CANTATA

[In spite of the high estimate of this work which has pre-
vailed among critics, Burns never included it with his published poems. In 1799, three years after his death, it first
appeared in print, at Glasgow. It was written, however,
toward the end of 1785 and was known to a number of
Burns's friends.

The story is that, as the poet and two companions, John
Richmond and James Smith (see page 136), were passing
"Poosie-Nansie's" ale-house in Mauchline one night, they
heard sounds of revelry that tempted them to investigate.
Within they found a picturesque group of vagabonds whose
appearance and actions suggested this "puissant and splendid
production," as Matthew Arnold called it. The principal
characters are a crippled soldier and a woman who journeys
with him about the country, begging; a "Merry-Andrew," or
wandering clown or juggler; a woman pickpocket who had
been a Highland beggar's companion; a little itinerant fiddler,
a tinker, and a ballad-maker. Each of these sings a song
(the "Bard" two songs), and the "recitativos" explain the
action or the scene between songs.

Some commentators have identified Burns himself with the
"Bard" because that character mentions or alludes to events
in his life which closely resemble events in Burns's life, and
because his songs express very well the views of "Burns the
rebel." This identification should not be taken too seriously,
however; it is very natural for a poet to apply his own ex-
periences or his own ideas to imagined characters.

Two of the songs should be compared with later songs in
which Burns used the same refrains—"Whistle owre the lave
o't" (compare page 205) and "For a' that, an' a' that" (compare page 227).]

### Recitativo

#### I

When lyart[1] leaves bestrow the yird,[2]
Or, wavering like the bauckie-bird,[3]
   Bedim cauld Boreas' blast;
When hailstanes drive wi' bitter skyte,[4]
And infant frosts begin to bite,
   In hoary cranreuch[5] drest;

---

1. **Lyart.** Faded.
2. **Yird.** Earth.
3. **Bauckie-bird.** Bat.

4. **Skyte.** Dash.
5. **Cranreuch.** Hoar-frost.

Ae[6] night at e'en a merry core
  O' randie, gangrel[7] bodies,
In Poosie-Nansie's* held the splore,[8]
  To drink their orra duddies:[9]
    Wi' quaffing and laughing
      They ranted an' they sang,
    Wi' jumping an' thumping
      The vera girdle[10] rang.

II

First, niest[11] the fire, in auld red rags,  ·
Ane sat, weel brac'd wi' mealy bags,
  And knapsack a' in order;
His doxy[12] lay within his arm;
Wi' usquebae[13] an' blankets warm
  She blinket on her sodger;
An' ay he gies the tozie[14] drab
  The tither skelpin[15] kiss,
While she held up her greedy gab,[16]
  Just like an aumous[17] dish;
    Ilk[18] smack still did crack still,
      Just like a cadger's[19] whip;
    Then staggering an' swaggering
      He roar'd this ditty up—

*Air*
*Tune*—"Soldier's Joy."

I

I am a son of Mars who have been in many wars,
  And show my cuts and scars wherever I come;
This here was for a wench, and that other in a trench,
  When welcoming the French at the sound of the drum.
Lal de daudle, etc.

6. **Ae.** One.
7. **Randie, gangrel.** Rowdy, vagrant.
8. **Splore.** Carousal.
9. **Orra duddies.** Extra rags.
10. **Girdle.** Griddle.
11. **Niest.** Next.
12. **Doxy.** Sweetheart.
13. **Usquebae.** Whisky.
14. **Tozie.** Tipsy.
15. **Tither skelpin.** Other smacking.
16. **Gab.** Mouth.
17. **Aumous.** Alms.
18. **Ilk.** Each.
19. **Cadger.** Peddler.

### II

My prenticeship I past where my leader breath'd his last,
    When the bloody die was cast on the heights of
        Abrám :*
And I servèd out my trade when the gallant game was
      play'd,
    And the Moro* low was laid at the sound of the drum.

### III

I lastly was with Curtis* among the floating batt'ries,
    And there I left for witness an arm and a limb;
Yet let my country need me, with Elliot* to head me,
    I'd clatter on my stumps at the sound of the drum.

### IV

And now tho' I must beg, with a wooden arm and leg,
    And many a tatter'd rag hanging over my bum,
I'm as happy with my wallet, my bottle and my callet,[20]
    As when I used in scarlet to follow a drum.

### V

What tho', with hoary locks, I must stand the winter
    shocks,
    Beneath the woods and rocks oftentimes for a home,
When the tother bag I sell, and the tother bottle tell,
    I could meet a troop of hell, at the sound of a drum.

### *Recitativo*

He ended; and the kebars sheuk,[21]
    Aboon[22] the chorus roar;
While frightened rattons[23] backward leuk,
    An' seek the benmost bore;[24]

20. **Callet.** Sweetheart.
21. **Kebars sheuk.** Rafters shook.
22. **Aboon.** Above.
23. **Rattons.** Rats.
24. **Benmost bore.** Inmost hole.

A fairy fiddler frae the neuk,[25]
   He skirl'd[26] out, encore!
But up arose the martial chuck,[27]
   An' laid the loud uproar.

[After the song of "the martial chuck," the narrative proceeds as follows:]

### *Recitativo*

Poor Merry-Andrew, in the neuk,
   Sat guzzling wi' a tinkler-hizzie,[28]
They mind't na wha the chorus teuk,[29]
   Between themselves they were sae busy:
At length, wi' drink an' courting dizzy,
   He stoiter'd[30] up an' made a face;
Then turn'd an' laid a smack on Grizzie,
   Syne[31] tun'd his pipes wi' grave grimace.

### *Air*
#### *Tune—"Auld Sir Symon."*

**I**

Sir Wisdom's a fool when he's fou;[32]
   Sir Knave is a fool in a session;[33]
He's there but a prentice I trow,
   But I am a fool by profession.

**II**

My grannie she bought me a beuk,
   An' I held awa[34] to the school;
I fear I my talent misteuk,
   But what will ye hae of a fool?

**III**

For drink I would venture my neck;
   A hizzie's the half of my craft;
But what could ye other expect
   Of ane that's avowedly daft?

\* \* \* \* \* \* \*

25. **Neuk.** Nook, corner.
26. **Skirl'd.** Shrieked.
27. **Martial chuck.** Soldier's darling.
28. **Tinkler-hizzie.** Tinker wench.
29. **Teuk.** Took.
30. **Stoiter'd.** Staggered.
31. **Syne.** Then.
32. **Fou.** Drunk (full).
33. **Session.** Court.
34. **Held awa.** Went away.

### V

Poor Andrew that tumbles for sport,
  Let naebody name wi' a jeer;
There's even, I'm tauld, i' the Court
  A tumbler ca'd the Premier.

### VI

Observ'd ye yon reverend lad
  Mak faces to tickle the mob?
He rails at our mountebank squad—
  It's rivalship just i' the job!

### VII

And now my conclusion I'll tell,
  For faith! I'm confoundedly dry:
The chiel[35] that's a fool for himsel,
  Guid Lord! he's far dafter than I.

*Recitativo*

Then niest[36] outspak a raucle carlin,[37]
Wha kent[38] fu' weel to cleek the sterlin,[39]
For monie a pursie she had hookèd,[40]
An' had in monie a well been doukèd.[41]
Her love had been a Highland laddie,
But weary fa'[42] the waefu' woodie![43]
Wi' sighs and sobs she thus began
To wail her braw[44] John Highlandman:

*Air*

*Tune*—"O, an ye were dead, Guidman."

### I

A Highland lad my love was born,
The Lalland[45] laws he held in scorn,
But he still was faithfu' to his clan,
My gallant, braw John Highlandman.

35. **Chiel.** Fellow.
36. **Niest.** Next.
37. **Raucle carlin.** Rough old woman.
38. **Kent.** Knew.
39. **Cleek the sterlin.** Snatch the money.
40. **Hookèd.** Caught, stolen.
41. **Doukèd.** Ducked.
42. **Weary fa'.** Woe betide.
43. **Woodie.** Gallows rope.
44. **Braw.** Fine.
45. **Lalland.** Lowland.

*Chorus*

Sing hey my braw John Highlandman!
Sing ho my braw John Highlandman!
There's not a lad in a' the lan'
Was match for my John Highlandman.


II

With his philibeg[46] an' tartan plaid,
An' guid claymore[47] down by his side,
The ladies' hearts he did trepan,
My gallant, braw John Highlandman.
          Sing hey, etc.


III

We rangèd a' from Tweed to Spey,*
An' liv'd like lords an' ladies gay,
For a Lalland face he fearèd none,
My gallant, braw John Highlandman.
          Sing hey, etc.


IV

They banish'd him beyond the sea,
But ere the bud was on the tree,
Adown my cheeks the pearls ran,
Embracing my John Highlandman.
          Sing hey, etc.


V

But, och! they catch'd him at the last,
And bound him in a dungeon fast.
My curse upon them every one—
They've hang'd my braw John Highlandman!
          Sing hey, etc.

46. **Philibeg.** Kilt.          47. **Claymore.**  Two-handed sword.

### VI

And now a widow I must mourn
The pleasures that will ne'er return;
No comfort but a hearty can,
When I think on John Highlandman.
   Sing hey, etc.


## Recitativo

### I

A pigmy scraper wi' his fiddle,
Wha us'd at trystes[48] an' fairs to driddle,[49]
Her strappin limb and gawsie[50] middle
  (He reach'd nae higher)
Had hol'd his heartie like a riddle,[51]
  An' blawn't[52] on fire.


### II

Wi' hand on hainch,[53] and upward e'e,[54]
He croon'd his gamut, one, two, three,
Then in an *arioso** key,
  The wee Apollo*
Set off wi' *allegretto* glee
  His *giga* solo.


## Air
Tune—"Whistle owre the lave o't."

### I

Let me ryke[55] up to dight[56] that tear,
An' go wi' me an' be my dear,
An' then your every care an' fear
  May whistle owre the lave[57] o't.

---

48. **Trystes.** Fairs, or cattle markets.
49. **Driddle.** Toddle.
50. **Gawsie.** Buxom.
51. **Hol'd . . like a riddle.** Perforated like a sieve.
52. **Blawn't.** Blown it.
53. **Hainch.** Hip (haunch).
54. **E'e.** Eye.
55. **Ryke.** Reach.
56. **Dight.** Wipe.
57. **Lave.** Rest.

*Chorus*

I am a fiddler to my trade,
An' a' the tunes that e'er I played,
The sweetest still to wife or maid
    Was Whistle owre the lave o't.

II

At kirns[58] an' weddins we'se[59] be there,
An' O, sae nicely's we will fare!
We'll bowse about till Daddie Care
    Sing Whistle owre the lave o't.
                    I am, etc.

III

Sae merrily's the banes we'll pyke,[60]
An' sun oursels about the dyke;
An' at our leisure, when ye like,
    We'll whistle owre the lave o't.
                    I am, etc.

IV

But bless me wi' your heav'n o' charms,
An' while I kittle[61] hair on thairms,[62]
Hunger, cauld, an' sic[63] harms
    May whistle owre the lave o't.
                    I am, etc.

*Recitativo*

I

Her charms had struck a sturdy caird,[64]
    As weel as poor gut-scraper;
He taks the fiddler by the beard,
    An' draws a roosty[65] rapier;
He swoor by a' was swearing worth,
    To speet[66] him like a pliver,[67]
Unless he would from that time forth
    Relinquish her for ever.

58. **Kirns.** Harvest-homes.
59. **We'se.** We shall.
60. **Pyke.** Pick.
61. **Kittle.** Tickle.
62. **Thairms.** Cat-gut.
63. **Sic.** Such.
64. **Caird.** Tinker.
65. **Roosty.** Rusty.
66. **Speet.** Spit.
67. **Pliver.** Plover.

### II

Wi' ghastly e'e, poor tweedle-dee
  Upon his hunkers[68] bended,
An' pray'd for grace wi' ruefu' face,
  An' so the quarrel ended.
But tho' his little heart did grieve
  When round the tinkler prest her,
He feign'd to snirtle[69] in his sleeve,
  When thus the caird address'd her:

*Air*
*Tune*—"Clout[70] the Cauldron."

### I

My bonie lass, I work in brass,
  A tinkler is my station;
I've travel'd round all Christian ground
  In this my occupation;
I've taen the gold, an' been enrolled
  In many a noble squadron;
But vain they search'd when off I march'd
  To go an' clout the cauldron.
      I've taen the gold, etc.

### II

Despise that shrimp, that wither'd imp,
  With a' his noise an' cap'rin;
An' take a share with those that bear
  The budget[71] and the apron!
And by that stowp![72] my faith an' houpe,[73]
  And by that dear Kilbaigie,[74]
If e'er ye want, or meet wi' scant,
  May I ne'er weet my craigie.[75]
      And by that stowp, etc.

---

68. **Hunkers.**  Hams.
69. **Snirtle.**  Snigger.
70. **Clout.**  Patch.
71. **Budget.**  Tool-bag.

72. **Stowp.**  A measure of drink.
73. **Houpe.**  Hope.
74. **Kilbaigie.**  A kind of whisky.
75. **Weet my craigie.**  Wet my throat.

*Recitativo*

I

The caird prevail'd—th' unblushing fair
    In his embraces sunk;
Partly wi' love o'ercome sae sair,[76]
    An' partly she was drunk:
Sir Violino, with an air
    That showed a man o' spunk,
Wish'd unison between the pair,
    An' made the bottle clunk[77]
        To their health that night.

\*   \*   \*   \*   \*   \*   \*

["Her lord, a wight of Homer's craft," interfered, however,
and the poem continues in relation to this new character:]

III

He was a care-defying blade
    As ever Bacchus listed![78]
Tho' Fortune sair upon him laid,
    His heart, she ever miss'd it.
He had no wish but—to be glad,
    Nor want but—when he thristed;[79]
He hated nought but—to be sad,
    An' thus the muse suggested
        His sang that night.

*Air*
*Tune*—"For a' that, an' a' that."

I

I am a Bard, of no regard
    Wi' gentle folks an' a' that;
But Homer-like, the glowrin byke,[80]
    Frae town to town I draw that.

76. **Sae sair.** So sorely.
77. **Clunk.** Make a hollow sound.
78. **Listed.** Enlisted.
79. **Thristed.** Thirsted.
80. **Glowrin byke.** Staring crowd.

*Chorus*

For a' that, an' a' that,
  An' twice as muckle's[81] a' that;
I've lost but ane, I've twa behin',
  I've wife eneugh for a' that.

II

I never drank the Muses' stank,[82]
  Castalia's* burn,[83] an' a' that;
But there it streams an' richly reams[84]—
  My Helicon* I ca' that.
            For a' that, etc.

III

Great love I bear to a' the fair,
  Their humble slave an' a' that;
But lordly will, I hold it still
  A mortal sin to thraw[85] that.
            For a' that, etc.

IV

In raptures sweet, this hour we meet
  Wi' mutual love an' a' that;
But for how lang the flie may stang,[86]
  Let inclination law[87] that.
            For a' that, etc.

V

Their tricks an' craft hae put me daft,
  They've taen me in, an' a' that;
But clear your decks, and here's "The Sex!"
  I like the jads[88] for a' that.

81. **Muckle's.**  Much as.
82. **Stank.**  Pond.
83. **Burn.**  Stream.
84. **Reams.**  Foams.  (The bard is speaking of the beverage before him.)
85. **Thraw.**  Thwart.
86. **Flie may stang.**  Fly may sting.
87. **Law.**  Regulate.
88. **Jads.**  Jades.

*Chorus*

For a' that, an' a' that,
    An' twice as muckle's a' that;
My dearest bluid, to do them guid,
    They're welcome till't[89] for a' that.

*Recitativo*

So sang the Bard—and Nansie's wa's[90]
Shook with a thunder of applause,
    Re-echoed from each mouth!
They toom'd their pocks,[91] they pawn'd their duds,
They scarcely left to coor[92] their fuds,[93]
    To quench their lowin[94] drouth.
Then owre again, the jovial thrang
    The poet did request
To lowse[95] his pack an' wale[96] a sang,
    A ballad o' the best;
        He rising, rejoicing,
            Between his twa Deborahs,*
        Looks round him, an' found them
            Impatient for the chorus:—

*Air*

*Tune*—"Jolly Mortals, fill your Glasses."

I

See the smoking bowl before us!
    Mark our jovial, ragged ring!
Round and round take up the chorus,
    And in raptures let us sing:

*Chorus*

A fig for those by law protected!
    Liberty's a glorious feast!
Courts for cowards were erected,
    Churches built to please the priest.

89. **Till't.**  To it.
90. **Wa's.**  Walls.
91. **Toom'd their pocks.**  Emptied
    their wallets.
92. **Coor.**  Cover.
93. **Fuds.**  Backs.
94. **Lowin.**  Flaming.
95. **Lowse.**  Untie.
96. **Wale.**  Choose.

II

What is title, what is treasure,
  What is reputation's care?
If we lead a life of pleasure,
  'Tis no matter how or where!
      A fig for, etc.

III

With the ready trick and fable,
  Round we wander all the day;
And at night, in barn or stable,
  Hug our doxies[97] on the hay.
      A fig for, etc.

IV

Does the train-attended carriage
  Thro' the country lighter rove?
Does the sober bed of marriage
  Witness brighter scenes of love?
      A fig for, etc.

V

Life is all a variorum,
  We regard not how it goes;
Let them cant about decorum,
  Who have character to lose.
      A fig for, etc.

VI

Here's to budgets, bags, and wallets!
  Here's to all the wandering train!
Here's our ragged brats and callets![98]
  One and all, cry out, Amen!

*Chorus*

A fig for those by law protected!
  Liberty's a glorious feast!
Courts for cowards were erected,
  Churches built to please the priest!

97. **Doxies.** Darlings.          98. **Callets.** Sweethearts.

# THE COTTER'S SATURDAY NIGHT*

### INSCRIBED TO R. AIKEN, ESQ.

"Let not Ambition mock their useful toil,
Their homely joys, and destiny obscure;
Nor Grandeur hear, with a disdainful smile,
The short and simple annals of the poor."
—GRAY.

[This is one of the poems Burns mentions in a letter of
February 17, 1786, as written between the previous November
and that date.

"R. Aiken, Esq.," to whom it is "inscribed," was the Ayr
lawyer mentioned in "Holy Willie's Prayer," who defended
Gavin Hamilton in his church trial.

Gilbert Burns wrote thus of the genesis of this poem:
"Robert had frequently remarked to me that he thought there
was something peculiarly venerable in the phrase, 'Let us
worship God,' used by a decent sober head of a family intro-
ducing family worship. To this sentiment of the author the
world is indebted for 'The Cotter's Saturday Night.' The
hint of the plan and title of the poem were taken from
Fergusson's 'Farmer's Ingle.'" Gilbert also said, "Although
the cotter .... is an exact copy of my father in his manners,
his family devotion, and his exhortations, yet the other parts
of the description do not apply to our family."]

### I

My lov'd, my honor'd, much respected friend[1]
    No mercenary bard his homage pays;
With honest pride, I scorn each selfish end,
    My dearest meed, a friend's esteem and praise:
    To you I sing, in simple Scottish lays,
The lowly train in life's sequester'd scene,
    The native feelings strong, the guileless ways,
What Aiken in a cottage would have been;
Ah! tho' his worth unknown, far happier there, I ween!

### II

November chill blaws loud wi' angry sugh;[1]
    The short'ning winter-day is near a close;
The miry beasts retreating frae the pleugh;
    The black'ning trains o' craws to their repose:
    The toil-worn Cotter frae his labor goes,

1. Sugh. Sough, a rushing sound.

This night his weekly moil is at an end,
    Collects his spades, his mattocks, and his hoes,
Hoping the morn in ease and rest to spend,
And weary, o'er the moor, his course does hameward bend.

### III

At length his lonely cot appears in view,
    Beneath the shelter of an agèd tree ;
Th' expectant wee-things, toddlin, stacher[2] through
    To meet their dad, wi' flichterin[3] noise and glee.
    His wee-bit ingle,[4] blinkin bonilie,
His clean hearth-stane, his thrifty wifie's smile,
    The lisping infant, prattling on his knee,
Does a' his weary kiaugh[5] and care beguile,
And makes him quite forget his labor and his toil.

### IV

Belyve[6] the elder bairns come drapping in,
    At service out, amang the farmers roun' ;
Same ca'[7] the pleugh, some herd, some tentie rin[8]
    A cannie[9] errand to a neebor town :
    Their eldest hope, their Jenny, woman grown,
In youthfu' bloom, love sparkling in her e'e,[10]
    Comes hame, perhaps to shew a braw[11] new gown,
Or deposite her sair-won[12] penny-fee,
To help her parents dear, if they in hardship be.

### V

With joy unfeign'd brothers and sisters meet,
    And each for other's weelfare kindly spiers :[13]
The social hours, swift-wing'd, unnotic'd fleet ;
    Each tells the uncos[14] that he sees or hears ;
    The parents partial eye their hopeful years ;

2. **Stacher.** Stagger.
3. **Flichterin.** Fluttering.
4. **Ingle.** Fireplace.
5. **Kiaugh.** Anxiety.
6. **Belyve.** Soon.
7. **Ca'.** Drive.
8. **Tentie rin.** Heedful run.
9. **Cannie.** Quiet.
10. **E'e.** Eye.
11. **Braw.** Fine.
12. **Sair-won.** Hard-earned.
13. **Spiers.** Asks.
14. **Uncos.** News (literally, strange things).

Anticipation forward points the view.

The mother, wi' her needle and her sheers,
Gars auld claes[15] look amaist as weel's the new;
The father mixes a' wi' admonition due.

## VI

Their master's and their mistress's command,
 The younkers[16] a' are warnèd to obey;
And mind their labors wi' an eydent[17] hand,
 And ne'er, tho' out o' sight, to jauk[18] or play:
"And O! be sure to fear the Lord alway!
And mind your duty, duly, morn and night!
 Lest in temptation's path ye gang[19] astray,
Implore His counsel and assisting might:
They never sought in vain that sought the Lord aright."

## VII

But hark! a rap comes gently to the door;
 Jenny, wha kens[20] the meaning o' the same,
Tells how a neebor lad cam o'er the moor,
 To do some errands, and convoy her hame.
 The wily mother sees the conscious flame
Sparkle in Jenny's e'e, and flush her cheek;
 With heart-struck, anxious care enquires his name,
While Jenny hafflins[21] is afraid to speak;
Weel pleas'd the mother hears, it's nae wild, worthless
 rake.

## VIII

Wi' kindly welcome, Jenny brings him ben;[22]
 A strappan youth, he takes the mother's eye;
Blythe Jenny sees the visit's no ill taen;[23]
 The father cracks[24] of horses, pleughs, and kye.[25]
 The youngster's artless heart o'erflows wi' joy,

15. **Gars auld claes.** Makes old clothes.
16. **Younkers.** Youngsters.
17. **Eydent.** Diligent.
18. **Jauk.** Trifle.
19. **Gang.** Go.
20. **Wha kens.** Who knows.
21. **Hafflins.** Partly (half).
22. **Ben.** Into the parlor.
23. **No ill taen.** Not ill taken.
24. **Cracks.** Talks.
25. **Kye.** Cows.

But blate an' laithfu',[26] scarce can weel behave;
   The mother, wi' a woman's wiles, can spy
What makes the youth sae bashfu' and sae grave;
Weel pleas'd to think her bairn's respected like the lave.[27]

### IX

O happy love! where love like this is found!
   O heart-felt raptures! bliss beyond compare!
I've pacèd much this weary, mortal round,
   And sage experience bids me this declare—
"If Heav'n a draught of heav'nly pleasure spare,
One cordial in this melancholy vale,
'Tis when a youthful, loving, modest pair,
In other's arms, breathe out their tender tale,
Beneath the milk-white thorn that scents the ev'ning
     gale."

### X

Is there, in human form, that bears a heart—
   A wretch! a villain! lost to love and truth!
That can, with studied, sly, ensnaring art,
   Betray sweet Jenny's unsuspecting youth?
   Curse on his perjur'd arts! dissembling smooth!
Are honor, virtue, conscience, all exil'd?
   Is there no pity, no relenting ruth,
Points to the parents fondling o'er their child?
Then paints the ruin'd maid, and their distraction wild!

### XI

But now the supper crowns their simple board,
   The healsome parritch,[28] chief o' Scotia's food;
The soupe[29] their only hawkie[30] does afford,
   That 'yont the hallan[31] snugly chows her cood:
   The dame brings forth, in complimental mood,

26. **Blate an' laithfu'.** Shy and bashful.
27. **Lave.** The rest.
28. **Healsome parritch.** Wholesome porridge.
29. **Soupe.** Milk.
30. **Hawkie.** Cow.
31. **'Yont the hallan.** Beyond the partition.

To grace the lad, her weel-hain'd kebbuck, fell;[32]
  And aft he's prest, and aft he ca's it guid;
The frugal wifie, garrulous, will tell
How 'twas a towmond[33] auld, sin' lint was i' the bell.[34]

### XII ✓

The cheerfu' supper done, wi' serious face,
  They, round the ingle,[35] form a circle wide;
The sire turns o'er, wi' patriarchal grace,
  The big ha'-Bible,[36] ance his father's pride:
His bonnet rev'rently is laid aside,
  His lyart haffets[37] wearing thin and bare;
Those strains that once did sweet in Zion glide,
He wales[38] a portion with judicious care;
And "Let us worship God!" he says with solemn air.

### XIII ✓

They chant their artless notes in simple guise;
  They tune their hearts, by far the noblest aim:
Perhaps *Dundee's*\* wild warbling measures rise,
  Or plaintive *Martyrs,* worthy of the name;
Or noble *Elgin* beets[39] the heavenward flame,
  The sweetest far of Scotia's holy lays:
Compar'd with these, Italian trills are tame;
The tickl'd ears no heart-felt raptures raise;
Nae unison hae they with our Creator's praise.

### XIV ✓

The priest-like father reads the sacred page,
  How Abram was the friend of God on high;
Or Moses bade eternal warfare wage
  With Amalek's ungracious progeny;
  Or how the royal Bard\* did groaning lie

32. **Weel-hain'd kebbuck, fell.** Well-saved, strong cheese.
33. **Towmond.** Twelve-month.
34. **Sin' lint was i' the bell.** Since flax was in flower.
35. **Ingle.** Fireplace.
36. **Ha'-Bible.** Hall Bible, family Bible.
37. **Lyart haffets.** Gray locks (on his temples).
38. **Wales.** Chooses.
39. **Beets.** Fans.

Beneath the stroke of Heaven's avenging ire;
  Or Job's pathetic plaint, and wailing cry;
Or rapt Isaiah's wild, seraphic fire;
  Or other holy seers that tune the sacred lyre.

### XV

Perhaps the Christian volume is the theme,
  How guiltless blood for guilty man was shed;
How He who bore in Heaven the second name,
  Had not on earth whereon to lay His head:
  How His first followers and servants sped;
The precepts sage they wrote to many a land:
  How he, who lone in Patmos banishèd,*
Saw in the sun a mighty angel stand,
And heard great Bab'lon's doom pronounc'd by Heav'n's
        command.

### XVI

Then kneeling down, to Heaven's Eternal King,
  The saint, the father, and the husband prays:
Hope "springs exulting on triumphant wing,"*
  That thus they all shall meet in future days,
  There ever bask in uncreated rays:
No more to sigh or shed the bitter tear,
  Together hymning their Creator's praise,
In such society, yet still more dear;
While circling Time moves round in an eternal sphere.

### XVII

Compar'd with this, how poor Religion's pride,
  In all the pomp of method, and of art,
When men display to congregations wide
  Devotion's ev'ry grace, except the heart!
  The Power, incens'd, the pageant will desert,
The pompous strain, the sacerdotal stole;⁴⁰
  But haply, in some cottage far apart,
May hear, well pleas'd, the language of the soul,
And in His Book of Life the inmates poor enroll.

40. **Sacerdotal stole.**  Priestly robe.

### XVIII

Then homeward all take off their sev'ral way;
  The youngling cottagers retire to rest;
The parent-pair their secret homage pay,
  And proffer up to Heaven the warm request,
  That He who stills the raven's clam'rous nest,
And decks the lily fair in flow'ry pride,
  Would, in the way His wisdom sees the best,
For them and for their little ones provide;
But chiefly, in their hearts with grace divine preside.

### XIX

From scenes like these old Scotia's grandeur springs,
  That makes her lov'd at home, rever'd abroad:
Princes and lords are but the breath of kings,
  "An honest man's the noblest work of God;"*
  And certes, in fair Virtue's heavenly road,
The cottage leaves the palace far behind;
  What is a lordling's pomp? a cumbrous load,
Disguising oft the wretch of human kind,
Studied in arts of Hell, in wickedness refin'd!

### XX

O Scotia! my dear, my native soil!
  For whom my warmest wish to Heaven is sent!
Long may thy hardy sons of rustic toil
  Be blest with health, and peace, and sweet content!
  And O! may Heaven their simple lives prevent
From Luxury's contagion, weak and vile!
  Then, howe'er crowns and coronets be rent,
A virtuous populace may rise the while,
And stand a wall of fire around their much-lov'd isle.

### XXI

O Thou! who pour'd the patriotic tide
  That stream'd thro' Wallace's* undaunted heart,
Who dar'd to, nobly, stem tyrannic pride,
  Or nobly die, the second glorious part,
  (The patriot's God peculiarly thou art,

His friend, inspirer, guardian, and reward!)
  O never, never Scotia's realm desert,
But still the patriot, and the patriot-bard
In bright succession raise, her ornament and guard!


# THE AULD FARMER'S NEW-YEAR MORNING SALUTATION TO HIS AULD MARE, MAGGIE

### ON GIVING HER THE ACCUSTOMED RIPP[1] OF CORN TO HANSEL[2] IN THE NEW-YEAR

[Presumably written about the New-Year of 1786.]


I

A Guid New-Year I wish thee, Maggie!
Hae, there's a ripp to thy auld baggie:[3]
Tho' thou's howe-backit[4] now, an' knaggie,[5]
          I've seen the day
Thou could hae gaen like ony staggie,[6]
          Out-owre the lay.[7]


II

Tho' now thou's dowie,[8] stiff, an' crazy,
An' thy auld hide as white's a daisie,
I've seen thee dappl't, sleek, an' glaizie,[9]
          A bonie gray:
He should been tight[10] that daur't to raize[11] thee,
          Ance in a day.


1. **Ripp.**  Handful.
2. **Hansel.**  Welcome with a gift.
3. **Baggie.**  Belly.
4. **Howe-backit.**  Sway-backed.
5. **Knaggie.**  Bony.
6. **Staggie.**  Colt.
7. **Out-owre the lay.**  Across the meadow.
8. **Dowie.**  Drooping.
9. **Glaizie.**  Glossy.
10. **Tight.**  Girt, prepared.
11. **Daur't to raize.**  Dared to excite.

### III

Thou ance was i' the foremost rank,
A filly buirdly, steeve, an' swank;[12]
An' set weel down a shapely shank
   As e'er tread yird,[13]
An' could hae flown out-owre a stank,[14]
   Like ony bird.

### IV

It's now some nine-an'-twenty year,
Sin' thou was my guid-father's meere;[15]
He gied me thee, o' tocher[16] clear,
   An' fifty mark;[17]
Tho' it was sma', 'twas weel-won gear,[18]
   An' thou was stark.[19]

### V

When first I gaed to woo my Jenny,
Ye then was trottin wi' your minnie;[20]
Tho' ye was trickie, slee,[21] an' funnie,
   Ye ne'er was donsie;[22]
But hamely, tawie,[23] quiet, an' cannie,[24]
   An' unco sonsie.[25]

### VI

That day, ye pranc'd wi' muckle[26] pride,
When ye bure[27] hame my bonie bride;
An' sweet an' gracefu' she did ride,
   Wi' maiden air!
Kyle-Stewart* I could bragged wide
   For sic[28] a pair.

12. **Buirdly, steeve, an' swank.** Stately, compact, and limber.
13. **Yird.** Earth.
14. **Stank.** Ditch or pool.
15. **Guid-father's meere.** Father-in-law's mare.
16. **o' tocher.** As dowry.
17. **Mark.** An old Scotch coin worth about 27 cents in American money.
18. **Gear.** Wealth.
19. **Stark.** Strong.
20. **Minnie.** Mother.
21. **Slee.** Sly.
22. **Donsie.** Hard to manage.
23. **Tawie.** Tractable.
24. **Cannie.** Gentle.
25. **Unco sonsie.** Very good-natured.
26. **Muckle.** Much.
27. **Bure.** Bore.
28. **Sic.** Such.

## VII

Tho' now ye dow but hoyte[29] and hoble,
An' wintle[30] like a saumont-coble,[31]
That day ye was a jinker[32] noble,
    For heels an' win'!
An' ran them till they a' did wauble,
    Far, far behin'.

## VIII

When thou an' I were young an' skiegh,[33]
An' stable-meals at fairs were driegh,[34]
How thou wad prance, an' snore, an' skriegh,[35]
    An' tak the road!
Town's-bodies ran, an' stood abeigh,[36]
    An' ca't thee mad.

## IX

When thou was corn't,[37] an' I was mellow,
We took the road ay like a swallow:
At brooses[38] thou had ne'er a fellow,
    For pith an' speed;
But ev'ry tail thou pay't them hollow,[39]
    Whare'er thou gaed.

## X

The sma', droop-rumpl't,[40] hunter cattle
Might aiblins waur't[41] thee for a brattle;[42]
But sax Scotch miles thou try't their mettle,
    An' gar't them whaizle:[43]
Nae whip nor spur, but just a wattle[44]
    O' saugh[45] or hazle.

29. **Dow but hoyte.** Can but amble crazily.
30. **Wintle.** Stagger
31. **Saumont-coble.** Salmon-boat.
32. **Jinker.** Goer.
33. **Skiegh.** Skittish.
34. **Driegh.** Dull.
35. **Snore an' skriegh.** Snort and neigh.
36. **Abiegh.** Aloof.
37. **Corn't.** Fed with corn (=oats).
38. **Brooses.** Wedding races.
39. **Ev'ry tail, etc.** Outran every other horse.
40. **Droop-rumpl't.** Short-rumped.
41. **Aiblins waur't.** Perhaps have beaten.
42. **Brattle.** Spurt.
43. **Gar't them whaizle.** Made them wheeze.
44. **Wattle.** Wand.
45. **Saugh.** Willow.

XI

Thou was a noble fittie-lan',[46]
As e'er in tug or tow[47] was drawn!
Aft thee an' I, in aught hours' gaun,[48]
          On guid March-weather,
Hae turn'd sax rood beside our han',
          For days thegither.

XII

Thou never braing't, an' fetch't, an' fliskit;[49]
But thy auld tail thou wad hae whiskit,
An' spread abreed thy weel-fill'd brisket,[50]
          Wi' pith an' pow'r;
Till sprittie knowes wad rair't an' riskit,[51]
          An' slypet owre.[52]

XIII

When frosts lay lang, an' snaws were deep,
An' threaten'd labor back to keep,
I gied thy cog[53] a wee-bit heap
          Aboon the timmer;[54]
I ken'd my Maggie wad na sleep
          For that, or simmer.[55]

XIV

In cart or car thou never reestit;[56]
The steyest brae[57] thou wad hae fac't it;
Thou never lap, an' sten't, and breastit,[58]
          Then stood to blaw;
But just thy step a wee thing hastit,
          Thou snoov't awa.[59]

46. **Fittie-lan'.** The near horse of the hindmost pair in plowing.
47. **Tug or tow.** Hide or rope traces.
48. **Aught hours' gaun.** Eight hours' going.
49. **Braing't, fetch't, fliskit.** Plunged, pulled irregularly, capered.
50. **Brisket.** Chest.
51. **Sprittie knowes wad rair't an' riskit.** Rooty hillocks would have roared and cracked.
52. **Slypet owre.** Fallen smoothly over.
53. **Gied thy cog.** Gave thy dish.
54. **Timmer.** Timber.
55. **Or simmer.** Ere summer.
56. **Reestit.** Balked.
57. **Steyest brae.** Steepest hill.
58. **Lap, sten't, breastit.** Leaped, sprang, jumped forward.
59. **Snoov't awa.** Jogged along.

### XV

My pleugh[60] is now thy bairn-time a',[61]
Four gallant brutes as e'er did draw;
Forbye sax mae[62] I've sell't awa,
      That thou hast nurst;
They drew me thretteen pund an' twa,
      The vera warst.

### XVI

Monie a sair daurk[63] we twa hae wrought,
An' wi' the weary warl' fought!
An' monie an anxious day I thought
      We wad be beat!
Yet here to crazy age we're brought,
      Wi' something yet.

### XVII

An' think na', my auld, trusty servan',
That now perhaps thou's less deservin,
An' thy auld days may end in starvin;
      For my last fow,[64]
A heapit stimpart,[65] I'll reserve ane
      Laid by for you.

### XVIII

We've worn to crazy years thegither;
We'll toyte[66] about wi' ane anither;
Wi' tentie[67] care I'll flit[68] thy tether
      To some hain'd rig,[69]
Whare ye may nobly rax your leather,[70]
      Wi' sma' fatigue.

---

60. **Pleugh.** Plow-team.
61. **Thy bairn-time a'.** All thy brood, issue.
62. **Forbye sax mae.** Besides six more.
63. **Sair daurk.** Hard day's work.
64. **Fow.** Bushel.
65. **Stimpart.** An eighth part.
66. **Toyte.** Totter.
67. **Tentie.** Attentive.
68. **Flit.** Shift.
69. **Hain'd rig.** Reserved ridge.
70. **Rax your leather.** Stretch your hide.

# THE TWA DOGS

### A TALE

[One of the poems composed between November, 1785, and
February, 1786; placed first in the Kilmarnock edition, and
in subsequent editions in which re-arrangement has not been
made.

Written in memory of a favorite dog, called Luath after
Cuchullin's dog in Ossian's *Fingal* (the Macpherson version),
which was killed the night before William Burnes's death in
1784.]

'Twas in that place o' Scotland's isle,
That bears the name of auld King Coil,*
Upon a bonie day in June,
When wearing thro' the afternoon,
5   Twa dogs, that were na thrang¹ at hame,
Forgather'd ance upon a time.

    The first I'll name, they ca'd him Cæsar,
Was keepit for his Honor's pleasure;
His hair, his size, his mouth, his lugs,²
10   Shew'd he was nane o' Scotland's dogs,
But whalpit³ some place far abroad,
Whare sailors gang to fish for cod.

    His lockèd, letter'd, braw⁴ brass collar
Shew'd him the gentleman and scholar;
15   But tho' he was o' high degree,
The fient⁵ a pride, nae pride had he;
But wad hae spent an hour caressin,
Ev'n wi' a tinkler⁶-gipsy's messin:⁷
At kirk or market, mill or smiddie,⁸
20   Nae tawted tyke,⁹ tho' e'er sae duddie,¹⁰
But he wad stan't, as glad to see him,
An' snuff'd at stanes an' hillocks wi' him.

---

1. **Thrang.** Busy.
2. **Lugs.** Ears.
3. **Whalpit.** Whelped, born.
4. **Braw.** Fine.
5. **Fient.** Fiend, devil.

6. **Tinkler.** Tinker.
7. **Messin.** Mongrel.
8. **Smiddie.** Smithy.
9. **Tawted tyke.** Matted cur.
10. **Duddie.** Ragged.

The tither[11] was a ploughman's collie,
A rhyming, ranting, raving billie,[12]
25  Wha for his friend an' comrade had him,
And in his freaks had Luath ca'd him,
After some dog in Highland sang,
Was made lang syne[13]—Lord knows how lang.
　　He was a gash[14] an' faithfu' tyke,
30  As ever lap a sheugh[15] or dyke.
His honest, sonsie, baws'nt[16] face
Ay gat him friends in ilka[17] place.
His breast was white, his touzie[18] back
Weel clad wi' coat o' glossy black;
35  His gawsie[19] tail, wi' upward curl,
Hung owre his hurdies[20] wi' a swirl.
　　Nae doubt but they were fain o' ither,[21]
And unco pack[22] an' thick thegither;
Wi' social nose whyles[23] snuff'd an' snowkit;[24]
40  Whyles mice an' moudieworts[25] they howkit;[26]
Whyles scour'd awa in lang excursion,
An' worry'd ither in diversion;
Until, wi' daffin[27] weary grown,
Upon a knowe[28] they sat them down,
45  An' there began a lang digression
About the lords o' the creation.

### CAESAR

I've aften wonder'd, honest Luath,
What sort o' life poor dogs like you have;
An' when the gentry's life I saw,
50  What way poor bodies liv'd ava.[29]

11. **Tither.** Other.
12. **Billie.** Fellow.
13. **Lang syne.** Long ago.
14. **Gash.** Wise.
15. **Lap a sheugh.** Leaped a ditch.
16. **Sonsie, baws'nt.** Pleasant, white-streaked.
17. **Ilka.** Every.
18. **Touzie.** Shaggy.
19. **Gawsie.** Big and jolly.
20. **Hurdies.** Crupper.
21. **Were fain o' ither.** Liked each other.
22. **Unco pack.** Very intimate.
23. **Whyles.** Sometimes.
24. **Snowkit.** Sniffed.
25. **Moudieworts.** Moles.
26. **Howkit.** Dug.
27. **Daffin.** Merriment.
28. **Knowe.** Knoll.
29. **Ava.** At all.

Our laird gets in his rackèd[30] rents,
His coals, his kain, an' a' his stents;[31]
He rises when he likes himsel;
His flunkies answer at the bell;
55　He ca's his coach; he ca's his horse;
He draws a bonie silken purse,
As lang's my tail, whare, thro' the steeks,[32]
The yellow-letter'd Geordie keeks.[33]

Frae morn to e'en it's nought but toiling
60　At baking, roasting, frying, boiling;
An' tho' the gentry first are stechin,[34]
Yet ev'n the ha' folk[35] fill their pechan[36]
Wi' sauce, ragouts, an' sic like trashtrie,[37]
That's little short o' downright wastrie.[38]

65　Our whipper-in, wee, blastit wonner,[39]
Poor, worthless elf, it eats a dinner,
Better than ony tenant man
His Honor has in a' the lan';
An' what poor cot-folk pit their painch in,[40]
70　I own it's past my comprehension.

LUATH

Trowth, Cæsar, whyles they're fash't[41] eneugh;
A cotter howkin[42] in a sheugh,[43]
Wi' dirty stanes biggin[44] a dyke,
Baring[45] a quarry, an sic like,
75　Himsel, a wife, he thus sustains,
A smytrie[46] o' wee duddie weans,[47]
An' nought but his han' darg,[48] to keep
Them right an' tight in thack an' rape.[49]

30. **Rackèd.** Extortionate.
31. **Kain, stents.** Rent in kind, dues.
32. **Steeks.** Stitches.
33. **Yellow-letter'd Geordie keeks.** Guinea peeps (a coin with a likeness of King George).
34. **Stechin.** Cramming.
35. **Ha' folk.** Hall folk, servants.
36. **Pechan.** Stomach.
37. **Trashtrie.** Trash, rubbish.
38. **Wastrie.** Waste.
39. **Whipper-in, etc.** A little, shriveled huntsman who kept the hounds whipped into the course.
40. **Pit their painch in.** Put in their paunch.
41. **Fash't.** Troubled.
42. **Howkin.** Digging.
43. **Sheugh.** Ditch.
44. **Biggin.** Building.
45. **Baring.** Clearing.
46. **Smytrie.** Brood.
47. **Duddie weans.** Ragged children.
48. **Han' darg.** Hand work.
49. **Thack an' rape.** Thatch and rope.

    An' when they meet wi' sair⁵⁰ disasters,
80 Like loss o' health or want o' masters,
    Ye maist wad think, a wee touch langer,
    An' they maun⁵¹ starve o' cauld and hunger:
    But, how it comes I never kend⁵² yet,
    They're maistly wonderfu' contented;
85 An' buirdly chiels,⁵³ an' clever hizzies,⁵⁴
    Are bred in sic a way as this is.

### CAESAR

    But then to see how ye're negleckit,
    How huff'd, an' cuff'd, an' disrespeckit!
    Lord, man, our gentry care as little
90 For delvers, ditchers, an' sic cattle;
    They gang as saucy by poor folk,
    As I wad by a stinking brock.⁵⁵
    I've notic'd, on our laird's court-day,
    An' mony a time my heart's been wae,⁵⁶
95 Poor tenant bodies, scant o' cash,*
    How they maun thole⁵⁷ a factor's snash ;⁵⁸
    He'll stamp an' threaten, curse an' swear,
    He'll apprehend them, poind their gear ;⁵⁹
    While they maun stan', wi' aspect humble,
100 An' hear it a', an' fear an' tremble !
    I see how folk live that hae riches ;
    But surely poor folk maun be wretches !

### LUATH

    They're nae sae wretched 's ane wad think ;
    Tho' constantly on poortith's⁶⁰ brink,
105 They're sae accustom'd wi' the sight,
    The view o't gies them little fright.

50. **Sair.** Sore.
51. **Maun.** Must.
52. **Kend.** Knew.
53. **Buirdly chiels.** Stout lads.
54. **Hizzies.** Girls.
55. **Brock.** Badger.
56. **Wae.** Sad.
57. **Maun thole.** Must endure.
58. **Snash.** Abuse.
59. **Poind their gear.** Seize their property.
60. **Poortith.** Poverty.

Then chance an' fortune are sae guided,
They're ay in less or mair provided;
An' tho' fatigu'd wi 'close employment,
A blink o' rest's a sweet enjoyment.

The dearest comfort o' their lives,
Their grushie weans[61] an' faithfu' wives;
The prattling things are just their pride,
That sweetens a' their fire-side.

An' whyles twalpennie worth o' nappy[62]
Can mak the bodies unco[63] happy;
They lay aside their private cares,
To mind the Kirk and State affairs;
They'll talk o' patronage an' priests,
Wi' kindling fury i' their breasts,
Or tell what new taxation's comin,
An' ferlie[64] at the folk in Lon'on.

As bleak-fac'd Hallowmass returns,
They get the jovial, ranting kirns,[65]
When rural life, of ev'ry station,
Unite in common recreation;
Love blinks, Wit slaps, an' social Mirth
Forgets there's Care upo' the earth.

That merry day the year begins,
They bar the door on frosty win's;
The nappy reeks wi' mantling ream,[66]
An' sheds a heart-inspiring steam;
The luntin[67] pipe, an' sneeshin mill,[68]
Are handed round wi' right guid will;
The cantie[69] auld folks crackin crouse,[70]
The young anes ranting thro' the house—
My heart has been sae fain to see them,
That I for joy hae barkit wi' them.

61. **Grushie weans.** Growing children.
62. **Nappy.** Ale.
63. **Unco.** Wonderfully.
64. **Ferlie.** Wonder.
65. **Kirns.** Harvest-homes.
66. **Ream.** Foam.
67. **Luntin.** Smoking.
68. **Sneeshin mill.** Snuff-box.
69. **Cantie.** Lively.
70. **Crackin crouse.** Talking merrily.

Still it's owre true that ye hae said,
140  Sic game is now owre aften[71] play'd.
There's monie a creditable stock
O' decent, honest, fawsont[72] folk,
Are riven out baith root an' branch,
Some rascal's pridefu' greed to quench,
145  Wha thinks to knit himsel the faster
In favor wi' some gentle master,
Wha, aiblins thrang[73] a-parliamentin,
For Britain's guid his saul indentin[74]—

### CAESAR

Haith,[75] lad, ye little ken about it;
150  For Britain's guid! guid faith! I doubt it.
Say, rather, gaun[76] as Premiers lead him,
An' saying aye or no's they bid him;
At operas an' plays parading,
Mortgaging, gambling, masquerading;
155  Or maybe, in a frolic daft,
To Hague or Calais taks a waft,
To mak a tour an' tak a whirl,
To learn *bon ton* an' see the worl'.
There, at Vienna or Versailles,
160  He rives[77] his father's auld entails;
Or by Madrid he taks the rout,
To thrum guitars an' fecht wi' nowt;[78]

\* \* \* \* \* \* \*

165  Then bouses drumly[79] German water,
To mak himsel look fair an' fatter.

\* \* \* \* \* \* \*

For Britain's guid! for her destruction!
170  Wi' dissipation, feud, an' faction.

71. **Owre aften.**  Too often.
72. **Fawsont.**  Seemly.
73. **Aiblins thrang.**  Perhaps busy.
74. **Indentin.**  Indenturing.
75. **Haith.**  Faith (a petty oath).
76. **Gaun.**  Going.
77. **Rives.**  Breaks.
78. **Fecht wi' nowt.**  Fight with bulls.
79. **Drumly.**  Muddy.

### LUATH

Hech, man! dear sirs! is that the gate[80]
They waste sae mony a braw estate!
Are we sae foughten[81] an' harass'd
For gear[82] to gang that gate at last?
175    O would they stay aback frae courts,
An' please themsels wi' countra sports,
It wad for ev'ry ane be better,
The laird, the tenant, an' the cotter!
For thae[83] frank, rantin, ramblin billies,[84]
Fient haet[85] o' them's ill-hearted fellows;
Except for breakin[86] o' their timmer,[87]
Or speakin lightly o' their limmer,[88]
Or shootin of a hare or moor-cock,
The ne'er a bit they're ill to poor folk.
185    But will ye tell me, master Cæsar,
Sure great folk's life's a life o' pleasure?
Nae cauld nor hunger e'er can steer[89] them,
The vera thought o't need na fear them.


### CAESAR

Lord, man, were ye but whyles whare I am,
190 The gentles, ye wad ne'er envy 'em.
   It's true, they need na starve or sweat,
Thro' winter's cauld, or simmer's heat;
They've nae sair[90] wark to craze their banes,
An' fill auld age wi' grips an' granes;[91]
195 But human bodies are sic fools,
For a' their colleges an' schools,

---

80. **Gate. Way.**
81. **Foughten.** Troubled.
82. **Gear.** Money.
83. **Thae.** Those.
84. **Billies.** Fellows.
85. **Fient haet.** Not one.
86. **Breakin.** Wasting.

87. **Timmer.** Timber.
88. **Limmer.** Sweetheart.
89. **Steer.** Stir, molest.
90. **Sair.** Hard.
91. **Grips an' granes.** Gripes an' groans.

That when nae real ills perplex them,
They mak enow themsels to vex them;
An' ay the less they hae to sturt[92] them,
200   In like proportion less will hurt them.
        A country fellow at the pleugh,
His acre's till'd, he's right eneugh;
A country girl at her wheel,
Her dizzen's dune,[93] she's unco weel;
205   But gentlemen, an' ladies warst,
Wi' ev'n down want o' wark are curst.
They loiter, lounging, lank, an' lazy;
Tho' deil haet[94] ails them, yet uneasy;
Their days insipid, dull, an' tasteless;
210   Their nights unquiet, lang, an' restless.
        An' ev'n their sports, their balls an' races,
Their galloping thro' public places,
There's sic parade, sic pomp an' art,
The joy can scarcely reach the heart.
215       The men cast out[95] in party matches,
Then sowther[96] a' in deep debauches.

          *    *    *    *    *    *    *

        The ladies arm-in-arm in clusters,
220   As great an' gracious a' as sisters;
But hear their absent thoughts o' ither,
They're a' run deils an' jads[97] thegither.
Whyles, owre the wee-bit cup an' platie,
They sip the scandal potion pretty;
225   Or lee-lang[98] nights, wi' crabbit leuks[99]
Pore owre the devil's pictur'd beuks;[100]
Stake on a chance a farmer's stackyard,
An' cheat like ony unhanged blackguard.

92. **Sturt.** Worry.
93. **Dizzen's dune.** Her dozen hanks of thread are spun.
94. **Deil haet.** Nothing (devil a bit).
95. **Cast out.** Quarrel.
96. **Sowther.** Solder, patch up.
97. **Run deils an' jads.** Downright devils and jades.
98. **Lee-lang.** Live-long.
99. **Crabbit leuks.** Crabbed looks.
100. **Devil's pictur'd beuks.** Playing-cards.

There's some exceptions, man an' woman;
230   But this is gentry's life in common.


By this, the sun was out of sight,
An' darker gloamin[101] brought the night;
The bum-clock[102] humm'd wi' lazy drone;
The kye[103] stood rowtin[104] i' the loan;[105]
235   When up they gat an' shook their lugs,[106]
Rejoic'd they were na *men,* but *dogs;*
An' each took aff his several way,
Resolv'd to meet some ither day.



## ADDRESS TO THE DEIL

"O Prince! O chief of many thronèd pow'rs,
That led th' embattl'd seraphim to war—"—MILTON.

[One of the poems completed between November, 1785, and February, 1786.

This poem "is, in part, a good-natured burlesque of the Miltonic ideal of Satan," and "a satiric thrust at the old Satanic dogma."]


I

O Thou! whatever title suit thee,
Auld Hornie, Satan, Nick, or Clootie,[1]
Wha in yon cavern grim an' sootie,
            Clos'd under hatches,
Spairges[2] about the brunstane cootie,[3]
            To scaud[4] poor wretches!

---

101. **Gloamin.** Twilight.
102. **Bum-clock.** Humming beetle.
103. **Kye.** Cows.
104. **Rowtin.** Lowing.
105. **Loan.** Lane.
106. **Lugs.** Ears.

1. **Clootie.** Hoofed one.
2. **Spairges.** Splashes.
3. **Brunstane cootie.** Brimstone dish.
4. **Scaud.** Scald.

## II

Hear me, auld Hangie, for a wee,
An' let poor damnèd bodies be;
I'm sure sma' pleasure it can gie,
   Ev'n to a deil,
To skelp[5] an' scaud poor dogs like me,
   An' hear us squeel!


## III

Great is thy pow'r an' great thy fame;
Far kend an' noted is thy name;
An' tho' yon lowin heuch's[6] thy hame,
   Thou travels far;
An' faith! thou's neither lag[7] nor lame,
   Nor blate nor scaur.[8]


## IV

Whyles,[9] ranging like a roarin lion,
For prey, a' holes an' corners tryin;
Whyles, on the strong-wing'd tempest flyin,
   Tirlin the kirks;[10]
Whyles, in the human bosom pryin,
   Unseen thou lurks.


## V

I've heard my rev'rend graunie say,
In lanely glens ye like to stray;
Or where auld, ruin'd castles, gray,
   Nod to the moon,
Ye fright the nightly wand'rer's way,
   Wi' eldritch[11] croon.


5. **Skelp.** Slap.
6. **Lowin heuch.** Flaming pit.
7. **Lag.** Backward.
8. **Blate, scaur.** Shy, afraid.

9. **Whyles.** Sometimes.
10. **Tirlin the kirks.** Unroofing the churches.
11. **Eldritch.** Unearthly.

## VI

When twilight did my graunie summon,
To say her pray'rs, douce,[12] honest woman!
Aft yont[13] the dyke she's heard you bummin,[14]
      Wi' eerie[15] drone;
Or, rustlin, thro' the boortrees[16] comin,
      Wi' heavy groan.

## VII

Ae[17] dreary, windy, winter night,
The stars shot down wi' sklentin[18] light,
Wi' you, mysel, I gat a fright,
      Ayont the lough;[19]
Ye, like a rash-buss,[20] stood in sight,
      Wi' wavin sugh.[21]

## VIII

The cudgel in my nieve[22] did shake,
Each bristl'd hair stood like a stake,
When, wi' an eldritch, stoor[23] "quaick, quaick,"
      Amang the springs,
Awa ye squatter'd[24] like a drake,
      On whistling wings.

## IX

Let warlocks[25] grim, an' wither'd hags,
Tell how wi' you, on ragweed nags,
They skim the muirs an' dizzy crags,
      Wi' wicked speed;
And in kirk-yards renew their leagues,
      Owre howkit[26] dead.

12. **Douce.** Grave.
13. **Yont.** Beyond.
14. **Bummin.** Humming.
15. **Eerie.** Uncanny.
16. **Boortrees.** Elders.
17. **Ae.** One.
18. **Sklentin.** Slanting.
19. **Ayont the lough.** Beyond the lake.
20. **Rash-buss.** Rush-bush.
21. **Sugh.** The rushing noise of wind or water.
22. **Nieve.** Fist.
23. **Eldritch, stoor.** Unearthly, harsh.
24. **Squatter'd.** Flapped.
25. **Warlocks.** Wizards.
26. **Howkit.** Dug up.

### X

Thence, countra wives, wi' toil and pain,
May plunge an' plunge the kirn[27] in vain;
For O! the yellow treasure's taen
      By witching skill;
An' dawtit, twal-pint hawkie's[28] gane
      As yell's the bill.[29]

\*   \*   \*   \*   \*   \*   \*   \*

### XII

When thowes[30] dissolve the snawy hoord,[31]
An' float the jinglin icy boord,[32]
Then water-kelpies[33] haunt the foord,
      By your direction,
An' nighted trav'llers are allur'd
      To their destruction.

### XIII

An' aft your moss-traversing spunkies[34]
Decoy the wight that late an' drunk is:
The bleezin,[35] curst, mischievous monkies
      Delude his eyes,
Till in some miry slough he sunk is,
      Ne'er mair to rise.

### XIV

When Masons' mystic word an' grip
In storms an' tempests raise you up,
Some cock or cat your rage maun[36] stop,
      Or, strange to tell!
The youngest brother ye wad whip
      Aff straught[37] to hell.

27. **Kirn.** Churn.
28. **Dawtit, twal-pint hawkie.** Petted, twelve-pint cow.
29. **As yell's the bill.** As dry as the bull.
30. **Thowes.** Thaws.
31. **Snawy hoord.** Snowy hoard.
32. **Boord.** Surface.
33. **Kelpies.** Water-spirits.
34. **Spunkies.** Will-o-the-wisps.
35. **Bleezin.** Blazing.
36. **Maun.** Must.
37. **Aff straught.** Off straight.

XV

Lang syne,[38] in Eden's bonie yard,
When youthfu' lovers first were pair'd,
An' all the soul of love they shar'd,
            The raptur'd hour,
Sweet on the fragrant flow'ry swaird,
            In shady bower:


XVI

Then you, ye auld, snick[39]-drawing dog!
Ye came to Paradise incog,
An' play'd on man a cursèd brogue,[40]
            (Black be your fa'![41])
An' gied the infant warld a shog,[42]
            'Maist ruin'd a'.


XVII

D'ye mind that day when, in a bizz,[43]
Wi' reekit[44] duds, an' reestit gizz,[45]
Ye did present your smoutie phiz[46]
            'Mang better folk,
An' sklented[47] on the man of Uzz[48]
            Your spitefu' joke?


XVIII

An' how ye gat him i' your thrall,
An' brak him out o' house an' hal',[49]
While scabs an' botches[50] did him gall,
            Wi' bitter claw;
An' lows'd[51] his ill-tongu'd wicked scawl,[52]
            Was warst ava?[53]

38. **Lang syne.** Long ago.
39. **Snick.** Latch.
40. **Brogue.** Trick.
41. **Fa'.** Fall, fate.
42. **Shog.** Shake.
43. **Bizz.** Flurry.
44. **Reekit.** Smoked.
45. **Reestit gizz.** Singed wig.
46. **Smoutie phiz.** Smutty face.
47. **Sklented.** Directed.
48. **Man of Uzz.** Job.
49. **Hal'.** Holding, possessions.
50. **Botches.** Pustules.
51. **Lows'd.** Loosed.
52. **Scawl.** Scold (his wife).
53. **Warst ava.** Worst of all.

### XIX

But a' your doings to rehearse,
Your wily snares an' fechtin[54] fierce,
Sin' that day Michael* did you pierce,
          Down to this time,
Wad ding[55] a Lallan[56] tongue, or Erse,[57]
          In prose or rhyme.


### XX

An' now, auld Cloots,[58] I ken ye're thinkin,
A certain Bardie's rantin,[59] drinkin,
Some luckless hour will send him linkin,[60]
          To your black pit;
But, faith! he'll turn a corner jinkin,[61]
          An' cheat you yet.


### XXI

But fare you weel, auld Nickie-ben!
O wad ye tak a thought an' men'![62]
Ye aiblins[63] might—I dinna ken—
          Still hae a stake[64]—
I'm wae[65] to think upo' yon den,
          Ev'n for your sake!

54. **Fechtin.**  Fighting.
55. **Ding.**  Baffle.
56. **Lallan.**  Lowland.
57. **Erse.**  Gaelic (Highland).
58. **Cloots.**  Hoofs.
59. **Rantin.**  Roistering.

60. **Linkin.**  Tripping.
61. **Jinkin.**  Dodging.
62. **An' men'.**  And mend.
63. **Aiblins.**  Perhaps.
64. **Stake.**  A chance in the game.
65. **Wae.**  Sad (woe).

## EPISTLE TO JAMES SMITH

"Friendship, mysterious cement of the soul!
Sweet'ner of Life, and solder of Society!
I owe thee much——"                        BLAIR.

[Written probably early in 1786, after Burns's decision to
publish his poems (see stanza vii).

Smith kept a small shop in Mauchline during the time of
his intimacy with Burns.  He was with the poet on the visit
to "Poosie-Nansie's" which resulted in "The Jolly Beggars,"
and was a steadfast friend during the trouble with the
Armour family.]

I

Dear Smith, the sleëst, paukie[1] thief,
That e'er attempted stealth or rief,[2]
Ye surely hae some warlock-breef[3]
        Owre human hearts;
For ne'er a bosom yet was prief[4]
        Against your arts.

II

For me, I swear by sun an' moon,
And ev'ry star that blinks aboon,[5]
Ye've cost me twenty pair o' shoon,[6]
        Just gaun[7] to see you;
And ev'ry ither pair that's done,
        Mair taen[8] I'm wi' you.

III

That auld, capricious carlin,[9] Nature,
To mak amends for scrimpit stature,
She's turn'd you off, a human creature
        On her first plan,
And in her freaks, on ev'ry feature,
        She's wrote the Man.

1. **Sleëst, paukie.**  Slyest, cunning.
2. **Rief.**  Robbery.
3. **Warlock-breef.**  Wizardry.
4. **Prief.**  Proof.
5. **Aboon.**  Above.
6. **Shoon.**  Shoes.
7. **Gaun.**  Going.
8. **Mair taen.**  More taken.
9. **Carlin.**  Beldam, witch.

### IV

Just now I've taen the fit o' rhyme,
My barmie[10] noddle's working prime,
My fancy yerkit[11] up sublime
          Wi' hasty summon:
Hae ye a leisure-moment's time
            To hear what's comin?

### V

Some rhyme a neebor's name to lash;
Some rhyme (vain thought!) for needfu' cash;
Some rhyme to court the countra clash,[12]
          An' raise a din;
For me, an aim I never fash;[13]
          I rhyme for fun.

### VI

The star that rules my luckless lot,
Has fated me the russet coat,
An' damn'd my fortune to the groat;
          But, in requit,
Has blest me with a random shot
          O' countra wit.

### VII

This while my notion's taen a sklent,[14]
To try my fate in guid, black prent;[15]
But still the mair I'm that way bent,
          Something cries "Hoolie![16]
I red[17] you, honest man, tak tent![18]
          Ye'll shaw[19] your folly.

10. **Barmie.**  Yeasty.
11. **Yerkit.**  Jerked.
12. **Clash.**  Idle talk.
13. **Fash.**  Trouble about.
14. **Sklent.**  Slant, turn.
15. **Prent.**  Print.
16. **Hoolie.**  Slowly.
17. **Red.**  Advise.
18. **Tent.**  Heed.
19. **Shaw.**  Show.

### VIII

"There's ither poets, much your betters,
Far seen in Greek, deep men o' letters,
Hae thought they had ensur'd their debtors,
   A' future ages;
Now moths deform, in shapeless tatters,
    Their unknown pages."

### IX

Then farewell hopes o' laurel-boughs,
To garland my poetic brows!
Henceforth I'll rove where busy ploughs
    Are whistling thrang,[20]
An' teach the lanely heights an' howes[21]
    My rustic sang.

### X

I'll wander on, wi' tentless[22] heed
How never-halting moments speed,
Till fate shall snap the brittle thread;
    Then, all unknown,
I'll lay me with th' inglorious dead,
    Forgot and gone!

### XI

But why o' death begin a tale?
Just now we're living sound and hale;
Then top and maintop crowd the sail,
    Heave Care o'er-side!
And large, before Enjoyment's gale,
    Let's tak the tide.

20. **Thrang.** Busily.          22. **Tentless.** Careless.
21. **Howes.** Hollows.

### XII

This life, sae far's I understand,
Is a' enchanted fairy-land,
Where Pleasure is the magic wand
   That, wielded right,
Maks hours like minutes, hand in hand,
   Dance by fu' light.

### XIII

The magic wand then let us wield;
For, ance that five-an'-forty's speel'd,[23]
See, crazy, weary, joyless Eild,[24]
   Wi' wrinkl'd face,
Comes hostin, hirplin,[25] owre the field,
   Wi' creepin pace.

### XIV

When ance life's day draws near the gloamin,
Then fareweel vacant, careless roamin;
An' fareweel cheerfu' tankards foamin,
   An' social noise;
An' fareweel dear deluding woman,
   The joy of joys!

### XV

O Life! how pleasant in thy morning,
Young Fancy's rays the hills adorning!
Cold-pausing Caution's lesson scorning,
   We frisk away,
Like school-boys, at th' expected warning,
   To joy an' play.

---

23. **Speel'd.** Climbed.
24. **Eild.** Age.

25. **Hostin, hirplin.** Coughing, limping.

XVI

We wander there, we wander here,
We eye the rose upon the brier,
Unmindful that the thorn is near,
              Among the leaves;
And tho' the puny wound appear,
              Short while it grieves.


XVII

Some, lucky, find a flow'ry spot,
For which they never toil'd nor swat;[26]
They drink the sweet and eat the fat,
              But[27] care or pain;
And, haply, eye the barren hut
              With high disdain.


XVIII

With steady aim, some Fortune chase;
Keen Hope does ev'ry sinew brace;
Thro' fair, thro' foul, they urge the race,
              And seize the prey:
Then canie,[28] in some cozie place,
              They close the day.


XIX

And others, like your humble servan',
Poor wights! nae rules nor roads observin,
To right or left eternal swervin,
              They zig-zag on;
Till, curst with age, obscure an' starvin,
              They aften groan.


26. **Swat.**  Sweated.              28. **Canie.**  Quiet.
27. **But.**  Without.

### XX

Alas! what bitter toil an' straining—
But truce with peevish, poor complaining!
Is Fortune's fickle *Luna* waning?
           E'en let her gang![29]
Beneath what light she has remaining,
           Let's sing our sang.


### XXI

My pen I here fling to the door,
And kneel, ye Pow'rs! and warm implore,
"Tho' I should wander *Terra* o'er,
           In all her climes,
Grant me but this, I ask no more,
           Ay rowth[30] o' rhymes.


### XXII

"Gie dreeping[31] roasts to countra lairds,
Till icicles hing frae their beards;
Gie fine braw claes[32] to fine life-guards,
           And maids of honor;
And yill[33] an' whisky gie to cairds,[34]
           Until they sconner.[35]


### XXIII

"A title, Dempster* merits it;
A garter gie to Willie Pitt;*
Gie wealth to some be-ledger'd cit,[36]
           In cent. per cent.
But give me real, sterling wit,
           And I'm content.

---

29. **Gang.** Go.
30. **Rowth.** Plenty.
31. **Gie dreeping.** Give dripping.
32. **Braw claes.** Handsome clothes.

33. **Yill.** Ale.
34. **Cairds.** Tinkers.
35. **Sconner.** Sicken.
36. **Cit.** Citizen.

### XXIV

"While ye are pleas'd to keep me hale,
I'll sit down o'er my scanty meal,
Be't water-brose or muslin-kail,[37]
        Wi' cheerfu' face,
As lang's the Muses dinna[38] fail
           To say the grace."

### XXV

An anxious e'e[39] I never throws
Behint my lug,[40] or by my nose;
I jouk[41] beneath Misfortune's blows
        As weel's I may;
Sworn foe to sorrow, care, and prose,
        I rhyme away.

### XXVI

O ye douce[42] folk that live by rule,*
Grave, tideless-blooded, calm an' cool,
Compar'd wi' you—O fool! fool! fool!
        How much unlike!
Your hearts are just a standing pool,
        Your lives, a dyke!

### XXVII

Nae hair-brained, sentimental traces
In your unletter'd, nameless faces!
In *arioso** trills and graces
        Ye never stray;
But *gravissimo,** solemn basses
        Ye hum away.

37. **Water-brose or muslin-kail.** Porridge made with water, or a broth
   of water, shelled barley, and
   greens.
38. **Dinna.** Do not.
39. **E'e.** Eye.
40. **Lug.** Ear.
41. **Jouk.** Duck.
42. **Douce.** Prudent.

## XXVIII

Ye are sae grave, nae doubt ye're wise;
Nae ferly[43] tho' ye do despise
The hairum-scairum, ram-stam[44] boys,
      The rattlin squad:
I see you upward cast your eyes—
      Ye ken[45] the road—

## XXIX

Whilst I—but I shall haud[46] me there,
Wi' you I'll scarce gang ony where—
Then, Jamie, I shall say nae mair,
      But quat[47] my sang,
Content wi' you to mak a pair,
      Whare'er I gang.

# TO A LOUSE

## ON SEEING ONE ON A LADY'S BONNET AT CHURCH

[Presumably written in 1786.
Noteworthy for the last stanza, the first four lines of which
are one of the most widely quoted passages in Burns's works.]

### I

Ha! whare ye gaun,[1] ye crowlin ferlie?[2]
Your impudence protects you sairly;[3]
I canna say but ye strunt[4] rarely,
      Owre gauze and lace;
Tho', faith! I fear ye dine but sparely
      On sic[5] a place.

43. **Ferly.** Wonder.
44. **Ram-stam.** Thoughtless.
45. **Ken.** Know.
46. **Haud.** Hold
47. **Quat.** Quit.

1. **Gaun.** Going.
2. **Ferlie.** Wonder.
3. **Sairly.** Sorely.
4. **Strunt.** Strut.
5. **Sic.** Such.

### II

Ye ugly, creepin, blastit wonner,[6]
Detested, shunn'd by saunt an' sinner,
How daur ye set your fit[7] upon her,
    Sae fine a lady?
Gae somewhere else and seek your dinner
    On some poor body.

### III

Swith![8] in some beggar's haffet[9] squattle:[10]
There ye may creep, and sprawl, and sprattle,[11]
Wi' ither kindred, jumping cattle,
    In shoals and nations;
Whare horn nor bane[12] ne'er daur unsettle
    Your thick plantations.

### IV

Now haud[13] you there, ye're out o' sight,
Below the fatt'rils,[14] snug an' tight;
Na, faith ye yet! ye'll no be right
    Till ye've got on it,
The vera tapmost, tow'rin height
    O' Miss's bonnet.

### V

My sooth! right bauld ye set your nose out,
As plump an' gray as onie groset:[15]
O for some rank, mercurial rozet,[16]
    Or fell,[17] red smeddum![18]
I'd gie you sic a hearty dose o't,
    Wad dress your droddum.[19]

6. **Wonner.** Wonder.
7. **Fit.** Foot.
8. **Swith.** Quick.
9. **Haffet.** Temples.
10. **Squattle.** Settle.
11. **Sprattle.** Scramble.
12. **Horn nor bane.** A comb (horn or bone).
13. **Haud.** Hold.
14. **Fatt'rils.** Ribbon-ends.
15. **Groset.** Gooseberry.
16. **Rozet.** Rosin.
17. **Fell.** Deadly.
18. **Smeddum.** Dust.
19. **Droddum.** Breech.

## VI

I wad na been surpris'd to spy
You on an auld wife's flainen toy;[20]
Or aiblins[21] some bit duddie[22] boy,
       On's wyliecoat;[23]
But Miss's fine Lunardi![24] fie!
       How daur[25] ye do't?

## VII

O Jenny, dinna[26] toss your head,
An' set your beauties a' abread![27]
Ye little ken what cursèd speed
       The blastie's[28] makin!
Thae[29] winks an' finger-ends, I dread,
       Are notice takin!

## VIII

O wad some Pow'r the giftie gie us
To see oursels as ithers see us!
It wad frae monie a blunder free us,
       An' foolish notion:
What airs in dress an' gait wad lea'e[30] us,
       An' ev'n devotion!

20. **Flainen toy.** Flannel cap.
21. **Aiblins.** Perhaps.
22. **Bit duddie.** Little ragged.
23. **Wyliecoat.** Undervest.
24. **Lunardi.** Balloon bonnet. Lunardi was the name of a famous balloonist.
25. **Daur.** Dare.
26. **Dinna.** Do not.
27. **Abread.** Abroad.
28. **Blastie.** Little wretch.
29. **Thae.** Those.
30. **Lea'e.** Leave.

# TO A MOUNTAIN DAISY

## ON TURNING ONE DOWN WITH THE PLOUGH IN APRIL, 1786

[Written after Burns was in trouble with the Armours and thought of going to the West Indies. Of course he himself is the "simple Bard" (stanza vii).]

### I

Wee, modest, crimson-tippèd flow'r,
Thou's met me in an evil hour;
For I maun[1] crush amang the stoure[2]
        Thy slender stem.
To spare thee now is past my pow'r,
        Thou bonie gem.

### II

Alas! it's no thy neebor sweet,
The bonie lark, companion meet!
Bending thee 'mang the dewy weet,[3]
        Wi' spreckl'd breast,
When upward-springing, blythe, to greet
        The purpling east.

### III

Cauld blew the bitter-biting north
Upon thy early, humble birth;
Yet cheerfully thou glinted forth
        Amid the storm,
Scarce rear'd above the parent-earth
        Thy tender form.

1. **Maun.** Must.
2. **Stoure.** Dust.

3. **Weet.** Wet.

IV

The flaunting flow'rs our gardens yield,
High shelt'ring woods and wa's[4] maun shield;
But thou, beneath the random bield[5]
        O' clod or stane,
Adorns the histie[6] stibble-field,
        Unseen, alane.


V

There, in thy scanty mantle clad,
Thy snawie bosom sun-ward spread,
Thou lifts thy unassuming head
        In humble guise;
But now the share uptears thy bed,
        And low thou lies!


VI

Such is the fate of artless maid,
Sweet flow'ret of the rural shade!
By love's simplicity betray'd,
        And guileless trust,
Till she, like thee, all soil'd, is laid
        Low i' the dust.


VII

Such is the fate of simple Bard,
On life's rough ocean luckless starr'd!
Unskillful he to note the card
        Of prudent lore,
Till billows rage, and gales blow hard,
        And whelm him o'er!

4. Wa's. Walls.
5. Bield. Shelter.
6. Histie. Barren.

### VIII

Such fate to suffering Worth is giv'n,
Who long with wants and woes has striv'n,
By human pride or cunning driv'n
    To mis'ry's brink;
Till, wrench'd of ev'ry stay but Heav'n,
    He, ruin'd, sink!

### IX

Ev'n thou who mourn'st the Daisy's fate,
That fate is thine—no distant date;
Stern Ruin's ploughshare drives, elate,
    Full on thy bloom,
Till crush'd beneath the furrow's weight
    Shall be thy doom!

## EPISTLE TO A YOUNG FRIEND
*May———, 1786.*

[This poem was addressed to Andrew Aiken, son of Robert
Aiken of Ayr, to whom "The Cotter's Saturday Night" was
dedicated. It is frankly didactic and not highly poetic; yet
it is excellent eighteenth-century verse and contains a number
of memorable lines. It has been criticized as inconsistent with
the poet's own practices. The last lines, however, show that
Burns made no hypocritical pretenses; like most purveyors of
good advice, he "knew better than he did."]

### I

I lang hae thought, my youthfu' friend,
    A something to have sent you,
Tho' it should serve nae ither end
    Than just a kind memento;
But how the subject-theme may gang,
    Let time and chance determine;
Perhaps it may turn out a sang;
    Perhaps turn out a sermon.

II

Ye'll try the world soon, my lad;
　　And, Andrew dear, believe me,
Ye'll find mankind an unco[1] squad,
　　And muckle[2] they may grieve ye:
For care and trouble set your thought,
　　Ev'n when your end's attainèd;
And a' your views may come to nought,
　　Where ev'ry nerve is strainèd;

III

I'll no say, men are villains a';
　　The real, harden'd wicked,
Wha hae nae check but human law,
　　Are to a few restricked;
But, och! mankind are unco weak,
　　An' little to be trusted;
If Self the wavering balance shake,
　　It's rarely right adjusted!

IV

Yet they wha fa' in Fortune's strife,
　　Their fate we should na censure;
For still, th' important end of life
　　They equally may answer:
A man may hae an honest heart,
　　Tho' poortith[3] hourly stare him;
A man may tak a neebor's part,
　　Yet hae nae cash to spare him.

V

Ay free, aff-han', your story tell,
　　When wi' a bosom crony;
But still keep something to yoursel
　　Ye scarcely tell to ony.

1. **Unco.**　Strange.
2. **Muckle.**　Much.

3. **Poortith.**　Poverty.

Conceal yoursel as weel's ye can
  Frae critical dissection ;
But keek[4] thro' ev'ry other man,
  Wi' sharpen'd, sly inspection.

VI

The sacred lowe[5] o' weel-plac'd love,
  Luxuriantly indulge it ;
But never tempt th' illicit rove,
  Tho' naething should divulge it :
I waive the quantum o' the sin,
  The hazard of concealing ;
But, och ! it hardens a' within,
  And petrifies the feeling !

VII

To catch Dame Fortune's golden smile,
  Assiduous wait upon her ;
And gather gear[6] by ev'ry wile
  That's justified by honor :
Not for to hide it in a hedge,
  Nor for a train-attendant ;
But for the glorious privilege
  Of being independent.

VIII

The fear o' Hell's a hangman's whip,
  To haud[7] the wretch in order ;
But where ye feel your honor grip,
  Let that ay be your border :
Its slightest touches, instant pause—
  Debar a' side pretences ;
And resolutely keep its laws,
  Uncaring consequences.

4. **Keek.** Peep.
5. **Lowe.** Flame.
6. **Gear.** Property.
7. **Haud.** Hold.

### IX

The great Creator to revere
  Must sure become the creature;
But still the preaching cant forbear,
  And ev'n the rigid feature:
Yet ne'er with wits profane to range
  Be complaisance extended;
An atheist-laugh's a poor exchange
  For Deity offended!


### X

When ranting round in Pleasure's ring,
  Religion may be blinded;
Or if she gie[8] a random sting,
  It may be little minded;
But when on life we're tempest-driv'n—
  A conscience but a canker—
A correspondence fix'd wi' Heav'n,
  Is sure a noble anchor!


### XI

Adieu, dear, amiable youth!
  Your heart can ne'er be wanting!
May prudence, fortitude, and truth,
  Erect your brow undaunting!
In ploughman phrase, "God send you speed,"
  Still daily to grow wiser;
And may ye better reck the rede,[9]
  Than ever did th' adviser!

8. **Gie.**  Give.
9. **Reck the rede.**  Heed the **advice.**

## A BARD'S EPITAPH

[Written during the period of despondency in 1786, shortly before the publication of the Kilmarnock edition; placed at the end of that edition as if intended for a sort of epilogue. The self-characterization and the self-pity of the lines are obvious.]

I

Is there a whim-inspirèd fool,
Owre[1] fast for thought, owre hot for rule,
Owre blate[2] to seek, owre proud to snool,[3]
          Let him draw near;
And owre this grassy heap sing dool,[4]
          And drap a tear.

II

Is there a Bard of rustic song,
Who, noteless, steals the crowds among,
That weekly this aréa throng,
          O, pass not by!
But, with a frater-feeling strong,
          Here heave a sigh.

III

Is there a man whose judgment clear
Can others teach the course to steer,
Yet runs, himself, life's mad career,
          Wild as the wave;
Here pause—and, thro' the starting tear,
          Survey this grave.

IV

The poor inhabitant below
Was quick to learn and wise to know,
And keenly felt the friendly glow,
          And softer flame;
But thoughtless follies laid him low,
          And stain'd his name!

1. **Owre.**  Too (over).
2. **Blate.**  Bashful.
3. **Snool.**  Cringe.
4. **Dool.**  Woe (dole).

V

Reader, attend! whether thy soul
Soars fancy's flights beyond the pole,
Or darkling grubs this earthly hole,
⠀⠀⠀⠀⠀In low pursuit;
Know, prudent, cautious self-control
⠀⠀⠀⠀⠀Is wisdom's root.


## ADDRESS OF BEELZEBUB

### TO THE EARL OF BREADALBANE, PRESIDENT OF THE HIGHLAND SOCIETY

[According to the old chronology which put the creation at 4004 B.C., the date of this poem—"1st June, Anno Mundi 5790"—must have been June 1, 1786. It was first printed in the *Edinburgh Magazine* in 1818. The following heading, originally prefixed to the poem, explains its meaning: "To the Right Honorable the Earl of Breadalbane, President of the Right Honorable the Highland Society, which met on the 23rd of May last, at the *Shakespeare*, Covent Garden, to concert ways and means to frustrate the designs of five hundred Highlanders who, as the Society were informed by Mr. McKenzie of Applecross, were so audacious as to attempt an escape from their lawful lords and masters whose property they were, by emigrating from the lands of Mr. Macdonald of Glengary to the wilds of Canada, in search of that fantastic thing—Liberty." The sustained and bitter irony must continually be kept in mind.]


Long life, my lord, an' health be yours,
Unskaith'd¹ by hunger'd Highland boors!
Lord grant nae duddie,² desperate beggar,
Wi' dirk, claymore,³ or rusty trigger,
5⠀May twin⁴ auld Scotland o' a life
She likes—as lambkins like a knife!

---

1. **Unskaith'd.** Unhurt.⠀⠀⠀⠀3. **Claymore.** A two-handed sword.
2. **Duddie.** Ragged.⠀⠀⠀⠀⠀⠀⠀4. **Twin.** Deprive.

Faith! you and Applecross were right
To keep the Highland hounds in sight!
I doubt na! they wad bid⁵ nae better
10  Than let them ance out owre the water!
Then up amang thae⁶ lakes and seas,
They'll mak what rules and laws they please:
Some daring Hancock, or a Franklin,*
May set their Highland bluid a-ranklin;
15  Some Washington again may head them,
Or some Montgomery,* fearless, lead them;
Till (God knows what may be effected
When by such heads and hearts directed)
Poor dunghill sons of dirt an' mire
20  May to Patrician rights aspire!
Nae sage North now, nor sager Sackville,*
To watch and premier o'er the pack vile!
An' whare will ye get Howes and Clintons*
To bring them to a right repentance—
25  To cowe the rebel generation,
An' save the honor o' the nation?
They, an' be damn'd! what right hae they
To meat, or sleep, or light o' day?
Far less to riches, pow'r, or freedom,
30  But what your lordship like to gie them?

But hear, my lord! Glengary, hear!
Your hand's owre light on them, I fear;
Your factors, grieves,⁷ trustees, and bailies,
I canna say but they do gaylies;⁸
35  They lay aside a' tender mercies,
An' tirl the hullions⁹ to the birses.¹⁰
Yet while they're only poind and herriet,¹¹
They'll keep their stubborn Highland spirit.

5. **Bid.** Ask, wish.
6. **Thae.** Those.
7. **Grieves.** Overseers.
8. **Gaylies.** Pretty well.

9. **Tirl the hullions.** Strip the slovens.
10. **Birses.** Bristles.
11. **Poind and herriet.** Distrained and harried.

But smash them! crush them a' to spails,[12]

40  An' rot the dyvors[13] i' the jails!

The young dogs, swinge[14] them to the labor;

Let wark an' hunger mak them sober!

The hizzies,[15] if they're aughtlins fawsont,[16]

Let them in Drury Lane* be lesson'd!

45  An' if the wives an' dirty brats

Come thiggin[17] at your doors an' yetts,[18]

Flaffin wi' duds,[19] an' grey wi' beas',[20]

Frightin awa your deuks an' geese,

Get out a horsewhip or a jowler,[21]

50  The langest thong, the fiercest growler,[22]

An' gar[23] the tatter'd gypsies pack

Wi' a' their bastards on their back!

Go on, my lord! I lang to meet you,

An' in my "house at hame" to greet you.

55  Wi' common lords ye shanna mingle:

The benmost neuk[24] beside the ingle,[25]

At my right han' assigned your seat,

'Tween Herod's hip an' Polycrate;*

Or (if you on your station tarrow[26])

60  Between Almagro and Pizarro,*

A seat, I'm sure ye're weel deservin't;

An' till ye come—your humble servant,

                                        BEELZEBUB.

12. **Spails.**  Chips.
13. **Dyvors.**  Bankrupts.
14. **Swinge.**  Scourge.
15. **Hizzies.**  Young women.
16. **Aughtlins fawsont.** At all decent.
17. **Thiggin.**  Begging.
18. **Yetts.**  Gates.
19. **Flaffin wi' duds.**  Flapping with rags.

20. **Beas'.**  Vermin.
21. **Jowler.**  A heavy-jawed dog.
22. **Growler.**  A surly dog.
23. **Gar.**  Make.
24. **Benmost neuk.**  Inmost corner
25. **Ingle.**  Fire.
26. **Tarrow.**  Tarry, hesitate.

## ADDRESS TO THE UNCO GUID[1]

### OR THE RIGIDLY RIGHTEOUS

> My Son, these maxims make a rule,
>    An' lump them ay thegither:
> The *Rigid Righteous* is a fool,
>    The *Rigid Wise* anither;
> The cleanest corn that ere was dight[2]
>    May hae some pyles o' caff[3] in;
> So ne'er a fellow creature slight
>    For random fits o' daffin.[4]
>                SOLOMON.—Eccles. ch. vii. verse 16.

[Probably written in 1786, but after the Kilmarnock edition appeared, as this poem was first published in the Edinburgh edition of 1787.

Related in thought to such work as "Holy Willie's Prayer." See also stanza xxvi of the "Epistle to James Smith" (page 142).]

### I

O ye wha are sae guid yoursel,
   Sae pious and sae holy,
Ye've nought to do but mark and tell
   Your neebor's fauts[5] and folly!
Whase life is like a weel-gaun[6] mill,
   Supplied wi' store o' water;
The heapet happer's[7] ebbing still,
   An' still the clap plays clatter.[8]

### II

Hear me, ye venerable core,[9]
   As counsel for poor mortals
That frequent pass douce[10] Wisdom's door
   For glaikit[11] Folly's portals;
I, for their thoughtless, careless sakes
   Would here propone defences—
Their donsie[12] tricks, their black mistakes,
   Their failings and mischances.

1. **Unco guid.** Remarkably good.
2. **Dight.** Winnowed.
3. **Pyles o' caff.** Grains of chaff.
4. **Daffin.** Fun.
5. **Fauts.** Faults.
6. **Weel-gaun.** Well going.
7. **Happer.** Hopper.
8. **Clap plays clatter.** Clapper makes a noise.
9. **Core.** Company (corps).
10. **Douce.** Sedate, grave.
11. **Glaikit.** Foolish, giddy.
12. **Donsie.** Unlucky.

### III

Ye see your state wi' theirs compar'd,
　　And shudder at the niffer,[13]
But cast a moment's fair regard,
　　What maks the mighty differ?
Discount what scant occasion gave,
　　That purity ye pride in,
And (what's aft mair[14] than a' the lave[15])
　　Your better art o' hidin.

### IV

Think, when your castigated pulse
　　Gies[16] now and then a wallop,
What ragings must his veins convulse,
　　That still eternal gallop!
Wi' wind and tide fair i' your tail,
　　Right on ye scud your sea-way;
But in the teeth o' baith to sail,
　　It maks an unco lee-way.

### V

See Social-life and Glee sit down,
　　All joyous and unthinking,
Till, quite transmugrify'd,[17] they're grown
　　Debauchery and Drinking:
O would they stay to calculate
　　Th' eternal consequences;
Or—your more dreaded hell to state—
　　Damnation of expenses!

### VI

Ye high, exalted, virtuous dames,
　　Tied up in godly laces,
Before ye gie poor Frailty names,
　　Suppose a change o' cases;

13. **Niffer.** Exchange.
14. **Aft mair.** Often more.
15. **Lave.** Rest.
16. **Gies.** Gives.
17. **Transmugrify'd.** Transformed.

A dear-lov'd lad, convenience snug,
    A treacherous inclination—
But, let me whisper i' your lug,[18]
    Ye're aiblins[19] nae temptation.


### VII

Then gently scan your brother man,
    Still gentler sister woman;
Tho' they may gang a kennin[20] wrang,
    To step aside is human:
One point must still be greatly dark,
    The moving *why* they do it;
And just as lamely can ye mark,
    How far perhaps they rue it.


### VIII

Who made the heart, 'tis He alone
    Decidedly can try us;
He knows each chord, its various tone,
    Each spring, its various bias:
Then at the balance let's be mute,
    We never can adjust it;
What's done we partly may compute
    But know not what's resisted.

18. Lug.  Ear.
19. Aiblins.  Perhaps.
20. Kennin.  Trifle.

## ADDRESS TO A HAGGIS

[Written rather early in Burns's first stay at Edinburgh; published in the *Caledonian Mercury* for December 19, 1786, then in the *Scots Magazine* for January, 1787, and in the first Edinburgh edition of Burns's poems.

A haggis is a sort of pudding made of sheep's entrails, onions, and oatmeal, boiled in a sheep's stomach; it is said to be a good antidote to whisky. "Painch, tripe, or thairm" (stanza i) were also used similarly in puddings.]

### I

Fair fa'[1] your honest, sonsie[2] face,
Great chieftain o' the puddin-race!
Aboon[3] them a' ye tak your place,
　　　　Painch,[4] tripe, or thairm:[5]
Weel are ye wordy[6] of a grace
　　　　As lang's my arm.

### II

The groaning trencher there ye fill,
Your hurdies[7] like a distant hill,
Your pin[8] wad help to mend a mill
　　　　In time o' need,
While thro' your pores the dews distil
　　　　Like amber bead.

### III

His knife see rustic Labor dight,[9]
An' cut you up wi' ready slight,
Trenching your gushing entrails bright,
　　　　Like onie ditch;
And then, O what a glorious sight,
　　　　Warm-reekin, rich!

1. **Fair fa'.** Benediction on.
2. **Sonsie.** Pleasant.
3. **Aboon.** Above.
4. **Painch.** Paunch.
5. **Thairm.** Intestine.
6. **Wordy.** Worthy.
7. **Hurdies.** Loins.
8. **Pin.** A long metal or wooden skewer.
9. **Dight.** Wipe.

### IV

Then, horn[10] for horn, they stretch an' strive;
Deil tak the hindmost, on they drive,
Till a' their weel-swall'd kytes belyve[11]
       Are bent like drums;
Then auld Guidman, maist like to rive,[12]
       "Bethankit!" hums.

### V

Is there that owre his French *ragout,*
Or *olio*[13] that wad staw[14] a sow,
Or *fricassee* wad mak her spew
       Wi' perfect sconner,[15]
Looks down wi' sneering, scornfu' view
       On sic' a dinner?

### VI

Poor devil! see him owre his trash,
As feckless[16] as a wither'd rash,[17]
His spindle shank a guid whip-lash,
       His nieve[18] a nit;[19]
Thro' bloody flood or field to dash,
       O how unfit!

### VII

But mark the Rustic, haggis-fed;
The trembling earth resounds his tread!
Clap in his walie nieve[20] a blade,
       He'll mak it whissle;
An' legs, an' arms, an' heads will sned,[21]
       Like taps o' thrissle.[22]

10. **Horn.** A horn spoon.
11. **Weel-swall'd kytes belyve.** Well-filled stomachs soon.
12. **Rive.** Burst.
13. **Olio.** Meat and vegetables stewed together.
14. **Staw.** Surfeit.
15. **Sconner.** Disgust.
16. **Feckless.** Weak.
17. **Rash.** Rush, reed.
18. **Nieve.** Fist.
19. **Nit.** Nut.
20. **Walie nieve.** Robust fist.
21. **Sned.** Crop, cut off.
22. **Taps o' thrissle.** Tops of thistle.

VIII

Ye Pow'rs wha mak mankind your care,
And dish them out their bill o' fare,
Auld Scotland wants nae skinking[23] ware
          That jaups in luggies;[24]
But, if ye wish her gratefu' pray'r,
          Gie her a haggis!


## A WINTER NIGHT

"Poor naked wretches, wheresoe'er you are,
  That bide the pelting of this pitiless storm!
  How shall your houseless heads, and unfed sides,
  Your loop'd and window'd raggedness, defend you
  From seasons such as these?"—SHAKESPEARE.

[Written probably late in 1786; first printed in the Edinburgh edition of 1787.
The quotation prefixed to the poem is from *King Lear*, and the rather grandiloquent English portion in irregular meter is little more than an elaboration of the passage from Shakespeare.]


When biting Boreas, fell and doure,[1]
Sharp shivers thro' the leafless bow'r;
When Phœbus gies a short-liv'd glow'r,
        Far south the lift,[2]
5 Dim-dark'ning thro' the flaky show'r,
        Or whirling drift:


Ae[3] night the storm the steeples rocked,
Poor Labor sweet in sleep was locked,
While burns,[4] wi' snawy wreaths up-choked,
10         Wild-eddying swirl,
Or, thro' the mining outlet bocked,[5]
        Down headlong hurl:

23. **Skinking.** Watery.
24. **Jaups in luggies.** Splashes in wooden dishes.
1. **Fell and doure.** Keen and severe.
2. **Lift.** Sky.
3. **Ae.** One.
4. **Burns.** Rivulets.
5. **Bocked.** Vomited.

List'ning the doors an' winnocks[6] rattle,
I thought me on the ourie[7] cattle,
15 Or silly sheep, wha bide this brattle[8]
　　　　　O' winter war,
And thro' the drift, deep-lairing, sprattle[9]
　　　　Beneath a scar.[10]


Ilk happing[11] bird, wee, helpless thing!
20 That, in the merry months o' spring,
Delighted me to hear thee sing,
　　　　　What comes o' thee?
Whare wilt thou cow'r[12] thy chittering[13] wing,
　　　　An' close thy e'e?[14]


25 Ev'n you, on murd'ring errands toil'd,
Lone from your savage homes exil'd,
The blood-stain'd roost and sheep-cote spoil'd
　　　　　My heart forgets,
While pityless the tempest wild
30　　　　　Sore on you beats.


Now Phœbe, in her midnight reign,
Dark-muffl'd, view'd the dreary plain;
Still crowding thoughts, a pensive train,
　　　　　Rose in my soul,
35 When on my ear this plaintive strain,
　　　　　Slow-solemn, stole—

---

6. **Winnocks.** Windows.
7. **Ourie.** Shivering.
8. **Brattle.** Onset.
9. **Lairing, sprattle.** Sinking, scramble.

10. **Scar.** Cliff.
11. **Ilk happing.** Each hopping.
12. **Cow'r.** Cover.
13. **Chittering.** Trembling.
14. **E'e.** Eye.

"Blow, blow, ye winds, with heavier gust!
And freeze, thou bitter-biting frost!
Descend, ye chilly, smothering snows!
40 Not all your rage, as now united, shows
    More hard unkindness unrelenting,
    Vengeful malice unrepenting,
Than heav'n-illumin'd Man on brother Man bestows!
See stern Oppression's iron grip,
45    Or mad Ambition's gory hand,
Sending, like blood-hounds from the slip,
    Woe, want, and murder o'er a land!
Ev'n in the peaceful rural vale,
Truth, weeping, tells the mournful tale,
50 How pamper'd Luxury, Flatt'ry by her side,
    The parasite empoisoning her ear,
    With all the servile wretches in the rear,
Looks o'er proud Property, extended wide;
    And eyes the simple, rustic hind,
55 Whose toil upholds the glitt'ring show—
    A creature of another kind,
    Some coarser substance, unrefin'd—
Plac'd for her lordly use, thus far, thus vile, below!
"Where, where is Love's fond, tender throe,
60 With lordly Honor's lofty brow,
    The pow'rs you proudly own?
Is there, beneath Love's noble name,
Can harbor, dark, the selfish aim,
    To bless himself alone!
65 Mark Maiden-innocence a prey
    To love-pretending snares:
This boasted Honor turns away,
Shunning soft Pity's rising sway,
Regardless of the tears and unavailing pray'rs!
70    Perhaps this hour, in Misery's squalid nest,

    She strains your infant to her joyless breast,
And with a mother's fears shrinks at the rocking
        blast!

    "Oh ye! who, sunk in beds of down,
      Feel not a want but what yourselves create,
75      Think, for a moment, on his wretched fate,
    Whom friends and fortune quite disown!
Ill-satisfy'd keen Nature's clam'rous call,
    Stretch'd on his straw, he lays himself to sleep;
While through the ragged roof and chinky wall,
80    Chill, o'er his slumbers, piles the drifty heap!
    Think on the dungeon's grim confine,
    Where Guilt and poor Misfortune pine!
    Guilt, erring man, relenting view!
    But shall thy legal rage pursue
85    The wretch, already crushèd low
    By cruel Fortune's undeservèd blow?
Affliction's sons are brothers in distress;
A brother to relieve, how exquisite the bliss!"

    I heard nae mair, for Chanticleer
90      Shook off the pouthery[15] snaw,
    And hail'd the morning with a cheer,
      A cottage-rousing craw.

    But deep this truth impress'd my mind—
      Thro' all His works abroad,
95    The heart benevolent and kind
      The most resembles God.

15. **Pouthery.** Powdery.

# EPISTLE TO MRS. SCOTT

## GUIDWIFE OF WAUCHOPE HOUSE, ROXBURGHSHIRE

[This poem was written in reply to a riming epistle from Mrs. Scott to Burns, dated February, 1787. Two years later the lady died (aged about sixty). After her death (in 1801) selections from her verses were published, and among them this poem of Burns's first appeared in print.

The allusion in stanza iii is to Burns's first love affair—with "Handsome Nell" (see page 187).]

I

I mind it weel, in early date,
When I was beardless, young, and blate,[1]
  An' first could thresh the barn,
Or haud a yokin[2] at the pleugh,
An', tho' forfoughten[3] sair eneugh,
  Yet unco[4] proud to learn;
When first amang the yellow corn
  A man I reckon'd was,
An' wi' the lave ilk[5] merry morn
  Could rank my rig and lass,[6]
    Still shearing, and clearing
    The tither stookèd raw,[7]
    Wi' clavers an' havers[8]
    Wearing the day awa:

II

E'en then, a wish (I mind its pow'r),
A wish that to my latest hour
  Shall strongly heave my breast,
That I for poor auld Scotland's sake
Some usefu' plan or book could make,
  Or sing a sang at least.

1. **Blate.** Bashful.
2. **Haud a yokin.** Hold a yoking (as much work as is done by draught animals at one time).
3. **Forfoughten.** Exhausted.
4. **Unco.** Very.
5. **Lave, ilk.** Rest, each.
6. **Rank my rig and lass.** A man and a woman would take a "ridge" of land.
7. **Tither stookèd raw.** Other stacked row.
8. **Clavers an' havers.** Gossip and nonsense.

The rough burr-thistle, spreading wide
  Amang the bearded bear,[9]
I turn'd the weeder-clips aside,
  An' spar'd the symbol dear.
    No nation, no station,
      My envy e'er could raise;
    A Scot still, but blot still,
      I knew nae higher praise.

### III

But still the elements o' sang
In formless jumble, right an' wrang,
  Wild floated in my brain;
'Till on that hairst[10] I said before,
My partner in the merry core,
  She roused the forming strain.
I see her yet, the sonsie quean[11]
  That lighted up my jingle,
Her witching smile, her pauky een[12]
  That gart[13] my heart-strings tingle;
    I fir'd, inspir'd,
      At ev'ry kindling keek,[14]
    But, bashing and dashing,[15]
      I fear'd ay to speak.

### IV

Hale to the sex! ilk guid chiel[16] says:
Wi' merry dance in winter days,
  An' we to share in common!
The gust[17] o' joy, the balm of woe,
The saul o' life, the heav'n below,
  Is rapture-giving woman.

9. **Bear.** Barley.
10. **Hairst.** Harvest.
11. **Sonsie quean.** Pleasant lass.
12. **Pauky een.** Mischievous eyes.
13. **Gart.** Made.
14. **Keek.** Peep.
15. **Bashing and dashing.** Abashed and ashamed.
16. **Ilk guid chiel.** Every good fellow.
17. **Gust.** Taste.

Ye surly sumphs,[18] who hate the name,
 Be mindfu' o' your mither;
She, honest woman, may think shame
 That ye're connected with her!
  Ye're wae[19] men, ye're nae men
   That slight the lovely dears;
  To shame ye, disclaim ye,
   Ilk honest birkie[20] swears.

V

For you, no[21] bred to barn and byre,[22]
Wha sweetly tune the Scottish lyre,
 Thanks to you for your line!
The marled[23] plaid ye kindly spare,
By me should gratefully be ware;[24]
 'Twad please me to the nine.*
I'd be mair vauntie[25] o' my hap,[26]
Douce[27] hingin owre my curple,[28]
Than onie ermine ever lap,[29]
 Or proud imperial purple.
  Farewell, then! lang hale[30] then,
   An' plenty be your fa'![31]
  May losses and crosses
   Ne'er at your hallan ca'![32]

R. BURNS.

18. **Sumphs.** Blockheads.
19. **Wae.** Woful.
20. **Birkie.** Fellow.
21. **No.** Not.
22. **Byre.** Cow-house.
23. **Marled.** Mottled.
24. **Ware.** Worn.
25. **Mair vauntie.** More proud.
26. **Hap.** Wrap.
27. **Douce.** Sedately.

28. **Curple.** Crupper.
29. **Onie ermine ever lap.** Any one who was ever covered with ermine.
30. **Hale.** Health.
31. **Fa'.** Lot (fall).
32. **Hallan ca'.** Cottage call. (A hallan is specifically a partition in a dwelling.)

# THE HUMBLE PETITION OF BRUAR WATER

### TO THE NOBLE DUKE OF ATHOLE

[Written during Burns's tour of the Highlands in 1787,
but first published in the 1793 edition of his poems. Prompted
by the fact that Bruar Falls, in Athol, were "exceedingly
picturesque and beautiful, but their effect ...... much impaired by the want of trees and shrubs." (R.B.) The compliment in the last stanza is due to Burns's entertainment by
the Duke of Athol.]

I

My lord, I know your noble ear
    Woe ne'er assails in vain;
Embolden'd thus, I beg you'll hear
    Your humble slave complain,
How saucy Phœbus' scorching beams,
    In flaming summer pride,
Dry-withering, waste my foamy streams,
    And drink my crystal tide.


II

The lightly-jumping, glowrin[1] trouts,
    That thro' my waters play,
If, in their random, wanton spouts,
    They near the margin stray;
If, hapless chance! they linger lang,
    I'm scorching up so shallow,
They're left the whitening stanes amang,
    In gasping death to wallow.


III

Last day I grat[2] wi' spite and teen,[3]
    As poet Burns came by,
That, to a bard, I should be seen
    Wi' half my channel dry;

1. **Glowrin.**  Staring.              3. **Teen.**  Vexation.
2. **Grat.**  Wept.

A panegyric rhyme, I ween,
　　Even as I was, he shor'd[4] me;
But had I in my glory been,
　　He, kneeling, wad ador'd me.


### IV

Here, foaming down the skelvy[5] rocks,
　　In twisting strength I rin;
There, high my boiling torrent smokes,
　　Wild-roaring o'er a linn:[6]
Enjoying large each spring and well,
　　As Nature gave them me,
I am, altho' I say't mysel,
　　Worth gaun a mile to see.


### V

Would, then, my noble master please
　　To grant my highest wishes,
He'll shade my banks wi' tow'ring trees
　　And bonic spreading bushes.
Delighted doubly, then, my lord,
　　You'll wander on my banks,
And listen mony a grateful bird
　　Return you tuneful thanks.


### VI

The sober lav'rock,[7] warbling wild,
　　Shall to the skies aspire;
The gowdspink,[8] Music's gayest child,
　　Shall sweetly join the choir;
The blackbird strong, the lintwhite[9] clear,
　　The mavis[10] mild and mellow,
The robin pensive Autumn cheer,
　　In all her locks of yellow.

---

4. **Shor'd.** Offered.
5. **Skelvy.** Sloping, shelving.
6. **Linn.** Waterfall.
7. **Lav'rock.** Lark.

8. **Gowdspink.** Goldfinch.
9. **Lintwhite.** Linnet.
10. **Mavis.** Thrush.

### VII

This, too, a covert shall ensure,
　To shield them from the storm;
And coward maukin[11] sleep secure,
　Low in her grassy form:
Here shall the shepherd make his seat,
　To weave his crown of flow'rs;
Or find a shelt'ring, safe retreat
　From prone-descending show'rs.

### VIII

And here, by sweet, endearing stealth,
　Shall meet the loving pair,
Despising worlds, with all their wealth,
　As empty idle care;
The flow'rs shall vie in all their charms
　The hour of heav'n to grace;
And birks[12] extend their fragrant arms
　To screen the dear embrace.

### IX

Here haply, too, at vernal dawn,
　Some musing bard may stray,
And eye the smoking, dewy lawn
　And misty mountain grey;
Or, by the reaper's nightly beam,
　Mild-chequering thro' the trees,
Rave to my darkly dashing stream,
　Hoarse-swelling on the breeze.

### X

Let lofty firs, and ashes cool,
　My lowly banks o'erspread,
And view, deep-bending in the pool,
　Their shadows' wat'ry bed:

11. **Maukin.** Rabbit.　　　12. **Birks.** Birches.

Let fragrant birks, in woodbines drest,
   My craggy cliffs adorn,
And, for the little songster's nest,
   The close embow'ring thorn.


### XI

So may old Scotia's darling hope,
   Your little angel band,
Spring, like their fathers, up to prop
   Their honor'd native land!
So may, thro' Albion's farthest ken,
   To social-flowing glasses,
The grace be—"Athole's honest men,
   And Athole's bonie lasses!"


## THE WOUNDED HARE

["On seeing a wounded hare limp by me, which a fellow
had just shot at"; sent in a letter to Mrs. Dunlop in April,
1789; published first in the edition of 1793.]


### I

Inhuman man! curse on thy barb'rous art,
   And blasted be thy murder-aiming eye;
   May never pity soothe thee with a sigh,
Nor never pleasure glad thy cruel heart!


### II

Go live, poor wanderer of the wood and field,
   The bitter little that of life remains!
   No more the thickening brakes and verdant plains
To thee shall home, or food, or pastime yield.

### III

Seek, mangled wretch, some place of wonted rest,
　　No more of rest, but now thy dying bed!
　　The sheltering rushes whistling o'er thy head,
The cold earth with thy bloody bosom prest.

### IV

Oft as by winding Nith I, musing, wait
　　The sober eve, or hail the cheerful dawn,
　　I'll miss thee sporting o'er the dewy lawn,
And curse the ruffian's aim, and mourn thy hapless fate.


## EPISTLE TO DR. BLACKLOCK

[Dr. Blacklock was an elderly blind, poet of Edinburgh whose letter to Burns soon after the appearance of his Kilmarnock edition decided the poet to go to Edinburgh instead of to Jamaica. The "epistle" was not published during Burns's lifetime, but was added by Currie in his edition of 1800. Stanzas ii and iii allude to the fact that Burns had sent a letter to Blacklock by his friend Robert Heron.]

Ellisland, 21st October, 1789.

### I

Wow, but your letter made me vauntie![1]
And are ye hale, and weel, and cantie?[2]
I kend[3] it still, your wee bit jauntie[4]
　　　　Wad bring ye to:
Lord send you ay as weel's I want ye,
　　　　And then ye'll do!

### II

The ill-thief[5] blaw the Heron south,
And never drink be near his drouth!
He tauld mysel by word o' mouth,
　　　　He'd tak my letter;
I lippen'd to the chiel[6] in trowth,
　　　　And bade[7] nae better.

1. **Vauntie.** Proud.
2. **Cantie.** Cheerful.
3. **Kend.** Knew.
4. **Wee bit jauntie.** Little trip (jaunt).
5. **Ill-thief.** Devil.
6. **Lippen'd to the chiel.** Trusted the fellow.
7. **Bade.** Asked.

### III

But aiblins[8] honest Master Heron
Had, at the time, some dainty fair one
To ware his theologic care on,
   And holy study,
And, tired o' sauls to waste his lear[9] on,
   E'en tried the body.

### IV

But what d'ye think, my trusty fier?[10]
I'm turn'd a gauger—Peace be here!
Parnassian queires,[11] I fear, I fear,
   Ye'll now disdain me,
And then my fifty pounds a year
   Will little gain me!

### V

Ye glaikit,[12] gleesome, dainty damies,
Wha by Castalia's wimplin[13] streamies*
Lowp,[14] sing, and lave your pretty limbies,
   Ye ken, ye ken,
That strang necessity supreme is
   'Mang sons o' men.

### VI

I hae a wife and twa wee laddies;
They maun hae brose[15] and brats[16] o' duddies;
Ye ken yoursels my heart right proud is—
   I need na vaunt—
But I'll sned besoms, thraw saugh woodies,[17]
   Before they want.

8. **Aiblins.** Perhaps.
9. **Lear.** Learning.
10. **Fier.** Comrade.
11. **Parnassian queires.** Choirs of Parnassus, the mountain of the Muses.
12. **Glaikit.** Foolish.
13. **Wimplin.** Meandering.
14. **Lowp.** Leap.
15. **Maun hae brose.** Must have porridge.
16. **Brats.** Bits.
17. **Sned besoms, thraw saugh woodies.** Cut brooms, twist willow-switches.

### VII

Lord help me thro' this warld o' care!
I'm weary, sick o't late and air![18]
Not but I hae a richer share
         Than monie ithers;
But why should ae[19] man better fare,
         And a' men brithers?

### VIII

Come, firm Resolve, take thou the van,
Thou stalk o' carl-hemp[20] in man!
And let us mind, faint heart ne'er wan
         A lady fair:
Wha does the utmost that he can
         Will whyles[21] do mair.

### IX

But to conclude my silly rhyme
(I'm scant o' verse and scant o' time),
To make a happy fireside clime
         To weans[22] and wife,
That's the true pathos and sublime
         Of human life.

### X

My compliments to sister Beckie,
And eke the same to honest Luckie;*
I wat she is a daintie chuckie[23]
         As e'er tread clay;
And gratefully, my guid auld cockie,[24]
         I'm yours for ay.
              ROBERT BURNS.

18. **Air.** Early.
19. **Ae.** One.
20. **Carl-hemp.** Male-hemp.
21. **Whyles.** Sometimes.
22 **Weans.** Children.

23. **Chuckie.** Mother hen (i. e., dear old lady).
24. **Cockie.** Diminutive of *cock* (rooster).

# ELEGY ON CAPTAIN MATTHEW HENDERSON

### A GENTLEMAN WHO HELD THE PATENT FOR HIS HONORS IMMEDIATELY FROM ALMIGHTY GOD!

*But now his radiant course is run,*
*For Matthew's course was bright;*
*His soul was like the glorious sun,*
*A matchless Heav'nly light.*

[Henderson was an army officer whom Burns met during his residence in Edinburgh, and who died November 21, 1788. Apparently Burns did not write this "Elegy" till the summer of 1790. At any rate, he sent copies of it to two different correspondents during July and August of that year, speaking of one of them as "a first fair copy." The poem was first published in the Edinburgh edition of 1793.]

### I

O Death! thou tyrant fell and bloody!
The meikle[1] devil wi' a woodie[2]
Haurl[3] thee hame to his black smiddie,[4]
      O'er hurcheon[5] hides,
And like stock-fish come o'er his studdie[6]
      Wi' thy auld sides!

### II

He's gane, he's gane! he's frae us torn,
The ae[7] best fellow e'er was born!
Thee, Matthew, Nature's sel shall mourn
      By wood and wild,
Where, haply, Pity strays forlorn,
      Frae man exil'd.

### III

Ye hills, near neebors o' the starns,[8]
That proudly cock your cresting cairns!
Ye cliffs, the haunts of sailing yearns[9]
      Where Echo slumbers!
Come join, ye Nature's sturdiest bairns,[10]
      My wailing numbers!

1. **Meikle.** Great.
2. **Woodie.** Rope.
3. **Haurl.** Drag.
4. **Smiddie.** Smithy.
5. **Hurcheon.** Hedgehog.
6. **Studdie.** Anvil.
7. **Ae.** One.
8. **Starns.** Stars.
9. **Yearns.** Eagles.
10. **Bairns.** Children.

IV

Mourn, ilka[11] grove the cushat kens![12]
Ye hazly shaws[13] and briery dens!
Ye burnies, wimplin[14] down your glens
        Wi' toddlin din,
Or foaming, strang, wi' hasty stens,[15]
        Frae lin to lin.[16]


V

Mourn, little harebells o'er the lea;
Ye stately foxgloves fair to see;
Ye woodbines hanging bonilie
        In scented bow'rs;
Ye roses on your thorny tree,
        The first o' flow'rs!


VI

At dawn, when ev'ry grassy blade
Droops with a diamond at his head,
At ev'n, when beans their fragrance shed
        I' th' rustling gale,
Ye maukins, whiddin[17] thro' the glade,
        Come join my wail.


VII

Mourn, ye wee songsters o' the wood;
Ye grouse that crap[18] the heather bud;
Ye curlews, calling thro' a clud;[19]
        Ye whistling plover;
And mourn, ye whirring paitrick[20] brood;
        He's gane for ever!

11. **Ilka.** Every.
12. **Cushat kens.** Wood-dove knows.
13. **Shaws.** Woods.
14. **Burnies wimplin.** Brooks meandering.
15. **Stens.** Leaps.
16. **Lin.** Waterfall.
17. **Maukins whiddin.** Hares scudding.
18. **Crap.** Crop, nibble.
19. **Clud.** Cloud.
20. **Paitrick.** Partridge.

### VIII

Mourn, sooty coots, and speckled teals;
Ye fisher herons, watching eels;
Ye duck and drake, wi' airy wheels
       Circling the lake;
Ye bitterns, till the quagmire reels,
       Rair[21] for his sake.


### IX

Mourn, clam'ring craiks[22] at close o' day,
'Mang fields o' flow'ring clover gay;
And when ye wing your annual way
       Frae our cauld shore,
Tell thae[23] far warlds wha lies in clay,
       Wham we deplore.


### X

Ye houlets,[24] frae your ivy bow'r
In some auld tree, or eldritch[25] tow'r,
What time the moon, wi' silent glow'r,
       Sets up her horn,[26]
Wail thro' the dreary midnight hour
       Till waukrife[27] morn!


### XI

O rivers, forests, hills, and plains!
Oft have ye heard my canty[28] strains:
But now, what else for me remains
       But tales of woe;
And frae my een[29] the drapping rains
       Maun[30] ever flow.

21. **Rair.** Roar.
22. **Craiks.** Corn-crakes (a kind of bird).
23. **Thae.** Those.
24. **Houlets.** Owlets.
25. **Eldritch.** Haunted.
26. **Sets up her horn.** Points the ends of her crescent upward.
27. **Waukrife.** Wakeful.
28. **Canty.** Cheerful.
29. **Een.** Eyes.
30. **Maun.** Must.

### XII

Mourn, Spring, thou darling of the year!
Ilk[31] cowslip cup shall kep[32] a tear:
Thou, Simmer, while each corny[33] spear
   Shoots up its head,
Thy gay, green, flow'ry tresses shear
   For him that's dead!


### XIII

Thou, Autumn, wi' thy yellow hair,
In grief thy sallow mantle tear!
Thou, Winter, hurling thro' the air
   The roaring blast,
Wide o'er the naked world declare
   The worth we've lost!


### XIV

Mourn him, thou Sun, great source of light!
Mourn, Empress of the silent night!
And you, ye twinkling starnies[34] bright,
   My Matthew mourn!
For through your orbs he's taen his flight,
   Ne'er to return.


### XV

O Henderson, the man! the brother!
And art thou gone, and gone forever?
And hast thou crost that unknown river,
   Life's dreary bound?
Like thee, where shall I find another,
   The world around?

31. **Ilk.** Each.
32. **Kep.** Catch.

33. **Corny.** Furnished with grains of corn.
34. **Starnies.** Little stars.

XVI

Go to your sculptur'd tombs, ye Great,
In a' the tinsel trash o' state!
But by thy honest turf I'll wait,
                    Thou man of worth!
And weep the ae[35] best fellow's fate
                    E'er lay in earth.


## TAM O' SHANTER

### A TALE

"Of Brownyis and of Bogillis full is this Buke."
                                    —GAWIN DOUGLAS.

[Written late in 1790 or early in 1791; published in the
*Edinburgh Magazine* for March, 1791, the *Edinburgh Herald*
of March 18, 1791; in Francis Grose's *Antiquities of Scotland*,
which appeared in April, 1791; and in the 1793 edition of
Burns's poems. "Tam o' Shanter" was really written for
Grose's *Antiquities*, after Burns had suggested to the antiquary
that Alloway Kirk deserved mention in the latter's book.
The poem was suggested by a legend which Burns had sent,
along with two others about Alloway Kirk, in a letter to
Grose before the poem was written. Alloway Kirk is only
a short distance from the cottage where Burns was born.]

When chapman billies[1] leave the street,
And drouthy neebors neebors meet;
As market-days are wearing late,
An' folk begin to tak the gate;[2]
5    While we sit bousing at the nappy,[3]
An' getting fou[4] and unco[5] happy,
We think na on the lang Scots miles,
The mosses, waters, slaps,[6] and styles,
That lie between us and our hame,
10   Whare sits our sulky, sullen dame,
Gathering her brows like gathering storm,
Nursing her wrath to keep it warm.

35. **Ae.**  One.
1. **Chapman billies.** Peddler fellows.
2. **Tak the gate.**  Take the road (go home).
3. **Nappy.**  Ale.
4. **Fou.**  Full, drunk.
5. **Unco.**  Very.
6. **Slaps.**  Gaps in fences.

This truth fand[7] honest Tam o' Shanter,
As he frae Ayr ae[8] night did canter
15 (Auld Ayr, wham ne'er a town surpasses,
For honest men and bonie lasses).


O Tam! hadst thou but been sae wise,
As taen thy ain wife Kate's advice!
She tauld thee weel thou was a skellum,[9]
20 A blethering,[10] blustering, drunken blellum;[11]
That frae November till October,
Ae market-day thou was nae sober;
That ilka melder[12] wi' the miller,
Thou sat as lang as thou had siller;
25 That ev'ry naig was ca'd a shoe on,[13]
The smith an thee gat roaring fou on;
That at the Lord's house, ev'n on Sunday,
Thou drank wi' Kirkton Jean* till Monday.
She prophesied that, late or soon,
30 Thou would be found deep drown'd in Doon,
Or catch'd wi' warlocks[14] in the mirk,[15]
By Alloway's auld haunted kirk.[16]


Ah, gentle dames! it gars me greet,[17]
To think how mony counsels sweet,
35 How mony lengthen'd, sage advices,
The husband frae the wife despises!


But to our tale: Ae market night,
Tam had got planted unco right,
Fast by an ingle, bleezing[18] finely,
40 Wi' reaming swats[19] that drank divinely;

7. **Fand.** Found.
8. **Ae.** One.
9. **Skellum.** Good-for-nothing.
10. **Blethering.** Chattering.
11. **Blellum.** Babbler.
12. **Ilka melder.** Every grinding.
13. **Ev'ry naig was ca'd a shoe on.**
   Every horse that was shod.
14. **Warlocks.** Wizards.
15. **Mirk.** Dark.
16. **Kirk.** Church.
17. **Gars me greet.** Makes me weep.
18. **Ingle, bleezing.** Fire, blazing.
19. **Reaming swats.** Foaming ale.

And at his elbow, Souter[20] Johnny,
His ancient, trusty, drouthy crony:
Tam lo'ed him like a vera brither;
They had been fou for weeks thegither.
45  The night drave on wi' sangs and clatter,
And ay the ale was growing better:
The landlady and Tam grew gracious,
Wi' favors secret, sweet, and precious:
The souter tauld his queerest stories;
50  The landlord's laugh was ready chorus:
The storm without might rair[21] and rustle,
Tam did na mind the storm a whistle.

Care, mad to see a man sae happy,
E'en drown'd himsel amang the nappy:[22]
55  As bees flee hame wi' lades o' treasure,
The minutes wing'd their way wi' pleasure:
Kings may be blest, but Tam was glorious,
O'er a' the ills o' life victorious!

But pleasures are like poppies spread—
60  You seize the flow'r, its bloom is shed;
Or like the snow falls in the river,*
A moment white—then melts for ever;
Or like the borealis race,
That flit ere you can point their place;
65  Or like the rainbow's lovely form,
Evanishing amid the storm.—
Nae man can tether time or tide;
The hour approaches Tam maun[23] ride;
That hour, o' night's black arch the key-stane,
70  That dreary hour he mounts his beast in;
And sic[24] a night he taks the road in,
As ne'er poor sinner was abroad in.

20. **Souter.** Shoemaker.          23. **Maun.** Must.
21. **Rair.** Roar.                 24. **Sic.** Such.
22. **Nappy.** Ale.

The wind blew as 'twad blawn its last;
The rattling show'rs rose on the blast;
75 The speedy gleams the darkness swallow'd;
Loud, deep, and lang the thunder bellow'd:
That night, a child might understand,
The Deil had business on his hand.

Weel mounted on his gray mare Meg,
80 A better never lifted leg,
Tam skelpit[25] on thro' dub[26] and mire,
Despising wind, and rain, and fire;
Whyles[27] holding fast his guid blue bonnet,
Whyles crooning o'er some auld Scots sonnet,
85 Whyles glow'ring round wi' prudent cares,
Lest bogles[28] catch him unawares:
Kirk-Alloway was drawing nigh,
Where ghaists and houlets[29] nightly cry.

By this time he was cross the ford,
90 Whare in the snaw the chapman smoor'd;[30]
And past the birks[31] and meikle[32] stane,
Whare drunken Charlie brak's neck-bane;
And thro' the whins,[33] and by the cairn,
Whare hunters fand the murder'd bairn;[34]
95 And near the thorn, aboon[35] the well,
Whare Mungo's mither hang'd hersel.
Before him Doon pours all his floods;
The doubling storm roars thro' the woods;
The lightnings flash from pole to pole;
100 Near and more near the thunders roll:
When, glimmering thro' the groaning trees,
Kirk-Alloway seem'd in a bleeze;[36]

25. **Skelpit.**  Hurried.
26. **Dub.**  Puddle.
27. **Whyles.**  Sometimes.
28. **Bogles.**  Hobgoblins.
29. **Houlets.**  Owlets.
30. **Chapman smoor'd.**  Peddler smothered.
31. **Birks.**  Birches.
32. **Meikle.**  Big.
33. **Whins.**  Gorse, furze.
34. **Bairn.**  Child.
35. **Aboon.**  Above.
36. **Bleeze.**  Blaze.

Thro' ilka bore[37] the beams were glancing,
And loud resounded mirth and dancing.

105     Inspiring bold John Barleycorn!
What dangers thou canst make us scorn!
Wi' tippenny,[38] we fear nae evil;
Wi' usquabae,[39] we'll face the devil!
The swats sae ream'd[40] in Tammie's noddle,
110 Fair play, he car'd na deils a boddle.[41]
But Maggie stood, right sair astonished,
Till, by the heel and hand admonish'd,
She ventur'd forward on the light;
And, vow! Tam saw an unco[42] sight!

115     Warlocks and witches in a dance:
Nae cotillion, brent new[43] frae France,
But hornpipes, jigs, strathspeys, and reels,
Put life and mettle in their heels.
A winnock-bunker[44] in the east,
120 There sat auld Nick, in shape o' beast;
A towzie tyke,[45] black, grim, and large,
To gie them music was his charge:
He screw'd the pipes and gart them skirl,[46]
Till roof and rafters a' did dirl.[47]
125 Coffins stood round, like open presses,
That shaw'd the dead in their last dresses;
And by some devilish cantraip slight,[48]
Each in its cauld hand held a light,
By which heroic Tam was able
130 To note upon the haly[49] table,

37. **Ilka bore.** Every crevice.
38. **Tippenny.** Twopence worth of ale.
39. **Usquabae.** Whisky.
40. **Swats sae ream'd.** Ale so foamed.
41. **Na deils a boddle.** Not a copper for devils.
42. **Unco.** Strange, wonderful.
43. **Brent new.** Brand-new.
44. **Winnock-bunker.** Window-seat.
45. **Towzie tyke.** Shaggy cur.
46. **Gart them skirl.** Made them shriek.
47. **Dirl.** Ring, vibrate.
48. **Cantraip slight.** Magic trick.
49. **Haly.** Holy.

A murderer's banes in gibbet airns;[50]
Twa span-lang, wee, unchristen'd bairns;
A thief, new-cutted frae a rape,
Wi' his last gasp his gab[51] did gape;
135    Five tomahawks, wi' bluid red-rusted;
Five scymitars, wi' murder crusted;
A garter which a babe had strangled;
A knife, a father's throat had mangled,
Whom his ain son o' life bereft—
140    The grey hairs yet stack[52] to the heft;
Wi' mair o' horrible and awfu',
Which ev'n to name wad be unlawfu'.


As Tammie glowr'd,[53] amaz'd and curious,
The mirth and fun grew fast and furious:
145    The piper loud and louder blew;
The dancers quick and quicker flew;
They reel'd, they set, they cross'd, they cleekit,[54]
Till ilka carlin[55] swat and reekit,[56]
And coost[57] her duddies to the wark,
150    And linket[58] at it in her sark![59]


Now Tam, O Tam! had thae[60] been queans,[61]
A' plump and strapping in their teens,
Their sarks, instead o' creeshie flannen,[62]
Been snaw-white seventeen hunder linen![63]
155    Thir breeks[64] o' mine, my only pair,
That ance were plush, o' guid blue hair,
I wad hae gi'en them off my hurdies,[65]
For ae blink o' the bonie burdies![66]

50. **Airns.** Irons.
51. **Gab.** Mouth.
52. **Stack.** Stuck.
53. **Glowr'd.** Stared.
54. **Cleekit.** Joined hands.
55. **Ilka carlin.** Every old woman.
56. **Reekit.** Steamed.
57. **Coost.** Cast off.
58. **Linket.** Tripped.
59. **Sark.** Shirt.
60. **Thae.** Those.
61. **Queans.** Girls.
62. **Creeshie flannen.** Greasy flannel.
63. **Seventeen hunder linen.** Very fine, woven in a reed of 1700 divisions.
64. **Thir breeks.** These breeches.
65. **Hurdies.** Hips.
66. **Burdies.** Maidens.

But wither'd beldams, auld and droll,
160 Rigwoodie[67] hags wad spean[68] a foal,
Louping an' flinging on a crummock,[69]
I wonder did na turn thy stomach.

But Tam kend what was what fu' brawlie :[70]
There was ae winsome wench and wawlie,[71]
165 That night enlisted in the core
(Lang after kend[72] on Carrick shore,
For mony a beast to dead she shot,
And perish'd mony a bonie boat,
And shook baith meikle[73] corn and bear,[74]
170 And kept the country-side in fear).
Her cutty[75] sark, o' Paisley harn,[76]
That while a lassie she had worn,
In longitude tho' sorely scanty,
It was her best, and she was vauntie.[77]
175 Ah! little kend thy reverend grannie,
That sark she coft[78] for her wee Nannie,
Wi' twa pund[79] Scots ('twas a' her riches),
Wad ever grac'd a dance of witches!

But here my Muse her wing maun cour ;[80]
180 Sic flights are far beyond her power ;
To sing how Nannie lap and flang[81]
(A souple jade she was and strang),
And how Tam stood, like ane bewitch'd,
And thought his very een enrich'd ;
185 Even Satan glowr'd,[82] and fidg'd fu' fain,[83]

67. **Rigwoodie.** Withered.
68. **Wad spean.** That would wean.
69. **Crummock.** Staff, cudgel.
70. **Fu' brawlie.** Very well.
71. **Wawlie.** Choice.
72. **Kend.** Known.
73. **Meikle.** Much.
74. **Bear.** Barley.
75. **Cutty.** Short.
76. **Harn.** A coarse linen.

77. **Vauntie.** Proud.
78. **Coft.** Bought.
79. **Twa pund.** Two pounds Scotch (about eighty cents).
80. **Cour.** Let down.
81. **Lap and flang.** Leaped and kicked.
82. **Glowr'd.** Stared.
83. **Fidg'd fu' fain.** Fidgeted with fondness.

And hotch'd[84] and blew wi' might and main;
Till first ae caper, syne[85] anither,
Tam tint[86] his reason a' thegither,
And roars out, "Weel done, Cutty-sark!"
190  And in an instant all was dark;
And scarcely had he Maggie rallied,
When out the hellish legion sallied.

As bees bizz out wi' angry fyke,[87]
When plundering herds[88] assail their byke;[89]
195  As open pussie's[90] mortal foes,
When, pop! she starts before their nose;
As eager runs the market-crowd,
When "Catch the thief!" resounds aloud;
So Maggie runs, the witches follow,
200  Wi' mony an eldritch[91] skreech and hollow.

Ah, Tam! ah, Tam! thou'll get thy fairin![92]
In hell they'll roast thee like a herrin!
In vain thy Kate awaits thy comin!
Kate soon will be a woefu' woman!
205  Now, do thy speedy utmost, Meg,
And win the key-stane of the brig;[93]*
There, at them thou thy tail may toss.
A running stream they dare na cross,
But ere the key-stane she could make,
210  The fient[94] a tail she had to shake!
For Nannie, far before the rest,
Hard upon noble Maggie prest,
And flew at Tam wi' furious ettle;[95]
But little wist she Maggie's mettle—
215  Ae spring brought off her master hale,
But left behind her ain gray tail:

| | |
|---|---|
| 84. **Hotch'd.** Jerked. | 90. **Pussie.** Hare, rabbit. |
| 85. **Syne.** Then. | 91. **Eldritch.** Unearthly. |
| 86. **Tint.** Lost. | 92. **Fairin.** Reward. |
| 87. **Fyke.** Fuss. | 93. **Brig.** Bridge. |
| 88. **Herds.** Herd-boys. | 94. **Fient.** Devil. |
| 89. **Byke.** Hive. | 95. **Ettle.** Effort. |

The carlin claught[96] her by the rump,
And left poor Maggie scarce a stump.

220 Now, wha this tale o' truth shall read,
Ilk man, and mother's son, take heed:
Whene'er to drink you are inclin'd,
Or cutty sarks run in your mind,
Think, ye may buy the joys o'er dear;
Remember Tam o' Shanter's mare.

# SONGS

## HANDSOME NELL

*Tune*—"I am a man unmarried."
[This is Burns's first poem, composed, he said, when he was fifteen, on inspiration which he described in several places: in his "Epistle to Mrs. Scott" (see page 165), in his *First Common Place Book*, in his autobiographical letter to Dr. Moore, etc.
First published in Johnson's *Musical Museum* in 1803.]

O, once I lov'd a bonie lass,
    Ay, and I love her still;
And whilst that virtue warms my breast,
    I'll love my handsome Nell.

As bonie lasses I hae seen,
    And monie full as braw;[1]
But for a modest, gracefu' mien
    The like I never saw.

A bonie lass, I will confess,
    Is pleasant to the e'e;[2]
But without some better qualities
    She's no a lass for me.

96. **Carlin claught.**  Witch clutched.     2. **E'e.**  Eye.
 1. **Braw.**  Fine

But Nelly's looks are blythe and sweet,
   And, what is best of a',
Her reputation is complete,
   And fair without a flaw.

She dresses ay sae clean and neat,
   Both decent and genteel;
And then there's something in her gait
   Gars[3] ony dress look weel.

A gaudy dress and gentle air
   May slightly touch the heart;
But it's innocence and modesty
   That polishes the dart.

'Tis this in Nelly pleases me,
   'Tis this enchants my soul;
For absolutely in my breast
   She reigns without control.


## MARY MORISON

[On the theory that this song relates to an early love affair of Burns which culminated in his rejection by the young lady about 1781, it is usually dated in that year; but the identity of the heroine is not proved—nor does it really matter. She was *not* "Highland Mary," however.

Sent to Thomson March 20, 1793, with a statement from Burns that it was "one of my juvenile works"; first printed in Currie's edition of 1800.]

O Mary, at thy window be!
   It is the wish'd, the trysted[1] hour.
Those smiles and glances let me see,
   That make the miser's treasure poor.
   How blithely wad I bide the stoure,[2]
A weary slave frae sun to sun,
   Could I the rich reward secure—
The lovely Mary Morison.

3. **Gars.** Makes.
1. **Trysted.** Agreed.

2. **Bide the stoure.** Bear the struggle.

Yestreen, when to the trembling string
   The dance gaed[3] thro' the lighted ha',
To thee my fancy took its wing;
   I sat, but neither heard nor saw.
   Tho' this was fair, and that was braw,[4]
And yon the toast of a' the town,
   I sigh'd and said amang them a':
"Ye are na Mary Morison!"

O Mary, canst thou wreck his peace
   Wha for thy sake wad gladly die?
Or canst thou break that heart of his
   Whase only faut[5] is loving thee?
   If love for love thou wilt na gie,[6]
At least be pity to me shown;
   A thought ungentle canna be
The thought o' Mary Morison.


## MY NANIE, O

*Tune*—"My Nanie, O."

[One of the few songs printed in the early editions of
Burns's poems; this and the next two were in the Edinburgh
edition of 1787. This song is copied in Burns's *First Common
Place Book* under the date April, 1784, and is generally believed
to have been written about two years earlier.

The proper name in the first line was originally Stinchar,
and so appears in all the early editions; but in a letter to
Thomson in 1792 Burns expressed a preference for Lugar as
more euphonious.

As in several cases, there is a dispute regarding the identity
of the heroine—which again does not really matter.]

Behind yon hills where Lugar* flows,
   'Mang moors an' mosses many, O,
The wintry sun the day has clos'd,
   And I'll awa to Nanie, O.

3. **Gaed.** Went.                    5. **Faut.** Fault.
4. **Braw.** Fine, handsome.          6. **Gie.** Give.

The westlin wind blaws loud an' shill;[1]
    The night's baith mirk[2] and rainy, O;
But I'll get my plaid, an' out I'll steal,
    An' owre the hill to Nanie, O.

My Nanie's charming, sweet, an' young;
    Nae artfu' wiles to win ye, O:
May ill befa' the flattering tongue
    That wad beguile my Nanie, O.

Her face is fair, her heart is true;
    As spotless as she's bonie, O;
The op'ning gowan,[3] wat wi' dew,
    Nae purer is than Nanie, O.

A country lad is my degree,
    An' few there be that ken[4] me, O;
But what care I how few they be?
    I'm welcome ay to Nanie, O.

My riches a's my penny-fee,
    An' I maun[5] guide it cannie,[6] O;
But warl's gear[7] ne'er troubles me,
    My thoughts are a', my Nanie, O.

Our auld guidman delights to view
    His sheep an' kye[8] thrive bonie, O;
But I'm as blythe that hauds[9] his pleugh,
    An' has nae care but Nanie, O.

Come weel, come woe, I care na by;[10]
    I'll tak what Heav'n will sen' me, O;
Nae ither care in life have I,
    But live, an' love my Nanie, O.

1. **Shill.** Shrill.
2. **Baith mirk.** Both dark.
3. **Gowan.** Daisy.
4. **Ken.** Know.
5. **Maun.** Must.
6. **Cannie.** Carefully.
7. **Warl's gear.** Worldly goods.
8. **Kye.** Cows.
9. **Hauds.** Holds.
10. **Care na by.** Care not.

# GREEN GROW THE RASHES[1]

## A FRAGMENT

[Entered in Burns's *First Common Place Book* under the
date of August (probably 1784); first printed in the Edinburgh edition, 1787.

After a paragraph in the *Common Place Book* on two classes
of young men, "the *grave* and the *merry*," Burns says this
"fragment," "as it is the genuine language of my heart, will
enable anybody to determine which of the classes I belong to."]

*Chor.*—Green grow the rashes, O;
　　　　Green grow the rashes, O;
　　　The sweetest hours that e'er I spend,
　　　Are spent amang the lasses, O.

There's nought but care on ev'ry han',
　　In ev'ry hour that passes, O:
What signifies the life o' man,
　　An' 'twere na for the lasses, O?
　　　　　Green grow, etc.

The warly[2] race may riches chase,
　　An' riches still may fly them, O;
An' tho' at last they catch them fast,
　　Their hearts can ne'er enjoy them, O.
　　　　　Green grow, etc.

But gie[3] me a cannie[4] hour at e'en,
　　My arms about my dearie, O;
An' warly cares, an' warly men,
　　May a' gae tapsalteerie,[5] O!
　　　　　Green grow, etc.

For you sae douce,[6] ye sneer at this,
　　Ye're nought but senseless asses, O:
The wisest man the warl' e'er saw,*
　　He dearly lov'd the lasses, O.
　　　　　Green grow, etc.

1. **Rashes.** Rushes.
2. **Warly.** Worldly.
3. **Gie.** Give.
4. **Cannie.** Quiet.

5. **Gae tapsalteerie.** Go upside-down.
6. **Douce.** Grave.

Auld Nature swears, the lovely dears
Her noblest work she classes, O:
Her prentice han' she try'd on man,
An' then she made the lasses, O.
            Green grow, etc.


## FAREWELL SONG TO THE BANKS OF AYR

*Tune*—"Roslin Castle."

[In Burns's autobiographic letter to Dr. Moore, dated
August 2, 1787, he explains the occasion of this song as follows: "I had taken the last farewell of my few friends; my
chest was on the road to Greenock; I had composed the
last song I should ever measure in Caledonia—The gloomy
night is gathering fast—when a letter from Dr. Blacklock to
a friend of mine overthrew all my schemes, by opening new
prospects to my poetic ambition." The time was the early
autumn of 1786. The poem appeared in the first Edinburgh
edition.]


The gloomy night is gath'ring fast,
Loud roars the wild, inconstant blast;
Yon murky cloud is foul with rain,
I see it driving o'er the plain;
The hunter now has left the moor,
The scatt'red coveys meet secure;
While here I wander, prest with care,
Along the lonely banks of Ayr.

The Autumn mourns her rip'ning corn,
By early Winter's ravage torn;
Across her placid, azure sky,
She sees the scowling tempest fly:
Chill runs my blood to hear it rave;
I think upon the stormy wave,
Where many a danger I must dare,
Far from the bonie banks of Ayr.

'Tis not the surging billow's roar,
'Tis not that fatal, deadly shore;
Tho' death in ev'ry shape appear,
The wretched have no more to fear:
But round my heart the ties are bound,
That heart transpierc'd with many a wound;
These bleed afresh, those ties I tear,
To leave the bonie banks of Ayr.

Farewell, old Coila's* hills and dales,
Her heathy moors and winding vales;
The scenes where wretched Fancy roves,
Pursuing past unhappy loves!
Farewell, my friends! farewell, my foes!
My peace with these, my love with those—
The bursting tears my heart declare,
Farewell, the bonie banks of Ayr!


## THE NIGHT WAS STILL

["Irvine's bairns" were the children of Dr. Lawrie, minister at Loudoun, at whose home Burns first heard the spinet played during the autumn of 1786. The manuscript of this song was first given to one of the daughters of Dr. Lawrie. The poem was not published until 1840.]

The night was still, and o'er the hill
    The moon shone on the castle wa';
The mavis[1] sang, while dew-drops hang
    Around her on the castle wa';
Sae merrily they danced the ring
    Frae e'enin' till the cock did craw;
And ay the o'erword[2] o' the spring[3]
    Was "Irvine's bairns[4] are bonie a'."

1. **Mavis.**  Thrush.
2. **O'erword.**  Refrain.
3. **Spring.**  A lively tune or song.
4. **Bairns.**  Children.

## McPHERSON'S FAREWELL

*Tune*—"McPherson's Rant."

[Published in Johnson's *Museum* in 1788, and usually thought to have been a result of Burns's Highland tour of the preceding fall.

The Poet's own note on this song is as follows: "Mc-Pherson, a daring robber in the beginning of this century, was condemned to be hanged at the assizes of Inverness. He is said, when under sentence of death, to have composed this tune, which he calls his own Lament, or Farewell." One stanza of an old poem on the theme strikingly resembles Burns's "chorus" and at the same time shows how he improved the old songs which he worked over.

"Then wantonly and rantingly
  I am resolved to die;
And with undaunted courage, I
  Shall mount this fatal tree."]

Farewell, ye dungeons dark and strong,
  The wretch's destinie!
McPherson's time will not be long
  On yonder gallows-tree.

*Chorus.*—Sae rantingly,[1] sae wantonly,
  Sae dauntingly gaed[2] he;
He play'd a spring,[3] and danc'd it round,
  Below the gallows-tree.

O, what is death but parting breath?
  On many a bloody plain
I've dar'd his face, and in this place
  I scorn him yet again!
    Sae rantingly, etc.

Untie these bands from off my hands,
  And bring to me my sword,
And there's no a man in all Scotland,
  But I'll brave him at a word.
    Sae rantingly, etc.

1. **Sae rantingly.** So jovially.
2. **Dauntingly gaed.** Dauntlessly went.
3. **Spring.** Lively tune.

I've liv'd a life of sturt[4] and strife;
   I die by treacherie;
It burns my heart I must depart,
   And not avengèd be.
       Sae rantingly, etc.

Now farewell, light, thou sunshine bright,
   And all beneath the sky!
May coward shame distain his name,
   The wretch that dare not die!
       Sae rantingly, etc.


## OF A' THE AIRTS[1] THE WIND CAN BLAW

*Tune*—"Miss Admiral Gordon's Strathspey."

[Said Burns of this song: "I composed [it] out of compliment to Mrs. Burns. *N.B.* It was during the honeymoon."
This means during the summer of 1788, probably soon after
the poet moved to Ellisland and while Mrs. Burns was still
in Ayrshire. First printed in Johnson's *Museum* in 1790.]

Of a' the airts[1] the wind can blaw
   I dearly like the west,
For there the bonie lassie lives,
   The lassie I lo'e best.
There wild-woods grow,* and rivers row,[2]
   And monie a hill between,
But day and night my fancy's flight
   Is ever wi' my Jean.

I see her in the dewy flowers,
   I see her sweet and fair.
I hear her in the tunefu' birds,
   I hear her charm the air.

4. **Sturt.** Trouble.

1. **Airts.** Directions.
2. **Row.** Roll.

There's not a bonie flower that springs
    By fountain, shaw,[3] or green;
There's not a bonie bird that sings,
    But minds me o' my Jean.


## O, WERE I ON PARNASSUS HILL

*Tune*—"My love is lost to me."

[This, like the preceding, was written at Ellisland in 1788 in compliment to Mrs. Burns, and was first published in Johnson's *Museum* in 1790.

Corsincon (stanza i) is a hill visible from Burns's home at Ellisland on the river Nith.]


O, were I on Parnassus* hill,
Or had o' Helicon* my fill,
That I might catch poetic skill
    To sing how dear I love thee!
But Nith maun[1] be my Muse's well,
My Muse maun be thy bonie sel',
On Corsincon I'll glowr and spell,[2]
    And write how dear I love thee.


Then come, sweet Muse, inspire my lay!
For a' the lee-lang[3] simmer's day
I couldna sing, I couldna say
    How much, how dear, I love thee.
I see thee dancing o'er the green,
Thy waist sae jimp,[4] thy limbs sae clean,
Thy tempting lips, thy roguish een[5]—
    By Heaven and Earth I love thee!


3. **Shaw.** Wood.
1. **Maun.** Must.
2. **Glowr and spell.** Stare and scan intently

3. **Lee-lang.** Live-long.
4. **Jimp.** Slender.
5. **Een.** Eyes.

By night, by day, a-field, at hame,
The thoughts o' thee my breast inflame,
And ay I muse and sing thy name—
        I only live to love thee.
Tho' I were doom'd to wander on,
Beyond the sea, beyond the sun,
Till my last weary sand was run,
        Till then—and then—I'd love thee!


## AULD LANG SYNE[1]

[In December, 1788, Burns wrote to Mrs. Dunlop: "Is not the Scotch phrase "Auld Lang Syne" exceedingly expressive? There is an old song and tune which has often thrilled through my soul ......I shall give you the verses on the other sheet." Nearly five years later, in September, 1793, he sent to Thomson the poem as we have it, with the following remarks: "The air is but mediocre; but the following song, the old song of the olden times, and which has never been in print, nor even in manuscript, until I took it down from an old man's singing, is enough to recommend any air." In spite of these statements, most of the poem is generally believed to be by Burns; at any rate it is a great improvement on some earlier poems on the same theme, one of them credited to Allan Ramsay. First published in Johnson's *Museum* in 1796.]


Should auld acquaintance be forgot,
    And never brought to mind?
Should auld acquaintance be forgot,
    And days o' lang syne?*


*Chorus.*—For auld lang syne, my jo,[2]
        For auld lang syne,
        We'll tak a cup o' kindness yet,
        For auld lang syne.

1. **Auld lang syne.**  A long time ago.       2. **Jo.**  Sweetheart.

And surely ye'll be your pint stowp[3]
And surely I'll be mine,
And we'll tak a cup o' kindness yet,
For auld lang syne.
For auld, etc.


We twa hae[4] run about the braes,[5]
And pou'd the gowans[6] fine;
But we've wander'd mony a weary fit,[7]
Sin' auld lang syne.
For auld, etc.


We twa hae paidl'd[8] i' the burn[9]
Frae morning sun till dine;[10]
But seas between us braid[11] hae roar'd
Sin' auld lang syne.
For auld, etc.


And there's a hand, my trusty fiere,[12]
And gie's[13] a hand o' thine,
And we'll tak a right gude-willie waught[14]
For auld lang syne.
For auld, etc.

3. **Be your pint stowp.** Pay for your pint measure.
4. **Twa hae.** Two have.
5. **Braes.** Hillsides.
6. **Pou'd the gowans.** Pulled the daisies.
7. **Fit.** Foot.
8. **Paidl'd.** Paddled.
9. **Burn.** Brook.
10. **Dine.** Dinner-time.
11. **Braid.** Broad.
12. **Fiere.** Comrade.
13. **Gie's.** Give us.
14. **Gude-willie waught.** Draught of good will.

## MY BONIE MARY

[Sent to Mrs. Dunlop in December, 1788, as "two other old stanzas that please me mightily"; but elsewhere Burns said "the first half stanza .... is old; the rest is mine." Published in Johnson's *Museum*, 1790.

The Berwick-law (Stanza i) was a height in Haddington-shire overlooking the Firth of Forth.]

Go, fetch to me a pint o' wine,
    And fill it in a silver tassie,[1]
That I may drink before I go
    A service to my bonie lassie!
The boat rocks at the pier o' Leith,
    Fu' loud the wind blaws frae[2] the Ferry,
The ship rides by the Berwick-law,
    And I maun[3] leave my bonie Mary.


The trumpets sound, the banners fly,
    The glittering spears are rankèd ready,
The shouts o' war are heard afar,
    The battle closes deep and bloody;
It's not the roar o' sea or shore
    Wad mak me langer wish to tarry,
Nor shouts o' war that's heard afar—
    It's leaving thee, my bonie Mary!

1. **Tassie.**  Goblet.
2. **Frae.**  From.
3. **Maun.**  Must.

## SWEET AFTON

[Sent to Mrs. Dunlop in February, 1789, with the statement that the song was written for Johnson's *Musical Museum* in compliment to the "small river Afton that flows into Nith"—the river beside which Burns's home at Ellisland was situated. Thus Gilbert Burns's notion that the poem referred to "Highland Mary" seems probably a mistake. Printed in Johnson's *Museum* in 1792.]

Flow gently, sweet Afton, among thy green braes![1]
Flow gently, I'll sing thee a song in thy praise!
My Mary's asleep by thy murmuring stream;
Flow gently, sweet Afton, disturb not her dream!

Thou stock-dove whose echo resounds thro' the glen,
Ye wild whistling blackbirds in yon thorny den,
Thou green-crested lapwing, thy screaming forbear;
I charge you, disturb not my slumbering fair.

How lofty, sweet Afton, thy neighboring hills,
Far mark'd with the courses of clear, winding rills!
There daily I wander, as noon rises high,
My flocks and my Mary's sweet cot in my eye.

How pleasant thy banks and green vallies below,
Where, wild in the woodlands, the primroses blow;
There oft, as mild Ev'ning weeps over the lea,
The sweet-scented birk[2] shades my Mary and me.

Thy crystal stream, Afton, how lovely it glides,
And winds by the cot where my Mary resides!
How wanton thy waters her snowy feet lave,
As, gathering sweet flow'rets, she stems thy clear wave!

Flow gently, sweet Afton, among thy green braes!
Flow gently, sweet river, the theme of my lays!
My Mary's asleep by thy murmuring stream;
Flow gently, sweet Afton, disturb not her dream!

**1. Braes.** Hillsides.            **2. Birk.** Birch.

## TO MARY IN HEAVEN

[Sent to Mrs. Dunlop in November, 1789, as "made the other day," and believed by the supporters of the "Highland Mary cult" to have been written on the third anniversary of Mary Campbell's death, October 20, 1789. Published in Johnson's *Museum* in 1790. See the Introduction, page 15.]

Thou ling'ring star with less'ning ray,
  That lov'st to greet the early morn,
Again thou usher'st in the day
  My Mary from my soul was torn.
O Mary, dear departed shade!
  Where is thy place of blissful rest?
See'st thou thy lover lowly laid?
  Hear'st thou the groans that rend his breast?


That sacred hour can I forget,
  Can I forget the hallow'd grove,
Where, by the winding Ayr, we met
  To live one day of parting love!
Eternity can not efface
  Those records dear of transports past,
Thy image at our last embrace—
  Ah! little thought we 'twas our last!


Ayr, gurgling, kiss'd his pebbled shore,
  O'erhung with wild woods thickening green;
The fragrant birch and hawthorn hoar
  Twin'd amorous round the raptur'd scene;
The flowers sprang wanton to be prest,
  The birds sang love on every spray,
Till too, too soon, the glowing west
  Proclaim'd the speed of wingèd day.

Still o'er these scenes my mem'ry wakes,
  And fondly broods with miser care.
Time but th' impression stronger makes,
  As streams their channels deeper wear.
My Mary, dear departed shade!
  Where is thy place of blissful rest?
See'st thou thy lover lowly laid?
  Hear'st thou the groans that rend his breast?


## JOHN ANDERSON, MY JO

[Published in Johnson's *Museum* in 1790; usually thought
to be a composition of 1789.

Notice that an elderly woman is assumed to be the
speaker.]

John Anderson my jo,[1] John,
  When we were first acquent,[2]
Your locks were like the raven,
  Your bonie brow was brent;[3]
But now your brow is beld,[4] John,
  Your locks are like the snaw,
But blessings on your frosty pow,[5]
  John Anderson my jo!

John Anderson my jo, John,
  We clamb the hill thegither;
And monie a cantie[6] day, John,
  We've had wi' ane anither:
Now we maun[7] totter down, John,
  And hand in hand we'll go,
And sleep thegither at the foot,
  John Anderson my jo!

| | |
|---|---|
| **1. Jo.** Sweetheart. | **4. Beld.** Bald. |
| **2. Acquent.** Acquainted. | **5. Pow.** Head. |
| **3. Brent.** Straight (not sloping from baldness). | **6. Cantie.** Lively. |
| | **7. Maun.** Must. |

## TAM GLEN

[Printed in Johnson's *Museum*, 1790, after previous appearances in periodicals in November and December, 1789. Burns's sister Mrs. Begg maintained that this was an old song which he had merely retouched, but no such old song has been found, and Burns's friend Riddell said this song was by Burns.
The speaker here is, of course, a young girl.]

My heart is a-breaking, dear tittie;[1]
   Some counsel unto me come len'.[2]
To anger them a' is a pity,
   But what will I do wi' Tam Glen?

I'm thinking, wi' sic a braw[3] fellow,
   In poortith[4] I might mak a fen'.[5]
What care I in riches to wallow,
   If I mauna[6] marry Tam Glen?

There's Lowrie the Laird o' Dumeller—
   "Guid day to you,"—brute! he comes ben;[7]
He brags and he blaws o' his siller,[8]
   But when will he dance like Tam Glen?

My minnie[9] does constantly deave[10] me,
   And bids me beware o' young men;
They flatter, she says, to deceive me,
   But wha can think sae o' Tam Glen?

My daddie says, gin[11] I'll forsake him,
   He'd gie me guid hunder marks ten;
But if it's ordain'd I maun take him,
   O, wha will I get but Tam Glen?

1. **Tittie.** Sister.
2. **Len'.** Lend.
3. **Sic a braw.** Such a fine.
4. **Poortith.** Poverty.
5. **Fen'.** Shift.
6. **Mauna.** Must not.
7. **Ben.** In (to the parlor).
8. **Siller.** Money (silver).
9. **Minnie.** Mother.
10. **Deave.** Deafen.
11. **Gin.** If.

Yestreen[12] at the valentines' dealing,
   My heart to my mou gied a sten,[13]
For thrice I drew ane without failing,
   And thrice it was written, "Tam Glen."

The last Halloween I was waukin[14]
   My droukit sark[15] sleeve, as ye ken;
His likeness came up the house staukin,[16]
   And the very grey breeks[17] o' Tam Glen!

Come, counsel, dear tittie, don't tarry!
   I'll gie[18] ye my bonie black hen,
Gif[19] ye will advise me to marry
   The lad I lo'e[20] dearly, Tam Glen.


## WILLIE BREW'D A PECK O' MAUT

[The meeting that suggested this rollicking song took place in the autumn of 1789. Burns made the following note on it: "The air is Masterton's [the "Allan" of the song]; the song mine. The occasion of it was this: Mr. Wm. Nicol, of the High School, Edinburgh, during the autumn vacation being at Moffat, honest Allan (who was at that time on a visit to Dalswinton) and I went to pay Nicol a visit. We had such a joyous time that Mr. Masterton and I agreed, each in our own way, that we should celebrate the business." Published in Johnson's *Museum*, 1790.]

O, Willie brew'd a peck o' maut,[1]
   And Rob and Allan cam to see;
Three blyther hearts, that lee-lang [2] night,
   Ye wadna found in Christendie.[3]

*Chorus.*—We are na fou,[4] we're nae that fou,
      But just a drappie[5] in our e'e;[6]
    The cock may craw,[7] the day may daw,[8]
    And ay we'll taste the barley bree.[9]

12. **Yestreen.** Last night.
13. **Gied a sten.** Gave a leap.
14. **Waukin.** Watching.
15. **Droukit sark.** Drenched shirt.
16. **Staukin.** Stalking.
17. **Breeks.** Breeches.
18. **Gie.** Give.
19. **Gif.** If.
20. **Lo'e.** Love.

1. **Maut.** Malt.
2. **Lee-lang.** Live-long.
3. **Christendie.** Christendom.
4. **Fou.** Full, drunk.
5. **Drappie.** Droplet.
6. **E'e.** Eye.
7. **Craw.** Crow.
8. **Daw.** Dawn.
9. **Bree.** Brew.

Here are we met, three merry boys,
   Three merry boys I trow are we;
And monie a night we've merry been,
   And monie mae[10] we hope to be!
     We are na fou, etc.


It is the moon, I ken[11] her horn,
   That's blinkin in the lift sae hie;[12]
She shines sae bright to wyle[13] us hame,
   But, by my sooth, she'll wait a wee![14]
     We are na fou, etc.


Wha first shall rise to gang[15] awa,
   A cuckold, coward loun[16] is he!
Wha first beside his chair shall fa',
   He is the king amang us three!
     We are na fou, etc.


## WHISTLE O'ER THE LAVE O'T

[Printed in Johnson's *Museum*, 1790. The refrain is from an old song and was used by Burns also in "The Jolly Beggars" (see page 103).]

First when Maggie was my care,
Heav'n, I thought, was in her air;
Now we're married, spier nae mair,[1]
   But whistle o'er the lave[2] o't!
Meg was meek, and Meg was mild,
Sweet and harmless as a child;
Wiser men than me's beguil'd—
   Whistle o'er the lave o't!

10. **Mae.** More.
11. **Ken.** Know.
12. **Lift sae hie.** Sky so high.
13. **Wyle.** Entice.
14. **Wee.** Bit.

15. **Gang.** Go.
16. **Loun.** Rascal (loon).
1. **Spier nae mair.** Ask no more.
2. **Lave.** Rest.

How we live, my Meg and me,
How we love, and how we gree,[3]
I care na by[4] how few may see—
 Whistle o'er the lave o't!
Wha I wish were maggots' meat,
Dish'd up in her winding-sheet,
I could write—but Meg maun[5] see't—
 Whistle o'er the lave o't!

## MY HEART'S IN THE HIGHLANDS

*Tune*—"Failte na Miosg."
[Burns said, "The first half stanza [of the chorus] of this song is old; the rest is mine."
Printed in Johnson's *Museum*, 1790.]

Farewell to the Highlands, farewell to the North,
The birthplace of valor, the country of worth;
Wherever I wander, wherever I rove,
The hills of the Highlands for ever I love.

*Chorus.*—My heart's in the Highlands, my heart is not here,
 My heart's in the Highlands a-chasing the deer,
 A-chasing the wild deer and following the roe—
 My heart's in the Highlands, wherever I go.

Farewell to the mountains high cover'd with snow,
Farewell to the straths[1] and green valleys below,
Farewell to the forests and wild-hanging woods,
Farewell to the torrents and loud-pouring floods!
 My heart's in the Highlands, etc.

3. **Gree.** Agree.
4. **Care na by.** Care nothing.
5. **Maun.** Must.
1. **Straths.** River bottoms.

## THE BANKS O' DOON

### SECOND VERSION

[There are three versions of this poem, varying considerably. The one most commonly known—"Ye banks and braes o' bonie Doon"—appeared in Johnson's *Museum* in 1792. It consists of two stanzas of eight lines each. In March, 1791, Burns sent to his friend Alexander Cunningham a set of words on the same theme, to a tune requiring "three stanzas of four lines each," or a long stanza of twelve lines. In this version, usually regarded as the first on the theme, there are two such twelve-line stanzas. The simpler version here printed was sent in a letter to John Ballantyne of Ayr, probably also of March, 1791, though by some critics dated four years earlier.

It should be noted that the poem is assumed to be sung by a woman who has been deserted by a "fause luver."]

Ye flowery banks o' bonie Doon,
　　How can ye blume sae fair?
How can ye chant, ye little birds,
　　And I sae fu' o' care?

Thou'll break my heart, thou bonie bird,
　　That sings upon the bough;
Thou minds[1] me o' the happy days
　　When my fause luve was true.

Thou'll break my heart, thou bonie bird,
　　That sings beside thy mate;
For sae I sat, and sae I sang,
　　And wist na[2] o' my fate.

Aft hae I rov'd by bonie Doon,
　　To see the woodbine twine;
And ilka[3] bird sang o' its luve,
　　And sae did I o' mine.

Wi' lightsome heart I pu'd[4] a rose,
　　Frae off its thorny tree;
And my fause luver staw[5] my rose,
　　But left the thorn wi' me.

1. **Minds.** Remindest.
2. **Wist na.** Knew not.
3. **Ilka.** Every.
4. **Pu'd.** Pulled.
5. **Staw.** Stole.

## AE FOND KISS, AND THEN WE SEVER

*Tune*—"Rory Dall's Port."

[Sent to "Clarinda" (Mrs. McLehose) in December, 1791,
as one of "some songs I have just been composing to different
tunes for the Collection of Songs, of which you have three
volumes, and of which you shall have the fourth." "Nancy"
is "Clarinda." The "collection of songs" was Johnson's
*Museum,* in which this appeared in 1792.

The last four lines of the second stanza were said by
Sir Walter Scott to contain "the essence of a thousand love
tales."]

Ae[1] fond kiss, and then we sever!
Ae farewell, and then for ever!
Deep in heart-wrung tears I'll pledge thee,
Warring sighs and groans I'll wage thee.
Who shall say that Fortune grieves him,
While the star of hope she leaves him?
Me, nae cheerfu' twinkle lights me;
Dark despair around benights me.

I'll ne'er blame my partial fancy—
Naething could resist my Nancy!
But to see her was to love her,
Love but her, and love for ever.
Had we never lov'd sae kindly,
Had we never loved sae blindly,
Never met—or never parted—
We had ne'er been broken-hearted.

Fare-thee-weel, thou first and fairest!
Fare-thee-weel, thou best and dearest!
Thine be ilka[2] joy and treasure,
Peace, Enjoyment, Love and Pleasure!
Ae fond kiss, and then we sever!
Ae farewell, alas, for ever!
Deep in heart-wrung tears I'll pledge thee,
Warring sighs and groans I'll wage thee.

1. **Ae.**  One.                    2. **Ilka.**  Every.

## BESSY AND HER SPINNIN-WHEEL

[A song of 1792, contributed to Johnson's *Museum*.]

O, leeze me on[1] my spinnin-wheel,
And leeze me on my rock[2] and reel,
Frae tap to tae[3] that cleeds[4] me bien,[5]
And haps me fiel[6] and warm at e'en!
I'll set me down and sing and spin,
While laigh[7] descends the simmer sun,
Blest wi' content, and milk and meal—
O, leeze me on my spinnin-wheel!

On ilka[8] hand the burnies[9] trot,
And meet below my theekit cot.[10]
The scented birk[11] and hawthorn white
Across the pool their arms unite,
Alike to screen the birdie's nest
And little fishes' caller[12] rest.
The sun blinks kindly in the biel',[13]
Where blythe I turn my spinnin-wheel.

On lofty aiks[14] the cushats[15] wail,
And Echo cons the doolfu' tale.
The lintwhites[16] in the hazel braes,
Delighted, rival ither's lays;
The craik[17] amang the claver[18] hay,
The paitrick[19] whirrin o'er the ley,[20]
The swallow jinkin[21] round my shiel,[22]
Amuse me at my spinnin-wheel.

1. **Leeze me on.** Dear to me is.
2. **Rock.** Distaff.
3. **Frae tap to tae.** From top to toe.
4. **Cleeds.** Clothes.
5. **Bien.** Comfortably.
6. **Haps me fiel.** Wraps me comfortably.
7. **Laigh.** Low.
8. **Ilka.** Every.
9. **Burnies.** Brooklets.
10. **Theekit cot.** Thatched cottage.
11. **Birk.** Birch.
12. **Caller.** Cool.
13. **Biel'.** Sheltered spot.
14. **Aiks.** Oaks.
15. **Cushats.** Doves.
16. **Lintwhites.** Linnets.
17. **Craik.** Corncrake (a kind of bird).
18. **Claver.** Clover.
19. **Paitrick.** Partridge.
20. **Ley.** Meadow.
21. **Jinkin.** Dodging.
22. **Shiel.** Shed.

Wi' sma' to sell and less to buy,
Aboon[23] distress, below envy,
O, wha wad leave this humble state
For a' the pride of a' the great?
Amid their flaring, idle toys,
Amid their cumbrous, dinsome[24] joys,
Can they the peace and pleasure feel
Of Bessy at her spinnin-wheel?


## WHEN SHE CAM BEN SHE BOBBÈD

[Printed in Johnson's *Museum*, 1792. The first two stanzas
vary only slightly from an old song.]

O, when she cam ben,[1] she bobbèd fu' law![2]
O, when she cam ben, she bobbèd fu' law!
And when she cam ben, she kiss'd Cockpen,
  And syne[3] she deny'd she did it at a'!

And was na Cockpen right saucy witha'?
And was na Cockpen right saucy witha',
In leaving the dochter o' a lord,
  And kissin a collier lassie an a'?

O, never look down, my lassie, at a'!
O, never look down, my lassie, at a'!
Thy lips are as sweet, and thy figure complete,
  As the finest dame in castle or ha'.

Tho' thou hast nae silk, and holland[4] sae sma',
Tho' thou hast nae silk, and holland sae sma',
Thy coat and thy sark[5] are thy ain handywark,
  And Lady Jean was never sae braw.[6]

23. **Aboon.** Above.
24. **Dinsome.** Noisy.

1. **Ben.** Into the parlor.
2. **Law.** Low.

3. **Syne.** Then.
4. **Holland.** A kind of linen or cotton cloth.
5. **Sark.** Shirt.
6. **Braw.** Handsome.

## THE DEIL'S AWA WI' THE EXCISEMAN

[In Cromek's *Reliques* it was declared that this song was written for "a festive meeting of all the Excise officers in Scotland;" but Lockhart believed this to be an error and presented an account of the writing of the poem which he obtained from the "private journal of one of the excisemen" concerned with Burns in the capture of a brig engaged in contraband traffic in Solway Firth. The gist of this account is that Burns composed the song in impatience at the slowness of some brother officers who had been dispatched for aid, while Burns with a few men was left to watch the brig. Published in Johnson's *Museum*, 1792.]

The Deil cam fiddlin thro' the town,
 And danc'd awa wi' th' Exciseman,
And ilka[1] wife cries, "Auld Mahoun,[2]
 I wish you luck o' the prize, man!"

*Chorus.*—The Deil's awa, the Deil's awa,
  The Deil's awa wi' the Exciseman!
 He's danc'd awa, he's danc'd awa,
  He's danc'd awa wi' the Exciseman.

"We'll mak our maut,[3] and we'll brew our drink,
 We'll laugh, sing, and rejoice, man,
And monie braw[4] thanks to the meikle[5] black Deil,
 That danc'd awa wi' the Exciseman."
    The Deil's awa, etc.

There's threesome reels, there's foursome reels,
 There's hornpipes and strathspeys, man,
But the ae[6] best dance e'er cam to the land
 Was "The Deil's awa wi' th' Exciseman."
    The Deil's awa, etc.

1. **Ilka.** Every.
2. **Mahoun.** Mahomet.
3. **Maut.** Malt.
4. **Braw.** Fine.
5. **Meikle.** Big.
6. **Ae.** One.

## SAW YE BONIE LESLEY

[Sent to Mrs. Dunlop as a new composition August 22, 1792; published first in Part II of Thomson's *Select Collection of Scottish Airs*, 1798.

"Bonie Lesley" was one of the two daughters of a gentleman of Ayrshire who, when on a trip to England with these daughters, stopped at Dumfries to call upon Burns. On their departure the poet mounted his horse "and accompanied them fourteen or fifteen miles, and dined and spent the day with them." The song illustrates how, when the fancy struck him, he could immortalize a chance acquaintance.]

O, saw ye bonie Lesley,
    As she gaed[1] o'er the Border?
She's gane,[2] like Alexander,
    To spread her conquests farther.

To see her is to love her,
    And love but her for ever;
For Nature made her what she is,
    And never made anither!

Thou art a queen, fair Lesley—
    Thy subjects, we before thee;
Thou art divine, fair Lesley—
    The hearts o' men adore thee.

The Deil he could na skaith[3] thee,
    Or aught that wad belang thee;
He'd look into thy bonie face,
    And say, "I canna wrang thee!"

The Powers aboon[4] will tent[5] thee,
    Misfortune sha'na steer[6] thee;
Thou'rt like themsel' sae lovely,
    That ill they'll ne'er let near thee.

1. **Gaed.**  Went.        4. **Aboon.**  Above.
2. **Gane.**  Gone.        5. **Tent.**  Guard.
3. **Skaith.**  Hurt.      6. **Steer.**  Molest.

Return again, fair Lesley,
    Return to Caledonie!
That we may brag we hae a lass,
    There's nane again sae bonie.


## HIGHLAND MARY

[Sent to Thomson November 14, 1792; not published till
Thomson's Part III appeared in 1799. Burns's remarks in
his letter to Thomson are as follows: "The foregoing song
pleases myself; I think it is in my happiest manner; you
will see at first glance that it suits the air. The subject
of the song is one of the most interesting passages of my
youthful days."]


Ye banks and braes[1] and streams around
    The castle of Montgomery,
Green be your woods, and fair your flowers,
    Your waters never drumlie![2]
There Simmer first unfald her robes,
    And there the langest tarry;
For there I took the last fareweel
    O' my sweet Highland Mary.

How sweetly bloom'd the gay, green birk,[3]
    How rich the hawthorn's blossom,
As underneath their fragrant shade,
    I clasp'd her to my bosom!
The golden hours on angel wings
    Flew o'er me and my dearie;
For dear to me as light and life
    Was my sweet Highland Mary.


1. **Braes.** Slopes.
2. **Drumlie.** Muddy.
3. **Birk.** Birch.

Wi' monie a vow and lock'd embrace
    Our parting was fu' tender;
And, pledging aft to meet again,
    We tore oursels asunder.
But O, fell Death's untimely frost,
    That nipt my flower sae early!
Now green's the sod, and cauld's the clay,
    That wraps my Highland Mary!


O, pale, pale now, those rosy lips
    I aft hae kiss'd sae fondly;
And clos'd for ay, the sparkling glance
    That dwalt on me sae kindly;
And mouldering now in silent dust,
    That heart that lo'ed me dearly!
But still within my bosom's core
    Shall live my Highland Mary.


## DUNCAN GRAY

[Sent to Thomson December 4, 1792; published by him in 1798. A different poem with the same title had appeared in Johnson's *Museum* in 1788.]


Duncan Gray cam here to woo—
    Ha, ha, the wooing o't!
On blythe Yule-night when we were fou[1]—
    Ha, ha, the wooing o't!
Maggie coost[2] her head fu' high,
Look'd asklent[3] and unco skeigh,[4]
Gart[5] poor Duncan stand abeigh[6]—
    Ha, ha, the wooing o't!


1. **Fou.** Full (drunk).
2. **Coost.** Cast.
3. **Asklent.** Askance.

4. **Unco skeigh.** Very skittish.
5. **Gart.** Made.
6. **Abeigh.** Aloof.

Duncan fleech'd[7] and Duncan pray'd—
  Ha, ha, the wooing o't!
Meg was deaf as Ailsa Craig[8]—
  Ha, ha, the wooing o't!
Duncan sigh'd baith out and in,
Grat[9] his een[10] baith bleer't[11] an' blin',
Spak o' lowpin[12] o'er a linn[13]—
  Ha, ha, the wooing o't!

Time and Chance are but a tide—
  Ha, ha, the wooing o't!
Slighted love is sair to bide[14]—
  Ha, ha, the wooing o't!
"Shall I, like a fool," quoth he,
"For a haughty hizzie[15] die?
She may gae to—France for me!"
  Ha, ha, the wooing o't!

How it comes, let doctors tell—
  Ha, ha, the wooing o't!
Meg grew sick, as he grew hale—
  Ha, ha, the wooing o't!
Something in her bosom wrings,
For relief a sigh she brings,
And O! her een they spak sic things!
  Ha, ha, the wooing o't!

Duncan was a lad o' grace—
  Ha, ha, the wooing o't!
Maggie's was a piteous case—
  Ha, ha, the wooing o't!
Duncan could na be her death,
Swelling pity smoor'd[16] his wrath;
Now they're crouse and canty[17] baith—
  Ha, ha, the wooing o't!

7. **Fleech'd.** Wheedled.
8. **Ailsa Craig.** A mountainous island off Ayrshire.
9. **Grat.** Wept.
10. **Een.** Eyes.
11. **Bleer't.** Bleared.
12. **Lowpin.** Leaping.
13. **Linn.** Waterfall.
14. **Sair to bide.** Hard to endure.
15. **Hizzie.** Hussy.
16. **Smoor'd.** Smothered.
17. **Crouse and canty.** Joyful and happy.

## WANDERING WILLIE

[Published by Thomson in his Part I, 1793. In Johnson's *Museum,* Vol. I, 1787, had appeared a song of the same title and in parts very similar. There are two versions by Burns, of which the one printed is his revision.]

Here awa, there awa, wandering Willie,
   Here awa, there awa, haud[1] awa hame;
Come to my bosom, my ae[2] only dearie,
   And tell me thou bring'st me my Willie the same.
Loud tho' the winter blew cauld at our parting;
   'Twas na the blast brought the tear in my e'e;
Welcome now Simmer, and welcome my Willie,
   The Simmer to Nature, my Willie to me!

Rest, ye wild storms, in the cave o' your slumbers—
   How your wild howling a lover alarms!
Wauken, ye breezes; row[3] gently, ye billows,
   And waft my dear laddie ance mair[4] to my arms.
But O, if he's faithless, and minds na his Nannie,
   Flow still between us, thou wide roaring main!
May I never see it, may I never trow it,
   But, dying, believe that my Willie's my ain![5]

1. **Haud.** Hold.
2. **Ae.** One.
3. **Row.** Roll.
4. **Ance mair.** Once more.
5. **Ain.** Own.

## BRAW LADS O' GALLA WATER

[A working over of an old song, sent to Thomson about
the same time as the revised version of "Wandering Willie."
Published by Thomson in 1793.]

Braw,[1] braw lads on Yarrow braes,[2]
   They rove amang the blooming heather;
But Yarrow braes nor Ettrick shaws[3]
   Can match the lads o' Galla Water.

But there is ane, a secret ane,
   Aboon[4] them a' I lo'e[5] him better;
And I'll be his, and he'll be mine,
   The bonie lad o' Galla Water.

Altho' his daddie was nae laird,
   And tho' I hae nae meikle tocher,[6]
Yet, rich in kindest, truest love,
   We'll tent[7] our flocks by Galla Water.

It ne'er was wealth, it ne'er was wealth,
   That coft[8] contentment, peace, and pleasure:
The bands and bliss o' mutual love,
   O, that's the chiefest warld's treasure.

1. **Braw.** Fine.
2. **Braes.** Hillsides.
3. **Shaws.** Woods.
4. **Aboon.** Above.
5. **Lo'e.** Love.

6. **Nae meikle tocher.** Not much dower.
7. **Tent.** Tend, watch.
8. **Coft.** Bought.

# WHISTLE AN' I'LL COME TO YE, MY LAD

[A short version, "written for this work by Robert Burns," appeared in Johnson's *Museum* in 1788. The complete song of the text was sent to Thomson in August, 1793, printed by him in 1799. The chorus is old. In August, 1795, Burns suggested to Thomson a change of the fourth line of the chorus to—
　　　　Thy Jeanie will venture wi' ye, my lad.
This was to avoid what he considered too many repetitions of the refrain. "Jeanie" here means Jean Lorimer, the heroine of several of his latest songs. See page 226.]

*Chorus.*—O, whistle an' I'll came to ye, my lad!
　　　　O, whistle an' I'll come to ye, my lad!
　　　　Tho' father an' mother an' a' should gae[1] mad,
　　　　O, whistle an' I'll came to ye, my lad!

But warily tent[2] when ye come to court me,
And come nae unless the back-yett[3] be a-jee;[4]
Syne[5] up the back-style, and let naebody see,
And come as ye were na comin to me,
And come as ye were na comin to me.
　　　　O, whistle an' I'll come, etc.

At kirk,[6] or at market, whene'er ye meet me,
Gang[7] by me as tho' that ye car'd na a flie;[8]
But steal me a blink o' your bonie black e'e,[9]
Yet look as ye were na lookin to me.
Yet look as ye were na lookin to me,
　　　　O, whistle an' I'll come, etc.

Ay vow and protest that ye care na for me,
And whyles[10] ye may lightly[11] my beauty a wee;
But court na anither, tho' jokin ye be,
For fear that she wyle[12] your fancy frae me,
For fear that she wyle your fancy frae me.
　　　　O, whistle an' I'll come, etc.

1. Gae.　Go.
2. Tent.　Take heed.
3. Yett.　Gate.
4. A-jee.　Ajar.
5. Syne.　Then.
6. Kirk.　Church.
7. Gang.　Go.
8. Flie.　Fly.
9. E'e.　Eye.
10. Whyles.　Sometimes.
11. Lightly.　Disparage.
12. Wyle.　Beguile.

## SCOTS, WHA HAE

[Sent to Thomson in September, 1793, with some remarks about the old tune, *Hey, Tuttie Taitie*, for which Burns intended the words. "There is a tradition," he says, "that it [this old tune] was Robert Bruce's march at the battle of Bannockburn. This thought, in my yesternight's evening walk, roused me to a pitch of enthusiasm on the theme of liberty and independence, which I threw into a kind of Scots ode, fitted to the air, that one might suppose to be the gallant royal Scot's address to his heroic followers on that eventful morning." This statement by Burns is inconsistent with the story of the composition of the poem which Carlyle mentions (page 260).

Thomson considered the tune Burns had in mind inferior, and urged the use of another tune which required two extra syllables in the last line of each stanza. Burns consented, and so when Thomson first printed the song (in 1799) it was much injured in effectiveness by the redundant syllables. In the meantime the poem as Burns first wrote it had become popular after appearing in a newspaper in May, 1794, and in a later volume of his work (1802) Thomson reprinted it with the tune Burns meant to use.]

Scots, wha hae wi' Wallace bled,
Scots, wham Bruce has aften led,
Welcome to your gory bed
      Or to victorie!

Now's the day, and now's the hour;
See the front o' battle lour;
See approach proud Edward's power—
      Chains and slaverie!

Wha will be a traitor knave?
Wha can fill a coward's grave?
Wha sae base as be a slave?
      Let him turn and flee!

Wha for Scotland's King and Law
Freedom's sword will strongly draw,
Freeman stand or freeman fa',
      Let him follow me!

By Oppression's woes and pains,
By your sons in servile chains,
We will drain our dearest veins
        But they shall be free!

Lay the proud usurpers low!
Tyrants fall in every foe!
Liberty's in every blow!
        Let us do or die!


## A RED, RED ROSE

[First published by Johnson in 1796, but generally placed
with the songs composed in 1794.
  Nearly all the ideas so beautifully put together here have
been found in old songs.]

My luve is like a red, red rose,
    That's newly sprung in June;
My luve is like the melodie,
    That's sweetly play'd in tune.

As fair art thou, my bonie lass,
    So deep in luve am I;
And I will luve thee still, my dear,
    Till a' the seas gang[1] dry.

Till a' the seas gang dry, my dear,
    And the rocks melt wi' the sun!
And I will luve thee still, my dear,
    While the sands o' life shall run.

And fare thee weel, my only luve,
    And fare thee weel a while!
And I will come again, my luve,
    Tho' it were ten thousand mile!

        1. Gang.  Go.

## MY NANIE'S AWA

*Tune*—"There'll never be peace till Jamie comes hame."

[Sent to Thomson in December, 1794; published by him in 1799. "Nanie" is "Clarinda"—Mrs. McLehose.]

Now in her green mantle blythe Nature arrays,
And listens the lambkins that bleat o'er the braes,[1]
While birds warble welcomes in ilka[2] green shaw,[3]
But to me it's delightless—my Nanie's awa.

The snawdrap and primrose our woodlands adorn,
And violets bathe in the weet[4] o' the morn;
They pain my sad bosom, sae sweetly they blaw,
They mind me o' Nanie—and Nanie's awa.

Thou lav'rock[5] that springs frae the dews of the lawn,
The shepherd to warn o' the grey-breaking dawn,
And thou mellow mavis[6] that hails the night-fa',
Give over for pity—my Nanie's awa.

Come Autumn, sae pensive in yellow and grey,
And soothe me wi' tidings o' Nature's decay!
The dark, dreary Winter and wild-driving snaw
Alane can delight me—now Nanie's awa.

1. **Braes.**  Hillsides.          4. **Weet.**  Wet.
2. **Ilka.**  Every.               5. **Lav'rock.**  Lark.
3. **Shaw.**  Wood.                6. **Mavis.**  Thrush.

## THE LOVELY LASS O' INVERNESS

[Published in Johnson's *Museum* in 1796. The date of composition is uncertain: some believe it to have been 1787, because in September of that year Burns visited the scene of the battle of Culloden; others make it 1794.

In Palgrave's *Golden Treasury* this song is given under the title, "Lament for Culloden." "Drumossie moor" is merely another name for "Cullodon lea," where the Highlanders under the Stuart Pretender were decisively defeated in 1746.]

The lovely lass of Inverness,
　　Nae joy nor pleasure can she see;
　For e'en to morn she cries "Alas!"
　　And ay the saut tear blin's her e'e.[1]

"Drumossie moor, Drumossie day—
　　A waefu' day it was to me!
For there I lost my father dear,
　　My father dear and brethren three.

"Their winding-sheet the bluidy clay,
　　Their graves are growin green to see,
And by them lies the dearest lad
　　That ever blest a woman's e'e.

"Now wae to thee, thou cruel lord,
　　A bluidy man I trow thou be;
For monie a heart thou hast made sair,[2]
　　That ne'er did wrang to thine or thee!"

1. **Blin's her e'e.**  Blinds her eye.
2. **Sair.**  Sore.

## CHARLIE, HE'S MY DARLING

[Published by Johnson in 1796; placed here because of the historical relation to the preceding poem. "Charlie" was the young Stuart prince, idol of many Highlanders, who was defeated at Culloden.]

'Twas on a Monday morning,
   Right early in the year,
That Charlie came to our town—
   The young Chevalier.

*Chorus.*—An' Charlie, he's my darling,
     My darling, my darling,
    Charlie, he's my darling—
     The young Chevalier.

As he was walking up the street,
   The city for to view,
O, there he spied a bonie lass
   The window looking thro'!
     An' Charlie, etc.

Sae light's he jumpèd up the stair,
   And tirl'd at the pin;[1]
And wha sae ready as hersel
   To let the laddie in!
     An' Charlie, etc.

He set his Jenny on his knee,
   All in his Highland dress;
For brawlie[2] weel he kend[3] the way
   To please a bonie lass.
     An' Charlie, etc.

It's up yon heathery mountain,
   An' down yon scroggy[4] glen,
We daur na gang[5] a-milking,
   For Charlie and his men.
     An' Charlie, etc.

1. **Tirl'd at the pin.** Rattled at a "rasping pin"—a sort of knocker.
2. **Brawlie.** Perfectly.
3. **Kend.** Knew.
4. **Scroggy.** Scrubby.
5. **Daur na gang.** Dare not go.

# CA' THE YOWES TO THE KNOWES

## *Second Version*

[In Johnson's *Museum* in 1790 appeared a version of this song which Burns said he had patched up from the singing of a friend of his. He attempted to improve his first version for Thomson in September, 1794, when he sent him the text printed below.]

*Chorus.*—Ca' the yowes[1] to the knowes,[2]
　　　　Ca' them where the heather grows,
　　　　Ca' them where the burnie rowes,[3]
　　　　　My bonie dearie.

Hark, the mavis'[4] e'ening sang,
Sounding Clouden's woods amang;
Then a-faulding[5] let us gang,[6]
　My bonie dearie.
　　Ca' the yowes, etc.

We'll gae[7] down by Clouden side,
Thro' the hazels, spreading wide
O'er the waves that sweetly glide
　To the moon sae clearly.
　　Ca' the yowes, etc.

Yonder Clouden's silent towers,
Where, at moonshine's midnight hours,
O'er the dewy bending flowers,
　Fairies dance sae cheery.
　　Ca' the yowes, etc.

Ghaist nor bogle[8] shalt thou fear;
Thou'rt to love and Heav'n sae dear,
Nocht of ill may come thee near,
　My bonie dearie.
　　Ca' the yowes, etc.

1. Yowes. Ewes.
2. Knowes. Knolls.
3. Burnie rowes. Brooklet rolls.
4. Mavis. Thrush.
5. A-faulding. Sheep-folding.
6. Gang. Go.
7. Gae. Go.
8. Ghaist nor bogle. Ghost nor goblin.

Fair and lovely as thou art,
Thou hast stown[9] my very heart;
I can die—but canna part,
   My bonie dearie.
      Ca' the yowes, etc.

# CONTENTED WI' LITTLE AND CANTIE WI' MAIR

*Tune*—"Lumps o' Pudding."

[Sent to Thomson in November, 1794, and printed by him in 1799.

In a letter written to Thomson in May, 1795, Burns says he intended this song as a picture of his own mind.]

Contented wi' little and cantie[1] wi' mair,
Whene'er I forgather wi' Sorrow and Care,
I gie[2] them a skelp[3] as they're creepin alang,
Wi' a cog[4] o' guid swats[5] and an auld Scottish sang.

I whyles[6] claw the elbow o' troublesome thought,
But man is a soger,[7] and life is a faught;[8]
My mirth and guid humor are coin in my pouch,[9]
And my Freedom's my lairdship nae monarch daur[10]
   touch.

A towmond[11] o' trouble, should that be my fa',[12]
A night o' guid fellowship sowthers[13] it a':
When at the blythe end o' our journey at last,
Wha the Deil ever thinks o' the road he has past?

Blind Chance, let her snapper and stoyte[14] on her way;
Be't to me, be't frae me, e'en let the jad gae![15]
Come Ease or come Travail, come Pleasure or Pain,
My warst word is, "Welcome, and welcome again!"

9. **Stown.** Stolen.

1. **Cantie.** Cheerful.
2. **Gie.** Give.
3. **Skelp.** Slap.
4. **Cog.** Bowl.
5. **Swats.** Ale.
6. **Whyles.** Sometimes.
7. **Soger.** Soldier.
8. **Faught.** Fight.
9. **Pouch.** Pocket.
10. **Daur.** Dare.
11. **Towmond.** Twelve-month.
12. **Fa'.** Lot.
13. **Sowthers.** Solders.
14. **Snapper and stoyte.** Stumble and stagger.
15. **Jad gae.** Jade go.

# LASSIE WI' THE LINT-WHITE LOCKS

*Tune*—"Rothiemurchie's Rant."

[Sent to Thomson in November, 1794, but first printed by Currie in 1800.

The heroine of this poem was Jean Lorimer, whom Burns also celebrated under the name Chloris, and in whose honor he partly rewrote "Whistle and I'll come to ye" (see page 218).]

*Chorus.*—Lassie wi' the lint-white[1] locks,
            Bonie lassie, artless lassie,
            Wilt thou wi' me tent[2] the flocks—
            Wilt thou be my dearie, O?

Now Nature cleeds[3] the flowery lea,
And a' is young and sweet like thee,
O, wilt thou share its joys wi' me.
        And say thou'lt be my dearie, O?
        Lassie wi' the, etc.

The primrose bank, the wimpling burn,[4]
The cuckoo on the milk-white thorn,
The wanton lambs at early morn
        Shall welcome thee, my dearie, O.
        Lassie wi' the, etc.

And when the welcome simmer shower
Has cheered ilk[5] drooping little flower.
We'll to the breathing woodbine-bower
        At sultry noon, my dearie, O.
        Lassie wi' the, etc.

When Cynthia lights, wi' silver ray,
The weary shearer's hameward way,
Thro' yellow waving fields we'll stray,
        And talk o' love, my dearie, O.
        Lassie wi' the, etc.

1. **Lint-white.** Flaxen.
2. **Tent.** Tend.
3. **Cleeds.** Clothes.
4. **Wimpling burn.** Meandering brook.
5. **Ilk.** Every.

And when the howling wintry blast
Disturbs my lassie's midnight rest,
Enclaspèd to my faithfu' breast,
    I'll comfort thee, my dearie, O.
      Lassie wi' the, etc.

## A MAN'S A MAN FOR A' THAT

*Tune*—"For A' That."

[Sent to Thomson in January, 1795; printed in the
*Glasgow Magazine* in August of the same year, and in a
number of other periodicals during the next few years.
"A great critic (Aikin) on songs says that love and wine
are the exclusive themes for song-writing. The following is
on neither subject and consequently is no song.... I do not
give you the foregoing song for your book, but merely by
way of *vive la bagatelle;* for the piece is not really poetry."
Thus Burns wrote of what has been called "the *Marseillaise* of
humanity."

Note that the same refrain was used in a song in "The
Jolly Beggars" (page 106).]

Is there for honest poverty
    That hings[1] his head, an' a' that?
The coward slave, we pass him by—
    We dare be poor for a' that!
For a' that, an' a' that,
    Our toils obscure, an' a' that,
The rank is but the guinea's stamp,
    The man's the gowd[2] for a' that.

What though on hamely fare we dine,
    Wear hoddin[3] grey, an' a' that?
Gie[4] fools their silks, and knaves their wine—
    A man's a man for a' that.
For a' that, an' a' that,
    Their tinsel show, an' a' that,
The honest man, tho' e'er sae poor,
    Is king o' men for a' that.

1. **Hings.** Hangs.
2. **Gowd.** Gold.
3. **Hoddin.** Coarse woolen cloth.
4. **Gie.** Give.

Ye see yon birkie ca'd[5] a lord,
　Wha struts, an' stares, an' a' that;
Tho' hundreds worship at his word,
　He's but a coof[6] for a' that.
For a' that, an' a' that,
　His ribband, star, an' a' that,
The man o' independent mind,
　He looks an' laughs at a' that.


A prince can mak a belted knight,
　A marquis, duke, an' a' that;
But an honest man's aboon[7] his might—
　Guid faith, he mauna fa'[8] that!
For a' that, an' a' that,
　Their dignities, an' a' that,
The pith o' sense an' pride o' worth
　Are higher rank than a' that.


Then let us pray that come it may,
　(As come it will for a' that)
That Sense and Worth, o'er a' the earth,
　Shall bear the gree,[9] an' a' that.
For a' that, an' a' that,
　It's coming yet for a' that,
That man to man, the world o'er,
　Shall brithers be for a' that.


5. **Birkie ca'd.** Fellow called.
6. **Coof.** Fool.
7. **Aboon.** Above.

8. **Mauna fa'.** Must not claim.
9. **Gree.** Prize.

## THE BRAW WOOER

[Sent to Thomson in June or July, 1795, and by him published in 1799.

The Gate-slack (stanza iv) is a romantic pass among the Lowther hills on the confines of Dumfriesshire; and Dalgarnock (stanza v) is near the river Nith.]

Last May a braw[1] wooer cam down the lang glen,
  And sair[2] wi' his love he did deave[3] me.
I said there was naething I hated like men—
  The deuce gae wi'm[4] to believe me, believe me—
  The deuce gae wi'm to believe me!

He spak o' the darts in my bonie black een,[5]
  And vow'd for my love he was diein.
I said, he might die when he liket for Jean—
  The Lord forgie[6] me for liein, for liein—
  The Lord forgie me for liein!

A weel-stockét mailen,[7] himsel for the laird,
  And marriage aff-hand were his proffers;
I never loot[8] on that I kenn'd it, or car'd,
  But I thought I might hae waur[9] offers, waur offers—
  But I thought I might hae waur offers.

But what wad ye think?—in a fortnight or less
  (The Deil tak his taste to gae near her!)
He up the Gate-slack to my black cousin, Bess—
  Guess ye how, the jad! I could bear her, could bear her—
  Guess ye how, the jad! I could bear her.

1. **Braw.** Fine.
2. **Sair.** Sorely.
3. **Deave.** Deafen.
4. **Gae wi'm.** Go with him.
5. **Een.** Eyes.
6. **Forgie.** Forgive.
7. **Mailen.** Farm.
8. **Loot.** Let.
9. **Waur.** Worse.

But a' the niest[10] week, as I petted wi' care,
   I gaed[11] to the tryste o' Dalgarnock;
And wha but my fine fickle wooer was there?
   I glowr'd[12] as I'd seen a warlock,[13] a warlock—
   I glowr'd as I'd seen a warlock.

But owre my left shouther[14] I gae[15] him a blink,
   Lest neebors might say I was saucy;
My wooer he caper'd as he'd been in drink,
   And vow'd I was his dear lassie, dear lassie—
   And vow'd I was his dear lassie.

I spier'd[16] for my cousin fu' couthy[17] and sweet,
   Gin[18] she had recover'd her hearin?
And how her new shoon[19] fit her auld shachl'd[20] feet?
   But heavens! how he fell a-swearin, a-swearin—
   But heavens! how he fell a-swearin!

He begged, for gudesake, I wad be his wife,
   Or else I wad kill him wi' sorrow;
So e'en to preserve the poor body in life,
   I think I maun[21] wed him tomorrow, tomorrow—
   I think I maun wed him tomorrow.

10. **Niest.** Next.
11. **Gaed.** Went.
12. **Glowr'd.** Stared.
13. **Warlock.** Wizard.
14. **Shouther.** Shoulder.
15. **Gae.** Gave.

16. **Spier'd.** Asked.
17. **Couthy.** Kindly.
18. **Gin.** If.
19. **Shoon.** Shoes.
20. **Shachl'd.** Shapeless.
21. **Maun.** Must.

## A LASS WI' A TOCHER[1]

*Tune*—"Ballinamona Ora."

[Sent to Thomson in February, 1796, and by him published
in 1799.]

Awa wi' your witchcraft o' Beauty's alarms,
The slender bit[2] beauty you grasp in your arms!
O, gie[3] me the lass that has acres o' charms!
O, gie me the lass wi' the weel-stockit farms!

   *Chorus.*—Then hey for a lass wi' a tocher,
       Then hey for a lass wi' a tocher,
       Then hey for a lass wi' a tocher,
       The nice yellow guineas for me!

Your Beauty's a flower, in the morning that blows,
And withers the faster, the faster it grows;
But the rapturous charm o' the bonie green knowes,[4]
Ilk[5] spring they're new deckit wi' bonie white yowes![6]
       Then hey for a lass, etc.

And e'en when this Beauty your bosom hath blest,
The brightest o' Beauty may cloy when possess'd;
But the sweet, yellow darlings wi' Geordie[7] impress'd,
The langer ye hae them, the mair they're carest!
       Then hey for a lass, etc.

1. **Tocher.** Dower.
2. **Bit.** Small.
3. **Gie.** Give.
4. **Knowes.** Knolls.
5. **Ilk.** Every.
6. **Yowes.** Ewes.
7. **Geordie.** King George III, whose image adorned golden guineas.

## O, WERT THOU IN THE CAULD BLAST

[Written during Burns's last illness in compliment to Jessie Lewars, the daughter of a fellow exciseman and a great help to Mrs. Burns at this time.]

O, wert thou in the cauld blast
 On yonder lea, on yonder lea,
My plaidie to the angry airt,[1]
 I'd shelter thee, I'd shelter thee;
Or did Misfortune's bitter storms
 Around thee blaw, around thee blaw,
Thy bield[2] should be my bosom,
 To share it a', to share it a'.

Or were I in the wildest waste,
 Sae black and bare, sae black and bare,
The desert were a Paradise,
 If thou wert there, if thou wert there;
Or were I monarch of the globe,
 Wi' thee to reign, wi' thee to reign,
The brightest jewel in my crown
 Wad be my queen, wad be my queen.

1. **Airt.** Wind.
2. **Bield.** Shelter.

# CARLYLE'S ESSAY ON BURNS

In the modern arrangements of society it is no uncommon thing that a man of genius must, like Butler, "ask for bread and receive a stone"*; for, in spite of our grand maxim of supply and demand,* it
5 is by no means the highest excellence that men are most forward to recognize. The inventor* of a spinning-jenny is pretty sure of his reward in his own day; but the writer of a true poem, like the apostle of a true religion, is nearly as sure of the contrary.
10 We do not know whether it is not an aggravation of the injustice, that there is generally a posthumous retribution. Robert Burns, in the course of Nature, might yet have been living; but his short life was spent in toil and penury; and he died, in the prime of
15 his manhood, miserable and neglected. And yet already a brave mausoleum* shines over his dust, and more than one splendid monument has been reared in other places to his fame; the street* where he languished in poverty is called by his name; the highest
20 personages in our literature have been proud to appear as his commentators and admirers; and here is the *sixth* narrative* of his *Life* that has been given to the world!

Mr. Lockhart thinks it necessary to apologize for
25 this new attempt on such a subject; but his readers, we believe, will readily acquit him; or, at worst, will censure only the performance of his task, not the choice of it. The character of Burns, indeed, is a theme that cannot easily become either trite or ex-
30 hausted; and will probably gain rather than lose in its dimensions by the distance to which it is removed by Time. No man, it has been said, is a hero* to his

233

valet; and this is probably true; but the fault is at least as likely to be the valet's as the hero's. For it is certain that to the vulgar eye few things are wonderful that are not distant. It is difficult for men
5 to believe that the man, the mere man whom they see—nay, perhaps painfully feel, toiling at their side through the poor jostlings of existence, can be made of finer clay than themselves. Suppose that some dining acquaintance of Sir Thomas Lucy's,* and neighbor
10 of John à Combe's,* had snatched an hour or two from the preservation of his game, and written us a Life of Shakespeare! What dissertations should we not have had—not on *Hamlet* and *The Tempest,* but on the wool-trade, and deer-stealing, and the libel and
15 vagrant laws; and how the Poacher became a Player; and how Sir Thomas and Mr. John had Christian bowels, and did not push him to extremities! In like manner, we believe, with respect to Burns, that till the companions of his pilgrimage, the Honorable Ex-
20 cise Commissioners,* and the Gentlemen of the Caledonian Hunt,* and the Dumfries Aristocracy, and all the Squires and Earls, equally with the Ayr Writers, and the New and Old Light Clergy* whom he had to do with, shall have become invisible in the darkness
25 of the Past, or visible only by light borrowed from *his* juxtaposition, it will be difficult to measure him by any true standard, or to estimate what he really was and did, in the eighteenth century, for his country and the world. It will be difficult, we say, but still
30 a fair problem for literary historians; and repeated attempts will give us repeated approximations.

His former Biographers have done something, no doubt, but by no means a great deal, to assist us. Dr. Currie and Mr. Walker, the principal of these
35 writers, have both, we think, mistaken one essen-

tially important thing—their own and the world's
true relation to their author, and the style in which
it became such men to think and to speak of such
a man. Dr. Currie loved the poet truly; more per-
5 haps than he avowed to his readers, or even to
himself; yet he everywhere introduces him with a
certain patronizing, apologetic air; as if the polite
public might think it strange and half unwarrant-
able that he, a man of science, a scholar and gentle-
10 man, should do such honor to a rustic. In all this,
however, we readily admit that his fault was not want
of love, but weakness of faith; and regret that the
first and kindest of all our poet's biographers should
not have seen further or believed more boldly what
15 he saw. Mr. Walker offends more deeply in the same
kind; and both err alike in presenting us with a de-
tached catalogue of his several supposed attributes,
virtues, and vices, instead of a delineation of the re-
sulting character as a living unity. This, however,
20 is not painting a portrait; but gauging the length
and breadth of the several features, and jotting down
their dimensions in arithmetical ciphers. Nay, it is
not so much as that; for we are yet to learn by what
arts or instruments the mind *could* be so measured
25 and gauged.

Mr. Lockhart, we are happy to say, has avoided
both these errors. He uniformly treats Burns as the
high and remarkable man the public voice has now
pronounced him to be; and in delineating him he
30 has avoided the method of separate generalities, and
rather sought for characteristic incidents, habits,
actions, sayings; in a word, for aspects which exhibit
the whole man, as he looked and lived among his
fellows. The book, accordingly, with all its de-
35 ficiencies, gives more insight, we think, into the true

character of Burns than any prior biography; though, being written on the very popular and condensed scheme of an article for *Constable's Miscellany*,* it has less depth than we could have wished and ex-
5 pected from a writer of such power; and contains rather more, and more multifarious, quotations than belong of right to an original production. Indeed, Mr. Lockhart's own writing is generally so good, so clear, direct, and nervous, that we seldom wish to see
10 it making place for another man's. However, the spirit of the work is throughout candid, tolerant, and anxiously conciliating; compliments and praises are liberally distributed, on all hands, to great and small; and, as Mr. Morris Birkbeck* observes of the society
15 in the backwoods of America, "the courtesies of polite life are never lost sight of for a moment." But there are better things than these in the volume; and we can safely testify not only that it is easily and pleas-antly read a first time, but may even be without diffi-
20 culty read again.

Nevertheless, we are far from thinking that the problem of Burns's Biography has yet been ade-quately solved. We do not allude so much to de-ficiency of facts or documents—though of these we
25 are still every day receiving some fresh accession—as to the limited and imperfect application of them to the great end of Biography. Our notions upon this subject may perhaps appear extravagant; but if an individual is really of consequence enough to
30 have his life and character recorded for public re-membrance, we have always been of opinion that the public ought to be made acquainted with all the in-ward springs and relations of his character. How did the world and man's life, from his particular position,
35 represent themselves to his mind? How did co-

existing circumstances modify him from without;
how did he modify these from within? With what
endeavors and what efficacy rule over them; with
what resistance and what suffering sink under them?
5 In one word, what and how produced was the effect
of society on him; what and how produced was his
effect on society? He who should answer these questions, in regard to any individual, would, as we believe, furnish a model of perfection in Biography.
10 Few individuals, indeed, can deserve such a study;
and many *lives* will be written, and, for the grati-
fication of innocent curiosity, ought to be written, and
read, and forgotten, which are not in this sense
*biographies.* But Burns, if we mistake not, is one
15 of these few individuals; and such a study, at least
with such a result, he has not yet obtained. Our
own contributions to it, we are aware, can be but
scanty and feeble; but we offer them with good will,
and trust they may meet with acceptance from those
20 they are intended for.

Burns first came upon the world as a prodigy;
and was, in that character, entertained by it, in the
usual fashion, with loud, vague, tumultuous wonder,
speedily subsiding into censure and neglect; till his
25 early and most mournful death again awakened an
enthusiasm for him, which, especially as there was
now nothing to be done and much to be spoken, has
prolonged itself even to our own time. It is true,
the "nine days"* have long since elapsed; and the
30 very continuance of this clamor proves that Burns
was no vulgar wonder. Accordingly, even in sober
judgments, where, as years passed by, he has come
to rest more and more exclusively on his own intrinsic
merits, and may now be well-nigh shorn of that casual
35 radiance, he appears not only as a true British poet,

but as one of the most considerable British men of the eighteenth century. Let it not be objected that he did little. He did much, if we consider where and how. If the work performed was small, we must remember that he had his very materials to discover; for the metal he worked in lay hid under the desert moor, where no eye but his* had guessed its existence; and we may almost say that with his own hand he had to construct the tools for fashioning it. For he found himself in deepest obscurity, without help, without instruction, without model, or with models only of the meanest sort. An educated man stands, as it were, in the midst of a boundless arsenal and magazine, filled with all the weapons and engines which man's skill has been able to devise from the earliest time; and he works, accordingly, with a strength borrowed from all past ages. How different is *his* state who stands on the outside of that storehouse and feels that its gates must be stormed, or remain forever shut against him! His means are the commonest and rudest; the mere work done is no measure of his strength. A dwarf behind his steam engine may remove mountains; but no dwarf will hew them down with a pickax; and he must be a Titan that hurls them abroad with his arms.

It is in this last shape that Burns presents himself. Born in an age the most prosaic Britain had yet seen, and in a condition the most disadvantageous, where his mind, if it accomplished aught, must accomplish it under the pressure of continual bodily toil, nay, of penury and desponding apprehension of the worst evils, and with no furtherance but such knowledge as dwells in a poor man's hut, and the rimes of a Fergusson or Ramsay* for his standard of beauty, he sinks not under all these impediments.

Through the fogs and darkness of that obscure region
his lynx eye discerns the true relations of the world
and human life; he grows into intellectual strength
and trains himself into intellectual expertness. Im-
5 pelled by the expansive movement of his own irre-
pressible soul he struggles forward into the general
view, and with haughty modesty lays down before us,
as the fruit of his labor, a gift which Time has now
pronounced imperishable. Add to all this, that his
10 darksome, drudging childhood and youth was by far
the kindliest era of his whole life, and that he died
in his thirty-seventh year—and then ask if it be
strange that his poems are imperfect and of small
extent, or that his genius attained no mastery in its
15 art. Alas, his Sun shone as through a tropical tor-
nado; and the pale Shadow of Death eclipsed it at
noon! Shrouded in such baleful vapors, the genius
of Burns was never seen in clear, azure splendor en-
lightening the world; but some beams from it did, by
20 fits, pierce through; and it tinted those clouds with
rainbow and orient colors into a glory and stern
grandeur which men silently gazed on with wonder
and tears!

We are anxious not to exaggerate, for it is expo-
25 sition rather than admiration that our readers require of us here; and yet to avoid some tendency to
that side is no easy matter. We love Burns and we
pity him; and love and pity are prone to magnify.
Criticism, it is sometimes thought, should be a cold
30 business; we are not so sure of this; but, at all
events, our concern with Burns is not exclusively that
of critics. True and genial as his poetry must appear, it is not chiefly as a poet, but as a man, that
he interests and affects us. He was often advised to
35 write a tragedy. Time and means were not lent him

for this; but through life he enacted a tragedy, and one of the deepest. We question whether the world has since witnessed so utterly sad a scene; whether Napoleon himself, left to brawl with Sir Hudson
5 Lowe,* and perish on his rock, "amid the melancholy main,"* presented to the reflecting mind such a "spectacle of pity and fear"* as did this intrinsically nobler, gentler, and perhaps greater soul, wasting itself away in a hopeless struggle with base entanglements, which
10 coiled closer and closer round him, till only death opened him an outlet. Conquerors are a class of men with whom, for most part, the world could well dispense; nor can the hard intellect, the unsympathizing loftiness, and high but selfish en-
15 thusiasm of such persons inspire us, in general, with any affection; at best it may excite amazement; and their fall, like that of a pyramid, will be beheld with a certain sadness and awe. But a true Poet, a man in whose heart resides some effluence of Wisdom,
20 some tone of the "Eternal Melodies,"* is the most precious gift that can be bestowed on a generation; we see him in a freer, purer development of whatever is noblest in ourselves; his life is a rich lesson to us; and we mourn his death as that of a benefactor who
25 loved and taught us.

Such a gift had Nature, in her bounty, bestowed on us in Robert Burns; but with queenlike indifference she cast it from her hand, like a thing of no moment; and it was defaced and torn asunder, as
30 an idle bauble, before we recognized it. To the ill-starred Burns was given the power of making man's life more venerable; but that of wisely guiding his own life was not given. Destiny—for so in our ignorance we must speak—his faults, the faults of
35 others, proved too hard for him; and that spirit

which might have soared, could it but have walked,
soon sank to the dust, its glorious faculties trodden
under foot in the blossom; and died, we may almost
say, without ever having lived. And so kind and
5 warm a soul, so full of inborn riches, of love to all
living and lifeless things! How his heart flows out
in sympathy over universal Nature; and in her bleak-
est provinces discerns a beauty and a meaning! The
"Daisy"* falls not unheeded under his plowshare;
10 nor the ruined nest of that "wee, cowrin, tim'rous
beastie,"* cast forth, after all its provident pains, to
"thole the sleety dribble and cranreuch cauld." The
"hoar visage" of Winter delights him; he dwells with
a sad and oft-returning fondness in these scenes of
15 solemn desolation; but the voice of the tempest becomes an anthem to his ears; he loves to walk in the
sounding woods, for "it raises his thoughts* to *Him
that walketh on the wings of the wind.*" A true
Poet-soul, for it needs but to be struck, and the sound
20 it yields will be music! But observe him chiefly as
he mingles with his brother men. What warm, all-
comprehending fellow-feeling; what trustful, boundless love; what generous exaggeration of the object
loved! His rustic friend, his nut-brown maiden are
25 no longer mean and homely, but a hero and a queen,
whom he prizes as the paragons of Earth. The rough
scenes of Scottish life, not seen by him in any Ar-
cadian illusion, but in the rude contradiction, in the
smoke and soil of a too harsh reality, are still lovely
30 to him; Poverty is indeed his companion, but Love
also, and Courage; the simple feelings, the worth, the
nobleness, that dwell under the straw roof, are dear
and venerable to his heart; and thus over the lowest
provinces of man's existence he pours the glory of
35 his own soul; and they rise, in shadow and sunshine,

softened and brightened into a beauty which other
eyes discern not in the highest. He has a just self-
consciousness, which too often degenerates into pride;
yet it is a noble pride, for defense, not for offense;
5 no cold, suspicious feeling, but a frank and social one.
The Peasant Poet bears himself, we might say, like
a King in exile; he is cast among the low and feels
himself equal to the highest; yet he claims no rank,
that none may be disputed to him. The forward he
10 can repel, the supercilious he can subdue; pretensions
of wealth or ancestry are of no avail with him; there
is a fire in that dark eye, under which the "insolence of condescension"* cannot thrive. In his
abasement, in his extreme need, he forgets not for a
15 moment the majesty of Poetry and Manhood. And yet,
far as he feels himself above common men, he wanders not apart from them, but mixes warmly in their
interests; nay, throws himself into their arms, and,
as it were, entreats them to love him. It is moving
20 to see how, in his darkest despondency, this proud
being still seeks relief from friendship; unbosoms
himself, often to the unworthy; and, amid tears,
strains to his glowing heart a heart that knows only
the name of friendship. And yet he was "quick to
25 learn,"* a man of keen vision, before whom common
disguises afforded no concealment. His understanding saw through the hollowness even of accomplished
deceivers; but there was a generous credulity in his
heart. And so did our Peasant show himself among
30 us, "a soul like an Æolian harp,* in whose strings the
vulgar wind, as it passed through them, changed
itself into articulate melody." And this was he for
whom the world found no fitter business* than quar-
reling with smugglers and vintners, computing excise
35 dues upon tallow, and gauging ale-barrels! In such

toils was that mighty Spirit sorrowfully wasted; and
a hundred years may pass on before another such is
given us to waste.

All that remains of Burns, the Writings he has
5 left, seem to us, as we hinted above, no more than
a poor, mutilated fraction of what was in him; brief,
broken glimpses of a genius that could never show
itself complete; that wanted all things for completeness—culture, leisure, true effort, nay, even
10 length of life. His poems are, with scarcely any exception, mere occasional effusions; poured forth with
little premeditation; expressing, by such means as
offered, the passion, opinion, or humor of the hour.
Never in one instance was it permitted him to grapple
15 with any subject with the full collection of his
strength, to fuse and mold it in the concentrated
fire of his genius. To try by the strict rules of Art
such imperfect fragments would be at once unprofitable and unfair. Nevertheless, there is something in
20 these poems, marred and defective as they are, which
forbids the most fastidious student of poetry to pass
them by. Some sort of enduring quality they must
have; for after fifty years of the wildest vicissitudes in
poetic taste they still continue to be read; nay, are
25 read more and more eagerly, more and more extensively; and this not only by literary virtuosos, and
that class upon whom transitory causes operate most
strongly, but by all classes, down to the most hard,
unlettered, and truly natural class, who read little,
30 and especially no poetry, except because they find
pleasure in it. The grounds of so singular and wide
a popularity, which extends, in a literal sense, from
the palace to the hut, and over all regions where the
English tongue is spoken, are well worth inquiring
35 into. After every just deduction, it seems to imply

some rare excellence in these works.  What is that excellence?

To answer this question will not lead us far.  The excellence of Burns is, indeed, among the rarest, 5 whether in poetry or prose; but, at the same time, it is plain and easily recognized—his *Sincerity*, his indisputable air of Truth.  Here are no fabulous woes or joys; no hollow, fantastic sentimentalities; no wiredrawn refinings, either in thought or feeling; the 10 passion that is traced before us has glowed in a living heart; the opinion he utters has risen in his own understanding, and been a light to his own steps. He does not write from hearsay, but from sight and experience; it is the scenes that he has lived and 15 labored amidst that he describes; those scenes, rude and humble as they are, have kindled beautiful emotions in his soul, noble thoughts, and definite resolves; and he speaks forth what is in him, not from any outward call of vanity or interest, but because his heart 20 is too full to be silent.  He speaks it with such melody and modulation as he can, "in homely, rustic jingle"*; but it is his own, and genuine.  This is the grand secret for finding readers and retaining them; let him who would move and convince others be first moved 25 and convinced himself.  Horace's rule, *Si vis me flere,** is applicable in a wider sense than the literal one. To every poet, to every writer, we might say:  Be true, if you would be believed.  Let a man but speak forth with genuine earnestness the thought, the emo- 30 tion, the actual condition of his own heart, and other men, so strangely are we all knit together by the tie of sympathy, must and will give heed to him.  In culture, in extent of view, we may stand above the speaker, or below him; but in either case his words, 35 if they are earnest and sincere, will find some response

within us; for in spite of all casual varieties in outward rank or inward, as face answers to face, so does
the heart of man to man.

This may appear a very simple principle, and one
which Burns had little merit in discovering. True,
the discovery is easy enough; but the practical appli-
ance is not easy; is indeed the fundamental difficulty
which all poets have to strive with, and which scarcely
one in the hundred ever fairly surmounts. A head
too dull to discriminate the true from the false, a
heart too dull to love the one at all risks and to hate
the other in spite of all temptations, are alike fatal
to a writer. With either, or, as more commonly
happens, with both of these deficiencies, combine a
love of distinction, a wish to be original, which is
seldom wanting; and we have Affectation, the bane of
literature, as Cant, its elder brother, is of morals.
How often does the one and the other front us, in
poetry as in life! Great poets themselves are not
always free of this vice; nay, it is precisely on a certain sort and degree of greatness that it is most
commonly ingrafted. A strong effort after excellence
will sometimes solace itself with a mere shadow of
success; he who has much to unfold will sometimes
unfold it imperfectly. Byron, for instance, was no
common man; yet if we examine his poetry with this
view, we shall find it far from faultless. Generally
speaking, we should say that it is not true. He re-
freshes us, not with the divine fountain, but too often
with vulgar, strong waters, stimulating indeed to the
taste, but soon ending in dislike, or even nausea. Are
his Harolds and Giaours,* we would ask, real men;
we mean, poetically consistent and conceivable men?
Do not these characters, does not the character of
their author, which more or less shines through them

all, rather appear a thing put on for the occasion—
no natural or possible mode of being, but something
intended to look much grander than nature? Surely,
all these stormful agonies, this volcanic heroism,
5 superhuman contempt, and moody desperation, with
so much scowling, and teeth-gnashing, and other sul-
phurous humor, is more like the brawling of a player
in some paltry tragedy, which is to last three hours,
than the bearing of a man in the business of life,
10 which is to last three-score and ten years. To our
minds there is a taint of this sort, something which
we should call theatrical, false, affected, in every one
of these otherwise so powerful pieces. Perhaps *Don
Juan,* especially the latter parts of it, is the only thing
15 approaching to a *sincere* work he ever wrote; the
only work where he showed himself, in any measure,
as he was; and seemed so intent on his subject as,
for moments, to forget himself. Yet Byron hated
this vice, we believe, heartily detested it; nay, he had
20 declared formal war against it in words. So difficult
is it even for the strongest to make this primary at-
tainment, which might seem the simplest of all: *to
read its own consciousness without mistakes,* without
errors involuntary or willful! We recollect no poet
25 of Burns's susceptibility who comes before us from
the first, and abides with us to the last, with such a
total want of affectation. He is an honest man and
an honest writer. In his successes and his failures,
in his greatness and his littleness, he is ever clear,
30 simple, true, and glitters with no luster but his own.
We reckon this to be a great virtue; to be, in fact, the
root of most other virtues, literary as well as moral.

Here, however, let us say, it is to the Poetry of
Burns that we now allude; to those writings which
35 he had time to meditate, and where no special rea-

son existed to warp his critical feeling or obstruct
his endeavor to fulfill it. Certain of his Letters, and
other fractions of prose composition, by no means
deserve this praise. Here, doubtless, there is not the
5 same natural truth of style; but, on the contrary,
something not only stiff, but strained and twisted; a
certain high-flown, inflated tone, the stilting emphasis of which contrasts ill with the firmness and
rugged simplicity of even his poorest verses. Thus
10 no man, it would appear, is altogether unaffected.
Does not Shakespeare himself sometimes premeditate
the sheerest bombast! But even with regard to these
Letters of Burns, it is but fair to state that he had
two excuses. The first was his comparative deficiency
15 in language. Burns, though for the most part he
writes with singular force and even gracefulness, is
not master of English prose, as he is of Scottish verse;
not master of it, we mean, in proportion to the depth
and vehemence of his matter. These Letters strike
20 us as the effort of a man to express something which
he has no organ fit for expressing. But a second
and weightier excuse is to be found in the peculiarity
of Burns's social rank. His correspondents are often
men whose relation to him he has never accurately
25 ascertained; whom, therefore, he is either forearming
himself against, or else unconsciously flattering, by
adopting the style he thinks will please them. At all
events, we should remember that these faults, even
in his Letters, are not the rule, but the exception.
30 Whenever he writes, as one would ever wish to do,
to trusted friends and on real interests, his style becomes simple, vigorous, expressive, sometimes even
beautiful. His letters to Mrs. Dunlop* are uniformly
excellent.

35     But we return to his Poetry. In addition to its

Sincerity, it has another peculiar merit, which indeed is but a mode, or perhaps a means, of the foregoing; this displays itself in his choice of subjects; or rather in his indifference as to subjects, and the 5 power he has of making all subjects interesting. The ordinary poet, like the ordinary man, is forever seeking in external circumstances the help which can be found only in himself. In what is familiar and near at hand, he discerns no form or comeliness; home is 10 not poetical, but prosaic; it is in some past, distant, conventional, heroic world that poetry resides for him; were he there and not here, were he thus and not so, it would be well with him. Hence our innumerable host of rose-colored Novels and iron- 15 mailed Epics, with their locality not on the Earth but somewhere nearer to the Moon. Hence our Virgins of the Sun,* and our Knights of the Cross, malicious Saracens in turbans, and copper-colored Chiefs in wampum, and so many other truculent figures from 20 the heroic times or the heroic climates, who on all hands swarm in our poetry. Peace be with them! But yet, as a great moralist proposed preaching to the men of this century, so would we fain preach to the poets, "a sermon on the duty of staying at home." 25 Let them be sure that heroic ages and heroic climates can do little for them. That form of life has attraction for us, less because it is better or nobler than our own, than simply because it is different; and even this attraction must be of the most transient 30 sort. For will not our own age, one day, be an ancient one, and have as quaint a costume as the rest; not contrasted with the rest, therefore, but ranked along with them, in respect of quaintness? Does Homer interest us now because he wrote of what 35 passed beyond his native Greece, and two centuries

before he was born; or because he wrote what passed
in God's world, and in the heart of man, which is the
same after thirty centuries? Let our poets look to
this: is their feeling really finer, truer, and their
5 vision deeper than that of other men—they have
nothing to fear, even from the humblest subject; is
it not so—they have nothing to hope but an ephemeral
favor, even from the highest.

The poet, we imagine, can never have far to seek
10 for a subject; the elements of his art are in him,
and around him on every hand; for him the Ideal
world is not remote from the Actual, but under it
and within it; nay, he is a poet precisely because
he can discern it there. Wherever there is a sky
15 above him and a world around him, the poet is in
his place; for here too is man's existence, with its
infinite longings and small acquirings; its ever-
thwarted, ever-renewed endeavors; its unspeakable
aspirations, its fears and hopes that wander through
20 Eternity; and all the mystery of brightness and of
gloom that it was ever made of, in any age or climate, since man first began to live. Is there not
the fifth act of a Tragedy in every deathbed, though
it were a peasant's, and a bed of heath? And are
25 wooings and weddings obsolete, that there can be
Comedy no longer? Or are men suddenly grown
wise, that Laughter must no longer shake his sides,
but be cheated of his Farce? Man's life and nature
is as it was, and as it will ever be. But the poet must
30 have an eye to read these things and a heart to understand them; or they come and pass away before him
in vain. He is a *vates,** a seer; a gift of vision has
been given him. Has life no meanings for him which
another cannot equally decipher, then he is no poet,
35 and Delphi* itself will not make him one.

In this respect, Burns, though not perhaps absolutely a great poet, better manifests his capability,
better proves the truth of his genius, than if he had
by his own strength kept the whole Minerva Press*
5 going, to the end of his literary course.   He shows
himself at least a poet of Nature's own making; and
Nature, after all, is still the grand agent in making
poets.   We often hear of this and the other external
condition being requisite for the existence of a poet.
10 Sometimes it is a certain sort of training; he must
have studied certain things, studied, for instance, "the
elder dramatists," and so learned a poetic language;
as if poetry lay in the tongue, not in the heart.
At other times we are told he must be bred in a cer-
15 tain rank, and must be on confidential footing with
the higher classes; because, above all things, he must
see the world.   As to seeing the world, we apprehend
this will cause him little difficulty, if he have but
eyesight to see it with.   Without eyesight, indeed, the
20 task might be hard.   The blind or the purblind man
"travels from Dan to Beersheba* and finds it all
barren."   But happily every poet is born *in* the world;
and sees it, with or against his will, every day and
every hour he lives.   The mysterious workmanship of
25 man's heart, the true light and the inscrutable darkness of man's destiny, reveal themselves not only in
capital cities and crowded saloons, but in every hut
and hamlet where men have their abode.   Nay, do not
the elements of all human virtues and all human
30 vices, the passions at once of a Borgia* and of a
Luther, lie written in stronger or fainter lines in the
consciousness of every individual bosom that has practiced honest self-examination?   Truly, this same
world may be seen in Mossgiel and Tarbolton,* if we
35 look well, as clearly as it ever came to light in
Crockford's* or the Tuileries* itself.

But sometimes still harder requisitions are laid on the poor aspirant to poetry; for it is hinted that he should have *been born* two centuries ago; inasmuch as poetry, about that date, vanished from the earth and became no longer attainable by men! Such cobweb speculations have, now and then, overhung the field of literature; but they obstruct not the growth of any plant there; the Shakespeare or the Burns, unconsciously, and merely as he walks onward, silently brushes them away. Is not every genius an impossibility till he appear? Why do we call him new and original, if *we* saw where his marble was lying, and what fabric he could rear from it? It is not the material but the workman that is wanting. It is not the dark *place* that hinders, but the dim *eye*. A Scottish peasant's life was the meanest and rudest of all lives till Burns became a poet in it and a poet of it, found it a *man's* life, and therefore significant to men. A thousand battlefields remain unsung; but the "Wounded Hare"* has not perished without its memorial; a balm of mercy yet breathes on us from its dumb agonies, because a poet was there. Our Halloween* had passed and repassed, in rude awe and laughter, since the era of the Druids; but no Theocritus,* till Burns, discerned in it the materials of a Scottish Idyl; neither was the "Holy Fair"* any Council of Trent* or Roman Jubilee;* but, nevertheless, Superstition and Hypocrisy and Fun having been propitious to him, in this man's hand it became a poem, instinct with satire and genuine comic life. Let but the true poet be given us, we repeat it; place him where and how you will; and true poetry will not be wanting.

Independently of the essential gift of poetic feeling, as we have now attempted to describe it, a cer-

tain rugged, sterling worth pervades whatever Burns
has written; a virtue, as of green fields and mountain breezes, dwells in his poetry; it is redolent of
natural life and hardy, natural men.    There is a
5 decisive strength in him, and yet a sweet, native
gracefulness; he is tender, he is vehement, yet without constraint or too visible effort; he melts the
heart, or inflames it, with a power which seems
habitual and familiar to him.    We see that in this
10 man there was the gentleness, the trembling pity
of a woman, with the deep earnestness, the force and
passionate ardor of a hero.    Tears lie in him, and
consuming fire; as lightning lurks in the drops of
the summer cloud.    He has a resonance in his bosom
15 for every note of human feeling; the high and the
low, the sad, the ludicrous, the joyful, are welcome
in their turns to his "lightly-moved and all-conceiv-
ing spirit."    And observe with what a fierce, prompt
force he grasps his subject, be it what it may!    How
20 he fixes, as it were, the full image of the matter in his
eye; full and clear in every lineament; and catches
the real type and essence of it, amid a thousand ac-
cidents and superficial circumstances, no one of
which misleads him!    Is it of reason: some truth to
25 be discovered?    No sophistry, no vain surface-logic
detains him; quick, resolute, unerring, he pierces
through into the marrow of the question; and speaks
his verdict with an emphasis that cannot be forgotten.
Is it of description; some visual object to be repre-
30 sented?    No poet of any age or nation is more graphic
than Burns; the characteristic features disclose
themselves to him at a glance; three lines from his
hand, and we have a likeness.    And, in that rough
dialect, in that rude, often awkward, meter, so clear
35 and definite a likeness!    It seems a draughtsman

working with a burnt stick; and yet the burin of a
Retzsch* is not more expressive or exact.

Of this last excellence, the plainest and most comprehensive of all, being indeed the root and founda-
5 tion of *every* sort of talent, poetical or intellectual,
we could produce innumerable instances from the
writings of Burns. Take these glimpses of a snow-
storm from his "Winter Night"* (the italics are
ours)[1]:

10       When biting Boreas, fell and doure,
      *Sharp shivers* thro' the leafless bow'r;
      And Phœbus *gies a short-liv'd glow'r,*
          *Far south the lift,*
      *Dim-dark'ning thro' the flaky show'r,*
15           *Or whirling drift:*

      Ae night the storm the steeples rocked,
      Poor Labor sweet in sleep was locked,
      While burns, *wi' snawy wreaths up-chok'd,*
          *Wild-eddying swirl,*
20           Or, thro' the mining outlet bocked,
          Down headlong hurl:

Are there not "descriptive touches" here? The de-
scriber *saw* this thing, the essential feature and true
likeness of every circumstance in it; saw, and not
25 with the eye only. "Poor labor locked in sweet
sleep"; the dead stillness of man, unconscious, van-
quished, yet not unprotected, while such strife of the
material elements rages, and seems to reign supreme
in loneliness; this is of the heart as well as of the
30 eye!—Look also at his image of a thaw, and prophesied fall of the "Auld Brig"*:

1. For definitions of Scottish words in these stanzas, see
page 161.

When heavy, dark, continued, a'-day rains
Wi' deepening deluges o'erflow the plains;
When from the hills where springs the brawling Coil,
Or stately Lugar's *mossy* fountains *boil*,
5  Or where the Greenock winds his *moorland* course,
Or haunted Garpal draws his feeble source,
Arous'd by blust'ring winds and *spotting* thowes,[1]
*In mony a torrent down his snaw-broo rowes;*[2]
*While crushing ice, borne on the roaring speat,*[3]
10 *Sweeps dams and mills and brigs a' to the gate;*
And from Glenbuck down to the Rottonkey,[4]
Auld Ayr is just one lengthen'd *tumbling* sea;
Then down ye'll hurl, Deil nor ye never rise!
And *dash the gumlie jaups*[5] *up to the pouring skies,*

15 The last line is in itself a Poussin*-picture of that
Deluge! The welkin has, as it were, bent down
with its weight; the "gumlie jaups" and the "pouring
skies" are mingled together; it is a world of rain and
ruin.—In respect of mere clearness and minute
20 fidelity the Farmer's commendation of his "Auld
Mare,"* in plow or in cart, may vie with Homer's
Smithy of the Cyclops, or yoking of Priam's Chariot.
Nor have we forgotten stout "Burn-the-Wind"* and
his brawny customers, inspired by "Scotch Drink";
25 but it is needless to multiply examples. One other
trait of a much finer sort we select from multitudes
of such among his Songs. It gives, in a single line,
to the saddest feeling the saddest environment and
local habitation:

30    *The pale Moon is setting* *beyond the white wave,*
*And Time is setting wi' me, O;*
Farewell, false friends! false lover, farewell!
I'll nae mair trouble them nor thee, O.

This clearness of sight we have called the founda-
35 tion of all talent; for, in fact, unless we *see* our ob-

---

1. **Thowes.** Thaws.
2. **Snaw-broo rowes.** Melted snow rolls.
3. **Speat.** Flood.

4. **Glenbuck. Rottonkey.** The source of the Ayr, and a small landing place above the large quay.
5. **Gumlie jaups.** Muddy splashes.

ject, how shall we know how to place or prize it, in
our understanding, our imagination, our affections?
Yet it is not in itself, perhaps, a very high excellence;
but capable of being united indifferently with the
5 strongest, or with ordinary powers. Homer surpasses
all men in this quality; but strangely enough, at no
great distance below him are Richardson and Defoe.*
It belongs, in truth, to what is called a lively mind;
and gives no sure indication of the higher endow-
10 ments that may exist along with it. In all the three
cases we have mentioned, it is combined with great
garrulity; their descriptions are detailed, ample, and
lovingly exact; Homer's fire bursts through, from
time to time, as if by accident; but Defoe and
15 Richardson have no fire. Burns, again, is not more
distinguished by the clearness than by the impetuous
force of his conceptions. Of the strength, the piercing emphasis with which he thought, his emphasis of
expression may give a humble but the readiest proof.
20 Who ever uttered sharper sayings than his, words
more memorable, now by their burning vehemence,
now by their cool vigor and laconic pith? A single
phrase depicts a whole subject, a whole scene. We
hear of "a gentleman that derived* his patent of
25 nobility direct from Almighty God." Our Scottish
forefathers in the battlefield struggled forward, he
says, "red-wat-shod,"* giving in this one word a full
vision of horror and carnage, perhaps too frightfully
accurate for Art!

30    In fact, one of the leading features in the mind of
Burns is this vigor of his strictly intellectual percep-
tions. A resolute force is ever visible in his judgments, and in his feelings and volitions. Professor
Stewart* says of him, with some surprise: "All the
35 faculties of Burns's mind were, as far as I could

judge, equally vigorous; and his predilection for
poetry was rather the result of his own enthusiastic
and impassioned temper than of a genius exclusively
adapted to that species of composition. From his
5 conversation I should have pronounced him to be
fitted to excel in whatever walk of ambition he had
chosen to exert his abilities." But this, if we mistake not, is at all times the very essence of a truly
poetical endowment. Poetry, except in such cases as
10 that of Keats,* where the whole consists in a weak-
eyed, maudlin sensibility, and a certain vague, random
tunefulness of nature, is no separate faculty, no organ
which can be superadded to the rest, or disjoined from
them; but rather the result of their general harmony
15 and completion. The feelings, the gifts, that exist
in the Poet are those that exist, with more or less development, in every human soul; the imagination
which shudders at the Hell of Dante is the same
faculty, weaker in degree, which called that picture
20 into being. How does the Poet speak to men with
power, but by being still more a man than they?
Shakespeare, it has been well observed, in the planning
and completing of his tragedies, has shown an Understanding, were it nothing more, which might have
25 governed states, or indited a *Novum Organum.** What
Burns's force of understanding may have been we
have less means of judging; it had to dwell among
the humblest objects; never saw Philosophy; never
rose, except by natural effort and for short intervals,
30 into the region of great ideas. Nevertheless, sufficient indication, if no proof sufficient, remains for
us in his works; we discern the brawny movements
of a gigantic though untutored strength; and can
understand how, in conversation, his quick, sure
35 insight into men and things may, as much as aught

else about him, have amazed the best thinkers of his time and country.

But, unless we mistake, the intellectual gift of Burns is fine as well as strong. The more delicate 5 relations of things could not well have escaped his eye, for they were intimately present to his heart. The logic of the senate and the forum is indispensable, but not all-sufficient; nay, perhaps the highest Truth is that which will the most certainly elude it. For 10 this logic works by words, and "the highest,"* it has been said, "cannot be expressed in words." We are not without tokens of an openness for this higher truth also, of a keen though uncultivated sense for it, having existed in Burns. Mr. Stewart, it will be re- 15 membered, "wonders," in the passage above quoted, that Burns had formed some distinct conception of the "doctrine of association." We rather think that far subtler things than the doctrine of association had from of old been familiar to him. Here, for instance:

20     We know nothing* [thus writes he], or next to nothing, of the structure of our souls; so we cannot account for those seeming caprices in them, that one should be par- ticularly pleased with this thing, or struck with that, which, on minds of a different cast, makes no extraordi- 25 nary impression. I have some favorite flowers in spring— among which are the mountain-daisy, the harebell, the fox- glove, the wild-brier rose, the budding birch, and the hoary hawthorn—that I view and hang over with particular de- light. I never hear the loud, solitary whistle of the curlew 30 in a summer noon, or the wild, mixing cadence of a troop of gray plover in an autumnal morning, without feeling an elevation of soul like the enthusiasm of devotion or poetry. Tell me, my dear friend, to what can this be owing? Are we a piece of machinery, which, like the Æolian harp, 35 passive, takes the impression of the passing accident; or do these workings argue something within us above the trodden clod? I own myself partial to such proofs of those awful and important realities: a God that made all things, man's immaterial and immortal nature, and a world 40 of weal or woe beyond death and the grave.

Force and fineness of understanding are often
spoken of as something different from general force
and fineness of nature, as something partly independent of them. The necessities of language so re-
5 quire it; but in truth these qualities are not distinct
and independent; except in special cases, and from
special causes, they ever go together. A man of
strong understanding is generally a man of strong
character; neither is delicacy in the one kind often
10 divided from delicacy in the other. No one, at all
events, is ignorant that in the Poetry of Burns keenness of insight keeps pace with keenness of feeling;
that his *light* is not more pervading than his *warmth*.
He is a man of the most impassioned temper; with
15 passions not strong only, but noble, and of the sort
in which great virtues and great poems take their
rise. It is reverence, it is love toward all Nature that
inspires him, that opens his eyes to its beauty, and
makes heart and voice eloquent in its praise. There
20 is a true, old saying, that "Love furthers knowledge"*;
but above all, it is the living essence of that knowledge which makes poets; the first principle of its
existence, increase, activity. Of Burns's fervid affection, his generous all-embracing Love, we have
25 spoken already, as of the grand distinction of his
nature, seen equally in word and deed, in his Life and
in his Writings. It were easy to multiply examples.
Not man only, but all that environs man in the material and moral universe, is lovely in his sight;
30 "the hoary hawthorn,"* the "troop of gray plover,"
the "solitary curlew," all are dear to him; all live
in this Earth along with him, and to all he is knit as
in mysterious brotherhood. How touching is it, for
instance, that, amidst the gloom of personal misery,
35 brooding over the wintry desolation without him and

within him, he thinks of the "ourie cattle" and "silly sheep" and their sufferings in the pitiless storm!

> I thought me* on the ourie cattle,
> Or silly sheep, wha bide this brattle
> 5              O' wintry war,
> Or thro' the drift, deep-lairing, sprattle
>        Beneath a scar.
>
> Ilk happing bird, wee, helpless thing!
> That, in the merry months o' spring,
> 10 Delighted me to hear thee sing,
>           What comes o' thee?
> Where wilt thou cow'r thy chittering wing,
>        An' close thy e'e?[1]

The tenant of the mean hut, with its "ragged roof 15 and chinky wall," has a heart to pity even these! This is worth several homilies on Mercy; for it is the voice of Mercy herself. Burns, indeed, lives in sympathy; his soul rushes forth into all realms of being; nothing that has existence can be indifferent to him. 20 The very Devil* he cannot hate with right orthodoxy:

> But fare you weel, auld Nickie-ben!
> O wad ye tak a thought and men'!
> Ye aiblins might—I dinna ken—
>           Still hae a stake—
> 25 I'm wae to think upo' yon den,
>           Ev'n for your sake![2]

" 'He is the father of curses and lies,'* said Dr. Slop; 'and is cursed and damned already.'—'I am sorry for it,' quoth my uncle Toby!"—A Poet without Love 30 were a physical and metaphysical impossibility.

But has it not been said, in contradiction to this principle, that "Indignation makes verses"*? It has been so said, and is true enough; but the contradiction is apparent, not real. The Indignation which makes 35 verses is, properly speaking, an inverted Love; the love of some right, some worth, some goodness, belong-

1. See page 162.
2. See page 135.

ing to ourselves or others, which has been injured, and
which this tempestuous feeling issues forth to defend
and avenge. No selfish fury of heart, existing there
as a primary feeling, and without its opposite, ever
5 produced much Poetry; otherwise, we suppose, the
Tiger were the most musical of all our choristers.
Johnson said he loved a good hater*; by which he
must have meant, not so much one that hated vio-
lently, as one that hated wisely; hated baseness from
10 love and nobleness. However, in spite of Johnson's
paradox, tolerable enough for once in speech, but
which need not have been so often adopted in print
since then, we rather believe that good men deal
sparingly in hatred, either wise or unwise; nay, that
15 a "good" hater is still a desideratum in this world.
The Devil, at least, who passes for the chief and best
of that class, is said to be nowise an amiable character.

Of the verses which Indignation makes, Burns has
also given us specimens; and among the best that
20 were ever given. Who will forget his "Dweller in
yon dungeon dark"*; a piece that might have been
chanted by the Furies of Æschylus?* The secrets of
the infernal Pit are laid bare; a boundless, baleful
"darkness visible"*; and streaks of hell-fire quivering
25 madly in its black, haggard bosom!

> Dweller in yon dungeon dark,
> Hangman of creation, mark!
> Who in widow-weeds appears,
> Laden with unhonored years,
> 30 Noosing with care a bursting purse,
> Baited with many a deadly curse?

Why should we speak of "Scots wha hae wi' Wallace
bled"*; since all know of it, from the king to the
meanest of his subjects? This dithyrambic was com-
35 posed on horseback; in riding in the middle of

tempests, over the wildest Galloway moor, in company with a Mr. Syme, who, observing the poet's looks, forbore to speak—judiciously enough, for a man composing "Bruce's Address" might be unsafe to trifle with. Doubtless this stern hymn was singing itself, as he formed it, through the soul of Burns; but to the external ear it should be sung with the throat of the whirlwind. So long as there is warm blood in the heart of Scotchman or man, it will move in fierce thrills under this war ode; the best, we believe, that was ever written by any pen.

Another wild, stormful Song, that dwells in our ear and mind with a strange tenacity, is "McPherson's Farewell."* Perhaps there is something in the tradition itself that coöperates. For was not this grim Celt, this shaggy Northland Cacus,* that "lived a life of sturt and strife, and died by treacherie"—was not he too one of the Nimrods and Napoleons of the earth, in the arena of his own remote, misty glens, for want of a clearer and wider one? Nay, was there not a touch of grace given him? A fiber of love and softness, of poetry itself, must have lived in his savage heart; for he composed that air the night before his execution; on the wings of that poor melody his better soul would soar away above oblivion, pain, and all the ignominy and despair, which, like an avalanche, was hurling him to the abyss! Here, also, as at Thebes,* and in Pelops' line, was material Fate matched against man's Free-will; matched in bitterest though obscure duel; and the ethereal soul sank not, even in its blindness, without a cry which has survived it. But who, except Burns, could have given words to such a soul; words that we never listen to without a strange, half-barbarous, half-poetic, fellow-feeling?

> Sae rantingly, sae wantonly,
>  Sae dauntingly gaed he;
> He play'd a spring, and danced it round,
>  Below the gallows-tree.[1]

5 Under a lighter disguise the same principle of
Love, which we have recognized as the great characteristic of Burns, and of all true poets, occasionally manifests itself in the shape of Humor. Everywhere, indeed, in his sunny moods, a full, buoyant
10 flood of mirth rolls through the mind of Burns;
he rises to the high, and stoops to the low, and is
brother and playmate to all Nature. We speak not
of his bold and often irresistible faculty of cari-
cature; for this is Drollery rather than Humor; but
15 a much tenderer sportfulness dwells in him; and
comes forth here and there, in evanescent and beautiful touches; as in his "Address to the Mouse,"* or
the "Farmer's Mare," or in his "Elegy on Poor
Mailie," which last may be reckoned his happiest
20 effort of this kind. In these pieces there are traits
of a Humor as fine as that of Sterne; yet altogether
different, original, peculiar—the Humor of Burns.

Of the tenderness, the playful pathos, and many
other kindred qualities of Burns's Poetry, much more
25 might be said; but now, with these poor outlines of
a sketch, we must prepare to quit this part of our
subject. To speak of his individual Writings, ade-
quately and with any detail, would lead us far beyond
our limits. As already hinted, we can look on but
30 few of these pieces as, in strict critical language, de-
serving the name of Poems; they are rimed eloquence, rimed pathos, rimed sense; yet seldom essentially melodious, aerial, poetical. "Tam o' Shanter"*
itself, which enjoys so high a favor, does not appear

1. See page 194.

to us at all decisively to come under this last
category. It is not so much a poem as a piece of
sparkling rhetoric; the heart and body of the story
still lies hard and dead. He has not gone back,
5 much less carried us back, into that dark, earnest,
wondering age when the tradition was believed and
when it took its rise; he does not attempt, by any
new-modeling of his supernatural ware, to strike
anew that deep, mysterious chord of human nature
10 which once responded to such things; and which
lives in us too, and will forever live, though silent
now, or vibrating with far other notes, and to far
different issues. Our German readers will understand us, when we say that he is not the Tieck but
15 the Musäus* of this tale. Externally it is all green and
living; yet look closer, it is no firm growth, but only
ivy on a rock. The piece does not properly cohere;
the strange chasm which yawns in our incredulous
imaginations between the Ayr public-house and the
20 gate of Tophet, is nowhere bridged over, nay, the
idea of such a bridge is laughed at; and thus the
Tragedy of the adventure becomes a mere drunken
phantasmagoria, or many-colored spectrum painted
on ale-vapors, and the Farce alone has any reality.
25 We do not say that Burns should have made much
more of this tradition; we rather think that, for
strictly poetical purposes, not much *was* to be made
of it. Neither are we blind to the deep, varied,
genial power displayed in what he has actually ac-
30 complished; but we find far more "Shakespearean"
qualities,* as these of "Tam o' Shanter" have been
fondly named, in many of his other pieces; nay, we
incline to believe that this latter might have been
written, all but quite as well, by a man who, in place
35 of genius, had only possessed talent.

Perhaps we may venture to say that the most
strictly poetical of all his "poems"* is one which does
not appear in Currie's Edition; but has been often
printed before and since, under the humble title of
5 "The Jolly Beggars."* The subject truly is among
the lowest in Nature; but it only the more shows our
Poet's gift in raising it into the domain of Art. To
our minds, this piece seems thoroughly compacted,
melted together, refined; and poured forth in one
10 flood of true *liquid* harmony. It is light, airy, soft
of movement; yet sharp and precise in its details;
every face is a portrait; that "raucle carlin," that
"wee Apollo," that "son of Mars," are Scottish, yet
ideal; the scene is at once a dream, and the very
15 Ragcastle of "Poosie Nansie." Further, it seems in
a considerable degree complete, a real self-support-
ing Whole, which is the highest merit in a poem. The
blanket of the Night is drawn asunder for a moment; in full, ruddy, flaming light, these rough tat-
20 terdemalions are seen in their boisterous revel; for
the strong pulse of Life vindicates its right to gladness even here; and when the curtain closes, we pro-
long the action without effort; the next day as the
last, our "Caird" and our "Balladmonger" are singing
25 and soldiering; their "brats and callets" are hawking,
begging, cheating; and some other night, in new combinations, they will wring from Fate another hour
of wassail and good cheer. Apart from the universal
sympathy with man which this again bespeaks in
30 Burns, a genuine inspiration and no inconsiderable
technical talent are manifested here. There is the
fidelity, humor, warm life, and accurate painting and
grouping of some Teniers,* for whom hostlers and
carousing peasants are not without significance. It
35 would be strange, doubtless, to call this the best of

Burns's writings; we mean to say only that it seems to us the most perfect of its kind, as a piece of poetical composition, strictly so called. In the "Beggar's Opera,"* in the "Beggar's Bush," as other critics have already remarked, there is nothing which, in real poetic vigor, equals this Cantata; nothing, as we think, which comes within many degrees of it.

But by far the most finished, complete, and truly inspired pieces of Burns are, without dispute, to be found among his Songs. It is here that, although through a small aperture, his light shines with least obstruction in its highest beauty, and pure, sunny clearness. The reason may be that Song is a brief, simple species of composition; and requires nothing so much for its perfection as genuine poetic feeling, genuine music of heart. Yet the Song has its rules equally with the Tragedy—rules which in most cases are poorly fulfilled, in many cases are not so much as felt. We might write a long essay on the Songs of Burns; which we reckon by far the best that Britain has yet produced; for, indeed, since the era of Queen Elizabeth, we know not that, by any other hand, aught truly worth attention has been accomplished in this department. True, we have songs enough "by persons of quality"*; we have tawdry, hollow, wine-bred madrigals; many a rimed speech "in the flowing and watery vein of Ossorius,* the Portugal Bishop," rich in sonorous words, and, for moral, dashed perhaps with some tint of a sentimental sensuality; all which many persons cease not from endeavoring to sing; though for most part, we fear, the music is but from the throat outward, or at best from some region far enough short of the *Soul;* not in which, but in a certain inane Limbo of the Fancy, or even in some vaporous debatable-land on the outskirts of the Nervous System, most of such madrigals and rimed speeches seem to have originated.

With the songs of Burns we must not name these things. Independently of the clear, manly, heart-felt sentiment that ever pervades *his* poetry, his Songs are honest in another point of view—in form, as well as in spirit. They do not *affect* to be set to music, but they actually and in themselves are music; they have received their life, and fashioned themselves together, in the medium of Harmony, as Venus rose from the bosom of the sea. The story, the feeling is not detailed, but suggested; not *said,* or spouted, in rhetorical completeness and coherence; but *sung,* in fitful gushes, in glowing hints, in fantastic breaks, in *warblings* not of the voice only, but of the whole mind. We consider this to be the essence of a song; and that no songs since the little careless catches, and, as it were, drops of song, which Shakespeare has here and there sprinkled over his plays, fulfill this condition in nearly the same degree as most of Burns's do. Such grace and truth of external movement, too, presupposes in general a corresponding force and truth of sentiment and inward meaning. The songs of Burns are not more perfect in the former quality than in the latter. With what tenderness he sings, yet with what vehemence and entireness! There is a piercing wail in his sorrow, the purest rapture in his joy; he burns with the sternest ire, or laughs with the loudest or slyest mirth; and yet he is sweet and soft, "sweet as the smile when fond lovers meet, and soft as their parting tear." If we further take into account the immense variety of his subjects; how, from the loud, flowing revel in "Willie Brew'd a Peck o' Maut,"* to the still, rapt enthusiasm of sadness for "Mary in

Heaven"*; from the glad, kind greeting of "Auld Lang Syne," or the comic archness of "Duncan Gray," to the fire-eyed fury of "Scots Wha Hae wi' Wallace Bled,"* he has found a tone and words for every mood 5 of man's heart—it will seem small praise if we rank him as the first of all our Song-writers; for we know not where to find one worthy of being second to him.

It is on his Songs, as we believe, that Burns's chief influence as an author will ultimately be found 10 to depend; nor, if our Fletcher's aphorism* is true, shall we account this a small influence. "Let me make the songs of a people," said he, "and you shall make its laws." Surely, if ever any Poet might have equaled himself with Legislators on this ground, it 15 was Burns. His Songs are already part of the mother tongue, not of Scotland only, but of Britain, and of the millions that in all ends of the earth speak a British language. In hut and hall, as the heart unfolds itself in many-colored joy and woe of ex- 20 istence, the *name,* the *voice* of that joy and that woe, is the name and voice which Burns has given them. Strictly speaking, perhaps no British man has so deeply affected the thoughts and feelings of so many men as this solitary and altogether private individual, 25 with means apparently the humblest.

In another point of view, moreover, we incline to think that Burns's influence may have been considerable; we mean, as exerted specially on the Literature of his country, at least on the Literature of 30 Scotland. Among the great changes which British, particularly Scottish, literature has undergone since that period, one of the greatest will be found to consist in its remarkable increase of nationality. Even the English writers, most popular in Burns's time, 35 were little distinguished for their literary patriotism, in this, its best sense. A certain attenuated cosmopolitanism had, in good measure, taken place of the old insular home-feeling; literature was, as it were, without any local environment; was not nourished 5 by the affections which spring from a native soil. Our Grays and Glovers* seemed to write almost as if *in vacuo;* the thing written bears no mark of place; it is not written so much for Englishmen, as for men; or rather, which is the inevitable result of this, 10 for certain Generalizations which philosophy termed men. Goldsmith is an exception; not so Johnson; the scene of his *Rambler** is little more English than that of his *Rasselas.*

But if such was in some degree the case with Eng-15 land, it was, in the highest degree, the case with Scotland. In fact, our Scottish literature had, at that period, a very singular aspect; unexampled, so far as we know, except perhaps at Geneva,* where the same state of matters appears still to continue. For a 20 long period after Scotland became British we had no literature; at the date when Addison and Steele were writing their *Spectators,* our good John Boston* was writing, with the noblest intent, but alike in defiance of grammar and philosophy, his *Fourfold State of* 25 *Man.* Then came the schisms in our National Church, and the fiercer schisms in our Body Politic: Theologic ink, and Jacobite blood, with gall enough in both cases, seemed to have blotted out the intellect of the country; however, it was only ob-30 scured, not obliterated. Lord Kames* made nearly the first attempt, and a tolerably clumsy one, at writing English; and ere long, Hume, Robertson, Smith,* and a whole host of followers, attracted hither the eyes of all Europe. And yet in this brilliant 35 resuscitation of our "fervid genius,"* there was nothing truly Scottish, nothing indigenous, except, perhaps, the natural impetuosity of intellect, which we sometimes claim, and are sometimes upbraided with, as a characteristic of our nation. It is curious to remark that Scotland, so full of writers, had no Scottish culture, nor indeed any English; our culture was almost exclusively French. It was by studying Racine and Voltaire, Batteux and Boileau, that Kames had trained himself to be a critic and philosopher; it was the light of Montesquieu and Mably that guided Robertson in his political speculations; Quesnay's lamp that kindled the lamp of Adam Smith. Hume was too rich a man to borrow; and perhaps he reacted on the French more than he was acted on by them; but neither had he aught to do with Scotland; Edinburgh, equally with La Flèche,* was but the lodging and laboratory in which he not so much morally *lived* as metaphysically *investigated*. Never, perhaps, was there a class of writers, so clear and well-ordered, yet so totally destitute, to all appearance, of any patriotic affection, nay, of any human affection whatever. The French wits of the period were as unpatriotic; but their general deficiency in moral principle, not to say their avowed sensuality and unbelief in all virtue, strictly so called, render this accountable enough. We hope there is a patriotism founded on something better than prejudice; that our country may be dear to us without injury to our philosophy; that in loving and justly prizing all other lands we may prize justly, and yet love before all others, our own stern Motherland, and the venerable Structure of social and moral Life, which Mind has through long ages been building up for us there. Surely there is nourishment for the better part of man's heart in all this; surely the roots

that have fixed themselves in the very core of man's
being may be so cultivated as to grow up not into
briers, but into roses, in the field of his life! Our
Scottish sages have no such propensities; the field
5 of their life shows neither briers nor roses; but only
a flat, continuous threshing-floor for Logic, whereon
all questions, from the "Doctrine of Rent"* to the
"Natural History of Religion," are threshed and
sifted with the same mechanical impartiality!

10     With Sir Walter Scott at the head of our literature
it cannot be denied that much of this evil is past,
or rapidly passing away; our chief literary men,
whatever other faults they may have, no longer live
among us like a French Colony, or some knot of
15 Propaganda Missionaries; but like natural-born subjects of the soil, partaking and sympathizing in all
our attachments, humors, and habits. Our literature
no longer grows in water but in mold, and with the
true, racy virtues of the soil and climate. How much
20 of this change may be due to Burns, or to any other
individual, it might be difficult to estimate. Direct
literary imitation of Burns was not to be looked for.
But his example, in the fearless adoption of domestic
subjects, could not but operate from afar; and cer-
25 tainly in no heart did the love of country ever burn
with a warmer glow than in that of Burns; " a tide of
Scottish prejudice,"* as he modestly calls this deep
and generous feeling, "had been poured along his
veins; and he felt that it would boil there till the
30 flood-gates shut in eternal rest." It seemed to him
as if *he* could do so little for his country and yet
would so gladly have done all. One small province
stood open for him—that of Scottish Song; and how
eagerly he entered on it; how devotedly he labored
35 there! In his toilsome journeyings this object never

quits him; it is the little happy-valley of his care-worn heart. In the gloom of his own affliction he eagerly searches after some lonely brother of the muse, and rejoices to snatch one other name from 5 the oblivion that was covering it! These were early feelings, and they abode with him to the end:

> . . . a wish* (I mind its pow'r),
>     A wish that to my latest hour
>         Shall strongly heave my breast,
> 10  That I for poor auld Scotland's sake,
>     Some usefu' plan or book could make,
>         Or sing a sang at least.
>     The rough burr-thistle, spreading wide
>         Amang the bearded bear,
> 15      I turn'd the weeder-clips aside,
>         An' spar'd the symbol dear.[1]

But to leave the mere literary character of Burns, which has already detained us too long. Far more interesting than any of his written works, as it ap-20 pears to us, are his acted ones—the Life he willed and was fated to lead among his fellow-men. These Poems are but like little rimed fragments scattered here and there in the grand, unrimed Romance of his earthly existence; and it is only when intercalated in 25 this at their proper places that they attain their full measure of significance. And this too, alas, was but a fragment! The plan of a mighty edifice had been sketched; some columns, porticos, firm masses of building stand completed; the rest more or less 30 clearly indicated; with many a far-stretching tend-ency, which only studious and friendly eyes can now trace toward the purposed termination. For the work is broken off in the middle—almost in the be-ginning—and rises among us, beautiful and sad, at 35 once unfinished and a ruin! If charitable judgment

1. See page 165.

was necessary in estimating his Poems, and justice required that the aim and the manifest power to fulfill it must often be accepted for the fulfillment; much more is this the case in regard to his Life, the sum 5 and result of all his endeavors, where his difficulties came upon him not in detail only, but in mass; and so much has been left unaccomplished, nay, was mistaken, and altogether marred.

Properly speaking, there is but one era in the life 10 of Burns, and that the earliest. We have not youth and manhood, but only youth; for to the end we discern no decisive change in the complexion of his character; in his thirty-seventh year he is still, as it were, in youth. With all that resoluteness of judg- 15 ment, that penetrating insight, and singular maturity of intellectual power exhibited in his writings, he never attains to any clearness regarding himself; to the last, he never ascertains his peculiar aim, even with such distinctness as is common among ordinary 20 men; and therefore never can pursue it with that singleness of will which insures success and some contentment to such men. To the last he wavers between two purposes: glorying in his talent, like a true poet, he yet cannot consent to make this his 25 chief and sole glory, and to follow it as the one thing needful, through poverty or riches, through good or evil report. Another far meaner ambition still cleaves to him; he must dream and struggle about a certain "Rock of Independence"*; which, natural and 20 even admirable as it might be, was still but a warring with the world, on the comparatively insignificant ground of his being more completely or less completely supplied with money than others; of his standing at a higher or at a lower altitude in gen- 35 eral estimation than others. For the world still

appears to him, as to the young, in borrowed colors;
he expects from it what it cannot give to any man;
seeks for contentment, not within himself, in action
and wise effort, but from without, in the kindness
5 of circumstances, in love, friendship, honor, pecuniary
ease. He would be happy, not actively and in himself,
but passively and from some ideal cornucopia of En-
joyments, not earned by his own labor but show-
ered on him by the beneficence of Destiny. Thus, like
10 a young man, he cannot gird himself up for any
worthy, well-calculated goal, but swerves to and fro,
between passionate hope and remorseful disappoint-
ment; rushing onward with a deep, tempestuous force,
he surmounts or breaks asunder many a barrier; trav-
15 els, nay, advances far, but advancing only under
uncertain guidance, is ever and anon turned from his
path; and to the last cannot reach the only true
happiness of a man, that of clear, decided Activity
in the sphere for which, by nature and circumstances,
20 he has been fitted and appointed.

We do not say these things in dispraise of Burns;
nay, perhaps, they but interest us the more in his
favor. This blessing is not given soonest to the
best; but rather, it is often the greatest minds that
25 are latest in obtaining it; for where most is to be
developed, most time may be required to develop it.
A complex condition had been assigned him from
without; as complex a condition from within; no
"preëstablished harmony" existed between the clay
30 soil of Mossgiel and the empyrean soul of Robert
Burns; it was not wonderful that the adjustment between them should have been long postponed, and his
arm long cumbered, and his sight confused, in so
vast and discordant an economy as he had been ap-
35 pointed steward over. Byron was, at his death, but

a year younger than Burns; and through life, as it
might have appeared, far more simply situated; yet
in him, too, we can trace no such adjustment, no such
moral manhood; but, at best, and only a little before
5 his end, the beginning of what seemed such.

By much the most striking incident in Burns's
Life is his journey to Edinburgh; but perhaps a still
more important one is his residence at Irvine, so
early as in his twenty-third year. Hitherto his life
10 had been poor and toilworn; but otherwise not un-
genial, and, with all its distresses, by no means unhappy. In his parentage, deducting outward circumstances, he had every reason to reckon himself
fortunate. His father was a man of thoughtful,
15 intense, earnest character, as the best of our peasants
are; valuing knowledge, possessing some, and, what
is far better and rarer, open-minded for more; a man
with a keen insight and devout heart; reverent
toward God, friendly therefore, at once, and fearless
20 toward all that God has made—in one word, though
but a hard-handed peasant, a complete and fully un-
folded *Man*. Such a father is seldom found in any
rank in society; and was worth descending far in
society to seek. Unfortunately, he was very poor;
25 had he been even a little richer, almost never so
little, the whole might have issued far otherwise.
Mighty events turn on a straw; the crossing of a
brook* decides the conquest of the world. Had this
William Burns's small seven acres of nursery-ground
30 anywise prospered, the boy Robert had been sent to
school, had struggled forward, as so many weaker
men do, to some university; come forth not as a
rustic wonder, but as a regular, well-trained intellectual workman, and changed the whole course of
35 British Literature—for it lay in him to have done

this! But the nursery did not prosper; poverty sank
his whole family below the help even of our cheap
school-system; Burns remained a hard-worked plowboy, and British literature took its own course.
5 Nevertheless, even in this rugged scene there is
much to nourish him. If he drudges, it is with his
brother, and for his father and mother, whom he
loves, and would fain shield from want. Wisdom
is not vanished from their poor hearth, nor the balm
10 of natural feeling; the solemn words, "Let us worship God,"* are heard there from a priest-like father;
if threatenings of unjust men throw mother and children into tears, these are tears not of grief only, but
of holiest affection; every heart in that humble group
15 feels itself the closer knit to every other; in their
hard warfare they are there together, a "little band
of brethren."* Neither are such tears, and the deep
beauty that dwells in them, their only portion. Light
visits the hearts as it does the eyes of all living;
20 there is a force, too, in this youth, that enables him
to trample on misfortune; nay, to bind it under his
feet to make him sport. For a bold, warm, buoyant
humor of character has been given him; and so the
thick-coming shapes of evil are welcomed with a gay,
25 friendly irony, and in their closest pressure he bates
no joy of heart or hope. Vague yearnings of ambition fail not, as he grows up; dreamy fancies hang
like cloud-cities around him; the curtain of Existence
is slowly rising, in many-colored splendor and gloom;
30 and the auroral light of first love is gilding his
horizon, and the music of song is on his path; and
so he walks

. . . . . in glory and in joy,*
Behind his plow, upon the mountain side.

We ourselves know from the best evidence, that up
to this date Burns was happy; nay, that he was the
gayest, brightest, most fantastic, fascinating being to
be found in the world; more so even than he ever after-
5 wards appeared. But now, at this early age, he quits
the paternal roof; goes forth into looser, louder, more
exciting society; and becomes initiated in those dis-
sipations, those vices, which a certain class of philosophers have asserted to be a natural preparative
10 for entering on active life; a kind of mud-bath, in
which the youth is, as it were, necessitated to steep
and, we suppose, cleanse himself, before the real toga
of Manhood can be laid on him. We shall not dispute
much with this class of philosophers; we hope they
15 are mistaken; for Sin and Remorse so easily beset
us at all stages of life, and are always such indifferent
company, that it seems hard we should, at any stage,
be forced and fated not only to meet but to yield
to them, and even serve for a term in their leprous
20 armada. We hope it is not so. Clear we are, at all
events, it cannot be the training one receives in this
Devil's service, but only our determining to desert
from it, that fits us for true manly Action. We become men, not after we have been dissipated, and
25 disappointed in the chase of false pleasure; but after
we have ascertained, in any way, what impassable bar-
riers hem us in through this life; how mad it is to
hope for contentment to our infinite soul from the
*gifts* of this extremely finite world; that a man must
30 be sufficient for himself; and that for suffering and
enduring there is no remedy but striving and doing.
Manhood begins when we have in any way made
truce with Necessity; begins even when we have surrendered to Necessity, as the most part only do; but
35 begins joyfully and hopefully only when we have

reconciled ourselves to Necessity; and thus, in reality, triumphed over it, and felt that in Necessity we are free. Surely, such lessons as this last, which, in one shape or other, is the grand lesson for every 5 mortal man, are better learned from the lips of a devout mother, in the looks and actions of a devout father, while the heart is yet soft and pliant, than in collision with the sharp adamant of Fate, attracting us to shipwreck us, when the heart is grown hard, 10 and may be broken before it will become contrite. Had Burns continued to learn this, as he was already learning it, in his father's cottage, he would have learned it fully, which he never did, and been saved many a lasting aberration, many a bitter hour and 15 year of remorseful sorrow.

It seems to us another circumstance of fatal import in Burns's history that at this time, too, he became involved in the religious quarrels of his district; that he was enlisted and feasted, as the fighting 20 man of the New-Light Priesthood, in their highly unprofitable warfare. At the tables of these free-minded clergy he learned much more than was needful for him. Such liberal ridicule of fanaticism awakened in his mind scruples about Religion itself, 25 and a whole world of Doubts, which it required quite another set of conjurors than these men to exorcise. We do not say that such an intellect as his could have escaped similar doubts at some period of his history; or even that he could, at a later period, 30 have come through them altogether victorious and unharmed; but it seems peculiarly unfortunate that this time, above all others, should have been fixed for the encounter. For now, with principles assailed by evil example from without, by "passions raging 35 like demons"* from within, he had little need of

skeptical misgivings to whisper treason in the heat of
the battle, or to cut off his retreat if he were already
defeated. He loses his feeling of innocence; his
mind is at variance with itself; the old divinity no
5 longer presides there; but wild Desires and wild Repentance alternately oppress him. Ere long, too, he
has committed himself before the world; his character
for sobriety, dear to a Scottish peasant as few cor-
rupted worldlings can even conceive, is destroyed in
10 the eyes of men; and his only refuge consists in
trying to disbelieve his guiltiness, and is but a refuge
of lies. The blackest desperation now gathers over
him, broken only by red lightnings of remorse. The
whole fabric of his life is blasted asunder; for now
15 not only his character, but his personal liberty, is
to be lost; men and Fortune are leagued for his hurt;
"hungry Ruin* has him in the wind." He sees no escape but the saddest of all—exile from his loved
country to a country in every sense inhospitable and
20 abhorrent to him. While the "gloomy night is
gathering fast,"* in mental storm and solitude, as well
as in physical, he sings his wild farewell to Scotland:

> Farewell, my friends; farewell, my foes!
> My peace with these, my love with those;
> 25 The bursting tears my heart declare;
> Adieu, my native banks of Ayr!

Light breaks suddenly in on him in floods; but still
a false, transitory light, and no real sunshine. He is
invited to Edinburgh; hastens thither with anticipat-
30 ing heart; is welcomed as in a triumph, and with
universal blandishment and acclamation; whatever is
wisest, whatever is greatest or loveliest there gathers
round him, to gaze on his face, to show him honor,
sympathy, affection. Burns's appearance among the
35 sages and nobles of Edinburgh must be regarded as

*which appears on all*

one of the most singular phenomena in modern
Literature; almost like the appearance of some Napoleon among the crowned sovereigns of modern
Politics. For it is nowise as a "mockery king,"* set
5 there by favor, transiently and for a purpose, that
he will let himself be treated; still less is he a mad
Rienzi,* whose sudden elevation turns his too weak
head; but he stands there on his own basis—cool,
unastonished, holding his equal rank from Nature
10 herself; putting forth no claim which there is not
strength *in* him, as well as about him, to vindicate.
Mr. Lockhart has some forcible observations on this
point:

It needs no effort of imagination [says he] to conceive
15 what the sensations of an isolated set of scholars (almost
all either clergymen or professors) must have been in the
presence of this big-boned, black-browed, brawny stranger,
with his great, flashing eyes, who, having forced his way
among them from the plow-tail at a single stride, mani-
20 fested in the whole strain of his bearing and conversation
a most thorough conviction that in the society of the most
eminent men of his nation he was exactly where he was
entitled to be; hardly deigned to flatter them by exhibiting
even an occasional symptom of being flattered by their
25 notice; by turns calmly measured himself against the most
cultivated understandings of his time in discussion; over-
powered the *bons mots* of the most celebrated convivialists
by broad floods of merriment, impregnated with all the
burning life of genius; astounded bosoms habitually en-
30 veloped in the thrice-piled folds of social reserve, by com-
pelling them to tremble—nay, to tremble visibly—beneath
the fearless touch of natural pathos; and all this without
indicating the smallest willingness to be ranked among
those professional ministers of excitement who are content
35 to be paid in money and smiles for doing what the spectators and auditors would be ashamed of doing in their
own persons, even if they had the power of doing it; and
last, and probably worst of all, who was known to be in the
habit of enlivening societies which they would have scorned
40 to approach, still more frequently than their own, with
eloquence no less magnificent; with wit, in all likelihood
still more daring; often enough, as the superiors whom he

fronted without alarm might have guessed from the beginning, and had ere long no occasion to guess, with wit pointed
at themselves.

The further we remove from this scene, the more
5 singular will it seem to us; details of the exterior
aspect of it are already full of interest. Most
readers recollect Mr. Walker's personal interviews
with Burns as among the best passages of his Narrative; a time will come when this reminiscence of
10 Sir Walter Scott's,* slight though it is, will also be
precious:

As for Burns [writes Sir Walter], I may truly say,
*Virgilium vidi tantum.** I was a lad of fifteen in 1786-7,
when he came first to Edinburgh, but had sense and feeling
15 enough to be much interested in his poetry, and would have
given the world to know him; but I had very little acquaintance with any literary people, and still less with the
gentry of the west country, the two sets that he most frequented. Mr. Thomas Grierson was at that time a clerk
20 of my father's. He knew Burns, and promised to ask him
to his lodgings to dinner, but had no opportunity to keep
his word; otherwise I might have seen more of this distinguished man. As it was, I saw him one day at the late
venerable Professor Ferguson's, where there were several
25 gentlemen of literary reputation, among whom I remember
the celebrated Mr. Dugald Stewart. Of course, we youngsters sat silent, looked, and listened. The only thing I
remember which was remarkable in Burns's manner was the
effect produced upon him by a print of Bunbury's, repre-
30 senting a soldier lying dead on the snow, his dog sitting
in misery on one side—on the other, his widow, with a
child in her arms. These lines were written beneath:

"Cold on Canadian hills, or Minden's plain,
    Perhaps that mother wept her soldier slain;
35    Bent o'er her babe, her eye dissolved in dew—
    The big drops, mingling with the milk he drew,
    Gave the sad presage of his future years,
    The child of misery, baptized in tears."

Burns seemed much affected by the print, or rather by
40 the ideas which it suggested to his mind. He actually shed
tears. He asked whose the lines were; and it chanced that

nobody but myself remembered that they occur in a half-
forgotten poem of Langborne's called by the unpromising
title of "The Justice of Peace." I whispered my information to a friend present; he mentioned it to Burns, who
5 rewarded me with a look and a word, which, though of mere
civility, I then received and still recollect with very great
pleasure.

His person was strong and robust; his manners rustic,
not clownish; a sort of dignified plainness and simplicity,
10 which received part of its effect perhaps from one's knowledge of his extraordinary talents. His features are represented in Mr. Nasmyth's picture; but to me it conveys the
idea that they are diminished, as if seen in perspective. I
think his countenance was more massive than it looks in
15 any of the portraits. I should have taken the poet, had I
not known what he was, for a very sagacious country farmer
of the old Scotch school, i. e., none of your modern agri-
culturists who keep laborers for their drudgery, but the
*douce gudeman* who held his own plow. There was a strong
20 expression of sense and shrewdness in all his lineaments;
the eye alone, I think, indicated the poetical character and
temperament. It was large, and of a dark cast, which
glowed (I say literally *glowed*) when he spoke with feeling
or interest. I never saw such another eye in a human head,
25 though I have seen the most distinguished men of my time.
His conversation expressed perfect self-confidence, without
the slightest presumption. Among the men who were the
most learned of their time and country, he expressed himself with perfect firmness, but without the least intrusive
30 forwardness; and when he differed in opinion, he did not
hesitate to express it firmly, yet at the same time with
modesty. I do not remember any part of his conversation distinctly enough to be quoted; nor did I ever see
him again, except in the street, where he did not recognize
35 me, as I could not expect he should. He was much caressed
in Edinburgh; but (considering what literary emoluments
have been since his day) the efforts made for his relief were
extremely trifling.

I remember, on this occasion I mention, I thought
40 Burns's acquaintance with English poetry was rather
limited; and also that, having twenty times the abilities
of Allan Ramsay and of Fergusson, he talked of them with
too much humility as his models; there was, doubtless, national predilection in his estimate.

45   This is all I can tell you about Burns. I have only to
add that his dress corresponded to his manner. He was
like a farmer dressed in his best to dine with the laird. I
do not speak *in malam partem** when I say I never saw a

man in company with his superiors in station or information more perfectly free from either the reality or the
affectation of embarrassment. I was told, but did not observe it, that his address to females was extremely deferen-
5 tial, and always with a turn either to the pathetic or
humorous, which engaged their attention particularly. I
have heard the late Duchess of Gordon remark this. I do
not know anything I can add to these recollections of forty
years since.

10 The conduct of Burns under this dazzling blaze
of favor; the calm, unaffected, manly manner in
which he not only bore it, but estimated its value,
has justly been regarded as the best proof that could
be given of his real vigor and integrity of mind. A
15 little natural vanity, some touches of hypocritical
modesty, some glimmerings of affectation, at least
some fear of being thought affected, we could have
pardoned in almost any man; but no such indication
is to be traced here. In his unexampled situation
20 the young peasant is not a moment perplexed; so
many strange lights do not confuse him, do not lead
him astray. Nevertheless, we cannot but perceive
that this winter did him great and lasting injury. A
somewhat clearer knowledge of men's affairs, scarcely
25 of their characters, it did afford him; but a sharper
feeling of Fortune's unequal arrangements in their
social destiny it also left with him. He had seen the
gay and gorgeous arena in which the powerful are
born to play their parts; nay, had himself stood in
30 the midst of it; and he felt more bitterly than ever
that here he was but a looker-on, and had no part or
lot in that splendid game. From this time a jealous,
indignant fear of social degradation takes possession
of him; and perverts, so far as aught could pervert,
35 his private contentment and his feelings toward his
richer fellows. It was clear to Burns that he had
talent enough to make a fortune, or a hundred for-

tunes, could he but have rightly willed this; it was
clear also that he willed something far different, and
therefore could not make one. Unhappy it was that
he had not power to choose the one and reject the
5 other, but must halt forever between two opinions,
two objects, making hampered advancement toward
either. But so is it with many men—we "long for
the merchandise, yet would fain keep the price";
and so stand chaffering with Fate, in vexatious alter-
10 cation, till the night come, and our fair is over!

The Edinburgh Learned of that period were in
general more noted for clearness of head than for
warmth of heart; with the exception of the good old
Blacklock,* whose help was too ineffectual, scarcely
15 one among them seems to have looked at Burns
with any true sympathy, or indeed much otherwise
than as at a highly curious *thing*. By the great also
he is treated in the customary fashion; entertained
at their tables and dismissed; certain modica of
20 pudding and praise are, from time to time, gladly
exchanged for the fascination of his presence; which
exchange once effected, the bargain is finished, and
each party goes his several way. At the end of this
strange season Burns gloomily sums up his gains
25 and losses, and meditates on the chaotic future. In
money he is somewhat richer; in fame and the show
of happiness, infinitely richer; but in the substance
of it, as poor as ever. Nay, poorer; for his heart is
now maddened still more with the fever of worldly
30 Ambition; and through long years the disease will
rack him with unprofitable sufferings, and weaken
his strength for all true and nobler aims.

What Burns was next to do or to avoid; how a man
so circumstanced was now to guide himself toward
35 his true advantage, might at this point of time have

been a question for the wisest. It was a question,
too, which apparently he was left altogether to answer for himself; of his learned or rich patrons it had
not struck any individual to turn a thought on this
5 so trivial matter. Without claiming for Burns the
praise of perfect sagacity, we must say that his Excise
and Farm scheme does not seem to us a very unrea-
sonable one; that we should be at a loss, even now,
to suggest one decidedly better. Certain of his ad-
10 mirers have felt scandalized at his ever resolving to
*gauge;* and would have had him lie at the pool,* till
the spirit of Patronage stirred the waters, that so,
with one friendly plunge, all his sorrows might be
healed. Unwise counselors! They know not the
15 manner of this spirit; and how, in the lap of most
golden dreams, a man might have happiness, were it
not that in the interim he must die of hunger! It
reflects credit on the manliness and sound sense of
Burns that he felt so early on what ground he was
20 standing; and preferred self-help, on the humblest
scale, to dependence and inaction, though with hope
of far more splendid possibilities. But even these
possibilities were not rejected in his scheme: he
might expect, if it chanced that he *had* any friend,
25 to rise, in no long period, into something even like
opulence and leisure; while again, if it chanced that
he had no friend, he could still live in security; and
for the rest, he "did not intend to borrow honor
from any profession."* We think, then, that his plan
30 was honest and well-calculated: all turned on the
execution of it. Doubtless it failed; yet not, we believe, from any vice inherent in itself. Nay, after
all, it was no failure of external means, but of internal, that overtook Burns. His was no bankruptcy
35 of the purse, but of the soul; to his last day, he owed
no man anything.

Meanwhile, he begins well—with two good and wise actions. His donation to his mother, munificent from a man whose income had lately been seven pounds a year, was worthy of him, and not more than
5 worthy. Generous also, and worthy of him, was his treatment of the woman whose life's welfare now depended on his pleasure. A friendly observer might have hoped serene days for him; his mind is on the true road to peace with itself; what clearness he still
10 wants will be given as he proceeds; for the best teacher of duties that still lie dim to us, is the Practice of those we see and have at hand. Had the "patrons of genius," who could give him nothing, but taken nothing from him, at least nothing more! The
15 wounds of his heart would have healed; vulgar ambition would have died away. Toil and Frugality would have been welcome,—since Virtue dwelt with them; and Poetry would have shone through them as of old; and in her clear, ethereal light, which was his
20 own by birthright, he might have looked down on his earthly destiny and all its obstructions, not with patience only, but with love.

But the patrons of genius would not have it so. Picturesque tourists,[1] all manner of fashionable
25 danglers after literature, and, far worse, all manner

1. There is one little sketch by certain "English gentlemen" of this class, which, though adopted in Currie's Narrative, and since then repeated in most others, we have all along felt an invincible disposition to regard as imaginary: "On a rock that projected into the stream, they saw a man employed in angling, of a singular appearance. He had a cap made of fox-skin on his head, a loose greatcoat fixed around him by a belt, from which depended an enormous Highland broad-sword. It was Burns." Now, we rather think, it was *not* Burns. For, to say nothing of the fox-skin cap, the loose and quite Hibernian watchcoat with the belt, what are we to make of this "enormous Highland broadsword" depending from him? More especially, as there is no word of parish constables on the outlook to see whether, as Dennis phrases it, he had an eye to his own midriff or that of the public! Burns, of all men, had the least need, and the least tendency, to seek for distinction either in his own eyes or those of others, by such poor mummeries. [The foregoing is Carlyle's note.]

of convivial Mæcenases,* hovered round him in his
retreat; and his good as well as his weak qualities
secured them influence over him. He was flattered
by their notice; and his warm, social nature made
5 it impossible for him to shake them off, and hold
on his way apart from them. These men, as we believe, were proximately the means of his ruin. Not
that they meant him any ill; they only meant themselves a little good; if he suffered harm, let *him* look
10 to it! But they wasted his precious time and his
precious talent; they disturbed his composure, broke
down his returning habits of temperance and assiduous, contented exertion. Their pampering was baneful to him; their cruelty, which soon followed, was
15 equally baneful. The old grudge against Fortune's
inequality awoke with new bitterness in their neighborhood; and Burns had no retreat but to the "Rock
of Independence,"* which is but an air castle after
all, that looks well at a distance, but will screen no
20 one from real wind and wet. Flushed with irregular
excitement, exasperated alternately by contempt of
others and contempt of himself, Burns was no longer
regaining his peace of mind, but fast losing it forever. There was a hollowness at the heart of his life,
25 for his conscience did not now approve what he was
doing.

Amid the vapors of unwise enjoyment, of bootless
remorse, and angry discontent with Fate, his true
loadstar, a life of Poetry, with Poverty, nay, with
30 Famine, if it must be so, was too often altogether
hidden from his eyes. And yet he sailed a sea where
without some such lodestar there was no right steer-
ing. Meteors of French Politics rise before him, but
these were not *his* stars. An accident this, which
35 hastened, but did not originate, his worst distresses.

In the mad contentions of that time he comes in collision with certain official Superiors; is wounded by them; cruelly lacerated, we should say, could a dead mechanical instrument, in any case, be called 5 cruel; and shrinks, in indignant pain, into deeper self-seclusion, into gloomier moodiness than ever. His life has now lost its unity; it is a life of fragments; led with little aim, beyond the melancholy one of securing its own continuance—in fits of wild, 10 false joy when such offered, and of black despondency when they passed away. His character before the world begins to suffer; calumny is busy with him; for a miserable man makes more enemies than friends. Some faults he has fallen into, and a thou-15 sand misfortunes; but deep criminality is what he stands accused of, and they that are *not* without sin cast the first stone at him! For is he not a well-wisher to the French Revolution, a Jacobin, and therefore in that one act guilty of all? These ac-20 cusations, political and moral, it has since appeared, were false enough; but the world hesitated little to credit them. Nay, his convivial Mæcenases themselves were not the last to do it. There is reason to believe that, in later years, the Dumfries Aristocracy 25 had partly withdrawn themselves from Burns, as from a tainted person no longer worthy of their acquaintance. That painful class, stationed in all provincial cities behind the outmost breastwork of Gentility, there to stand siege and do battle against the in-30 trusions of Grocerdom and Grazierdom, had actually seen dishonor in the society of Burns, and branded him with their veto; had, as we vulgarly say, *cut* him! We find one passage in this Work of Mr. Lockhart's, which will not out of our thoughts:

*Forsaking of his friends*

A gentleman of that county, whose name I have already more than once had occasion to refer to, has often told me that he was seldom more grieved than when, riding into Dumfries one fine summer's evening about this time to at-
5 tend a county ball, he saw Burns walking alone, on the shady side of the principal street of the town, while the opposite side was gay with successive groups of gentlemen and ladies, all drawn together for the festivities of the night, not one of whom appeared willing to recognize him.
10 The horseman dismounted, and joined Burns, who, on his proposing to cross the street, said: "Nay, nay, my young friend, that's all over now," and quoted, after a pause, some verses of Lady Grizzel Baillie's pathetic ballad:

"His bonnet stood ance fu' fair on his brow,
15    His auld ane look'd better than mony ane's[1] new;
But now he lets 't wear ony way it will hing,
And casts himsel dowie[2] upon the corn-bing.[3]

O, were we young as we ance hae been,
We suld hae been galloping down on yon green,
20    And linking it ower the lily-white lea!
*And werena my heart light, I wad die.*"[4]

It was little in Burns's character to let his feelings on certain subjects escape in this fashion. He, immediately after reciting these verses, assumed the sprightliness of his
25 most pleasing manner; and taking his young friend home with him, entertained him very agreeably till the hour of the ball arrived.

Alas! when we think that Burns now sleeps "where bitter indignation can no longer lacerate his heart,"[5]
30 and that most of those fair dames and frizzled gentlemen already lie at his side, where the breastwork of gentility is quite thrown down—who would not sigh over the thin delusions and foolish toys that divide heart from heart, and make man unmerciful to
35 his brother!

---

1. **Mony ane's.** Many a one that is.
2. **Dowie.** Sad.
3. **Bing.** Heap.
4. **Die.** Pronounced dē.
5. **Ubi saeva indignatio cor ulterius nequit.** Swift's epitaph.

It was not now to be hoped that the genius of
Burns would ever reach maturity or accomplish
aught worthy of itself. His spirit was jarred in its
melody; not the soft breath of natural feeling, but
5 the rude hand of Fate, was now sweeping over the
strings. And yet what harmony was in him, what
music even in his discords! How the wild tones
had a charm for the simplest and the wisest; and
all men felt and knew that here also was one of the
10 Gifted! "If he entered an inn* at midnight, after
all the inmates were in bed, the news of his arrival
circulated from the cellar to the garret; and ere ten
minutes had elapsed, the landlord and all his guests
were assembled!" Some brief, pure moments of
15 poetic life were yet appointed him, in the composition of his Songs. We can understand how he
grasped at this employment; and how, too, he
spurned all other reward for it but what the labor
itself brought him. For the soul of Burns, though
20 scathed and marred, was yet living in its full moral
strength, though sharply conscious of its errors and
abasement; and here in his destitution and degradation was one act of seeming nobleness and self-
devotedness left even for him to perform. He felt,
25 too, that with all the "thoughtless follies"* that had
"laid him low," the world was unjust and cruel to
him; and he silently appealed to another and calmer
time. Not as a hired soldier, but as a patriot, would
he strive for the glory of his country; so he cast
30 from him the poor sixpence a day, and served zeal-
ously as a volunteer. Let us not grudge him this
last luxury of his existence; let him not have appealed
to us in vain! The money was not necessary to him;
he struggled through without it; long since, these
35 guineas would have been gone; and now the high-

mindedness of refusing them will plead for him in all
hearts forever.

We are here arrived at the crisis of Burns's life,
for matters had now taken such a shape with him
5 as could not long continue. If improvement was
not to be looked for, Nature could only for a limited
time maintain this dark and maddening warfare
against the world and itself. We are not medically
informed whether any continuance of years was, at
10 this period, probable for Burns; whether his death
is to be looked on as in some sense an accidental
event, or only as the natural consequence of the
long series of events that had preceded. The latter
seems to be the likelier opinion; and yet it is by no
15 means a certain one. At all events, as we have said,
*some* change could not be very distant. Three gates
of deliverance, it seems to us, were open for Burns:
clear poetical activity; madness; or death. The first,
with longer life, was still possible, though not prob-
20 able, for physical causes were beginning to be concerned in it; and yet Burns had an iron resolution,
could he but have seen and felt, that not only his
highest glory, but his first duty, and the true medi-
cine for all his woes lay here. The second was still
25 less probable; for his mind was ever among the clear-
est and firmest. So the milder third gate was opened
for him; and he passed, not softly, yet speedily, into
that still country where the hailstorms and fire-
showers do not reach, and the heaviest laden way-
30 farer at length lays down his load!

Contemplating this sad end of Burns, and how he
sank unaided by any real help, uncheered by any
wise sympathy, generous minds have sometimes
figured to themselves, with a reproachful sorrow,
35 that much might have been done for him; that by

counsel, true affection, and friendly ministrations,
he might have been saved to himself and the world.
We question whether there is not more tenderness
of heart than soundness of judgment in these sug-
5 gestions. It seems dubious to us whether the richest,
wisest, most benevolent individual could have lent
Burns any effectual help. Counsel, which seldom
profits anyone, he did not need; in his understanding, he knew the right from the wrong, as well, per-
10 haps, as any man ever did; but the persuasion
which would have availed him lies not so much in the
head as in the heart, where no argument or expostula-
tion could have assisted much to implant it. As to
money again, we do not believe that this was his
15 essential want; or well see how any private man
could, even presupposing Burns's consent, have bestowed on him an independent fortune, with much
prospect of decisive advantage. It is a mortifying
truth, that two men, in any rank of society, could
20 hardly be found virtuous enough to give money, and
to take it as a necessary gift, without injury to the
moral entireness of one or both. But so stands the
fact. Friendship, in the old heroic sense of that
term, no longer exists; except in the cases of kindred
25 or other legal affinity it is in reality no longer expected, or recognized as a virtue among men. A
close observer of manners* has pronounced "Patronage," that is, pecuniary or other economic furtherance, to be "twice cursed"; cursing him that gives,
30 and him that takes! And thus, in regard to outward matters also it has become the rule, as in regard to inward it always was and must be the rule,
that no one shall look for effectual help to another;
but that each shall rest contented with what help he
35 can afford himself. Such, we say, is the principle

of modern Honor; naturally enough growing out of
that sentiment of Pride, which we inculcate and en-
courage as the basis of our whole social morality.
Many a poet has been poorer than Burns; but no one
5 was ever prouder; we may question whether, without
great precautions, even a pension from Royalty would
not have galled and encumbered, more than actually
assisted him.

Still less, therefore, are we disposed to join with
10 another class of Burns's admirers, who accuse the
higher ranks among us of having ruined Burns by
their selfish neglect of him. We have already stated
our doubts whether direct pecuniary help, had it been
offered, would have been accepted, or could have
15 proved very effectual. We shall readily admit, however, that much was to be done for Burns; that many
a poisoned arrow might have been warded from his
bosom; many an entanglement in his path cut
asunder by the hand of the powerful; and light
20 and heat, shed on him from high places, would have
made his humble atmosphere more genial; and the
softest heart then breathing might have lived and
died with some fewer pangs. Nay, we shall grant
further, and for Burns it is granting much, that,
25 with all his pride, he would have thanked, even with
exaggerated gratitude, any one who had cordially be-
friended him; patronage, unless once cursed, needed
not to have been twice so. At all events, the poor
promotion he desired in his calling might have been
30 granted; it was his own scheme, therefore likelier
than any other to be of service. All this it might
have been a luxury, nay, it was a duty, for our
nobility to have done. No part of all this, however,
did any of them do; or apparently attempt, or wish
35 to do; so much is granted against them. But what

then is the amount of their blame? Simply that
they were men of the world, and walked by the principles of such men; that they treated Burns as
other nobles and other commoners had done other
5 poets; as the English did Shakespeare; as King
Charles and his Cavaliers did Butler,* as King Philip
and his Grandees did Cervantes.*  Do men gather
grapes of thorns; or shall we cut down our thorns*
for yielding only a *fence* and haws?  How, indeed,
10 could the "nobility and gentry* of his native land"
hold out any help to this "Scottish Bard, proud of
his name and country"?  Were the nobility and
gentry so much as able rightly to help themselves?
Had they not their game to preserve; their borough
15 interests to strengthen; dinners, therefore, of various kinds to eat and give?  Were their means more
than adequate to all this business, or less than adequate?  Less than adequate, in general; few of them
in reality were richer than Burns; many of them
20 were poorer; for sometimes they had to wring their
supplies, as with thumbscrews, from the hard hand,
and, in their need of guineas, to forget their duty of
mercy—which Burns was never reduced to do.  Let
us pity and forgive them.  The game they preserved
25 and shot, the dinners they ate and gave, the borough
interests they strengthened, the *little* Babylons they
severally builded by the glory of their might, are all
melted or melting back into the primeval Chaos, as
man's merely selfish endeavors are fated to do; and
30 here was an action extending, in virtue of its worldly
influence, we may say, through all time; in virtue of
its moral nature, beyond all time, being immortal as
the Spirit of Goodness itself; this action was offered
them to do, and light was not given them to do it.
35 Let us pity and forgive them.  But better than pity,

let us go and *do otherwise.* Human suffering did not
end with the life of Burns; neither was the solemn
mandate, "Love one another,* bear one another's bur-
dens," given to the rich only, but to all men. True,
5 we shall find no Burns to relieve, to assuage by our
aid or our pity; but celestial natures, groaning under
the fardels of a weary life, we shall still find; and
that wretchedness which Fate has rendered *voiceless*
and *tuneless,* is not the least wretched, but the most.
10      Still, we do not think that the blame of Burns's
failure lies chiefly with the world. The world, it
seems to us, treated him with more, rather than with
less, kindness than it usually shows to such men. It
has ever, we fear, shown but small favor to its
15 Teachers; hunger and nakedness, perils and revilings,
the prison, the cross, the poison-chalice have, in most
times and countries, been the market price it has
offered for Wisdom, the welcome with which it has
greeted those who have come to enlighten and purify.
20 Homer and Socrates, and the Christian Apostles, belong to old days; but the world's Martyrology was
not completed with these. Roger Bacon and Galileo*
languish in priestly dungeons; Tasso* pines in the cell
of a madhouse; Camoëns* dies begging on the streets
25 of Lisbon. So neglected, so "persecuted they the
Prophets,"* not in Judea only, but in all places where
men have been. We reckon that every poet of Burns's
order is, or should be, a prophet and teacher to his
age; that he has no right to expect great kindness
30 from it, but rather is bound to do it great kindness;
that Burns, in particular, experienced fully the usual
proportion of the world's goodness; and that the
blame of his failure, as we have said, lies not chiefly
with the world.
35      Where, then, does it lie? We are forced to answer:

With himself; it is his inward, not his outward, misfortunes that bring him to the dust. Seldom, indeed, is it otherwise; seldom is a life morally wrecked but the grand cause lies in some internal mal-arrange-
5 ment, some want less of good fortune than of good guidance. Nature fashions no creature without implanting in it the strength needful for its action and duration; least of all does she so neglect her masterpiece and darling, the poetic soul. Neither can we
10 believe that it is in the power of *any* external circumstances utterly to ruin the mind of a man; nay, if proper wisdom be given him, even so much as to affect its essential health and beauty. The sternest sum total of all worldly misfortunes is Death; noth-
15 ing more *can* lie in the cup of human woe; yet many men, in all ages, have triumphed over Death, and led it captive, converting its physical victory into a moral victory for themselves, into a real and immortal consecration for all that their past life had achieved.
20 What has been done, may be done again; nay, it is but the degree and not the kind of such heroism that differs in different seasons; for without some portion of this spirit, not of boisterous daring, but of silent fearlessness, of Self-denial in all its forms, no good
25 man, in any scene or time, has ever attained to be good.

We have already stated the error of Burns; and mourned over it rather than blamed it. It was the want of unity in his purpose, of consistency in
30 his aims; the hapless attempt to mingle in friendly union the common spirit of the world with the spirit of poetry, which is of a far different and altogether irreconcilable nature. Burns was nothing wholly; and Burns could be nothing, no man formed as he
35 was can be anything, by halves. The heart, not of a

mere hot-blooded, popular Versemonger, or poetical
*Restaurateur,** but of a true Poet and Singer, worthy
of the old, religious, heroic times, had been given him;
and he fell in an age, not of heroism and religion, but
5 of skepticism, selfishness, and triviality, when true
Nobleness was little understood, and its place supplied by a hollow, dissocial, altogether barren and un-
fruitful principle of Pride. The influences of that
age, his open, kind, susceptible nature, to say noth-
10 ing of his highly untoward situation, made it more
than usually difficult for him to cast aside, or rightly
subordinate; the better spirit that was within him
ever sternly demanded its rights, its supremacy; he
spent his life in endeavoring to reconcile these two;
15 and lost it, as he must lose it, without reconciling
them.

Burns was born poor; and born also to continue
poor, for he would not endeavor to be otherwise;
this it had been well could he have once for all ad-
20 mitted, and considered as finally settled. He was
poor, truly; but hundreds even of his own class and
order of minds have been poorer, yet have suffered
nothing deadly from it; nay, his own father had a
far sorer battle with ungrateful destiny than his
25 was; and he did not yield to it, but died courageously
warring, and to all moral intents prevailing, against
it. True, Burns had little means, had even little
time for poetry, his only real pursuit and vocation;
but so much the more precious was what little he had.
30 In all these external respects his case was hard;
but very far from the hardest. Poverty, incessant
drudgery, and much worse evils, it has often been
the lot of Poets and wise men to strive with, and their
glory to conquer. Locke* was banished as a traitor;
35 and wrote his *Essay on the Human Understanding*

sheltering himself in a Dutch garret. Was Milton rich* or at his ease when he composed *Paradise Lost?* Not only low, but fallen from a height; not only poor, but impoverished; in darkness and with dangers 5 compassed round, he sang his immortal song, and found fit audience, though few. Did not Cervantes* finish his work, a maimed soldier and in prison? Nay, was not the *Araucana,* * which Spain acknowledges as its Epic, written without even the aid of 10 paper; on scraps of leather, as the stout fighter and voyager snatched any moment from that wild warfare?

And what, then, had these men, which Burns wanted? Two things; both which, it seems to us, 15 are indispensable for such men. They had a true, religious principle of morals; and a single, not a double, aim in their activity. They were not self-seekers and self-worshipers; but seekers and worshipers of something far better than Self. Not per-20 sonal enjoyment was their object; but a high, heroic idea of Religion, of Patriotism, of heavenly Wisdom, in one or the other form, ever hovered before them; in which cause they neither shrank from suffering, nor called on the earth to witness it as something 25 wonderful; but patiently endured, counting it blessedness enough so to spend and be spent. Thus the "golden calf of Self-love,"* however curiously carved, was not their Deity; but the Invisible Goodness, which alone is man's reasonable service. This feel-30 ing was as a celestial fountain, whose streams refreshed into gladness and beauty all the provinces of their otherwise too desolate existence. In a word, they willed one thing, to which all other things were subordinated and made subservient; and therefore they 35 accomplished it. The wedge will rend rocks; but its edge must be sharp and single; if it be double, the wedge is bruised in pieces, and will rend nothing.

Part of this superiority these men owed to their age; in which heroism and devotedness were still 5 practiced, or at least not yet disbelieved in; but much of it likewise they owed to themselves. With Burns, again, it was different. His morality, in most of its practical points, is that of a mere worldly man; enjoyment, in a finer or coarser shape, is the only 10 thing he longs and strives for. A noble instinct sometimes raises him above this; but an instinct only, and acting only for moments. He has no Religion; in the shallow age where his days were cast, Religion was not discriminated from the New and 15 Old Light *forms* of Religion; and was, with these, becoming obsolete in the minds of men. His heart, indeed, is alive with a trembling adoration, but there is no temple in his understanding. He lives in darkness and in the shadow of doubt. His religion, at 20 best, is an anxious wish; like that of Rabelais,* "a great Perhaps."

He loved Poetry warmly, and in his heart; could he but have loved it purely, and with his whole undivided heart, it had been well. For Poetry, as Burns 25 could have followed it, is but another form of Wisdom, of Religion; is itself Wisdom and Religion. But this also was denied him. His poetry is a stray, vagrant gleam, which will not be extinguished within him, yet rises not to be the true light of his path, 30 but is often a wildfire that misleads him. It was not necessary for Burns to be rich; to be, or to seem, "independent"; but it *was* necessary for him to be at one with his own heart; to place what was highest in his nature highest also in his life: "to seek within 35 himself for that consistency and sequence, which ex-

ternal events would forever refuse him." He was
born a poet; poetry was the celestial element of his
being, and should have been the soul of his whole
endeavors.    Lifted into that serene ether, whither
5 he had wings given him to mount, he would have
needed no other elevation; poverty, neglect, and all
evil save the desecration of himself and his Art, were
a small matter to him; the pride and the passions of
the world lay far beneath his feet; and he looked
10 down alike on noble and slave, on prince and beggar,
and all that wore the stamp of man, with clear recognition, with brotherly affection, with sympathy, with
pity.    Nay, we question whether, for his culture as a
Poet, poverty and much suffering for a season were
15 not absolutely advantageous.    Great men, in looking
back over their lives, have testified to that effect.  "I
would not for much," says Jean Paul,* "that I had
been born richer."    And yet Paul's birth was poor
enough; for, in another place, he adds:  "The
20 prisoner's allowance is bread and water; and I had
often only the latter."    But the gold that is refined
in the hottest furnace comes out the purest; or, as
he has himself expressed it, "the canary-bird sings
sweeter the longer it has been trained in a darkened
25 cage."

A man like Burns might have divided his hours
between poetry and virtuous industry; industry which
all true feeling sanctions, nay, prescribes, and which
has a beauty, for that cause, beyond the pomp of
30 thrones; but to divide his hours between poetry and
rich men's banquets was an ill-starred and inauspi-
cious attempt.    How could he be at ease at such banquets?    What had he to do there, mingling his music
with the coarse roar of altogether earthly voices;
35 brightening the thick smoke of intoxication with fire

lent him from heaven? Was it his aim to *enjoy* life?
Tomorrow he must go drudge as an Exciseman! We
wonder not that Burns became moody, indignant, and
at times an offender against certain rules of society;
5 but rather that he did not grow utterly frantic, and
run *amuck* against them all.  How could a man, so
falsely placed, by his own or others' fault, ever know
contentment or peaceable diligence for an hour? What
he did, under such perverse guidance, and what he
10 forbore to do, alike fill us with astonishment at the
natural strength and worth of his character.

Doubtless there was a remedy for this perverse-
ness; but not in others—only in himself; least of
all in simple increase of wealth and worldly "respect-
15 ability."  We hope we have now heard enough about
the efficacy of wealth for poetry, and to make poets
happy.  Nay, have we not seen another instance of it
in these very days?  Byron, a man of an endowment
considerably less ethereal than that of Burns, is born
20 in the rank not of a Scottish plowman, but of an
English peer; the highest worldly honors, the fairest
worldly career, are his by inheritance; the richest
harvest of fame he soon reaps, in another province,
by his own hand.  And what does all this avail him?
25 Is he happy; is he good; is he true?  Alas, he has a
poet's soul, and strives toward the Infinite and the
Eternal; and soon feels that all this is but mount-
ing to the housetop to reach the stars!  Like Burns,
he is only a proud man; might, like him, have
30 "purchased a pocket copy* of Milton to study the
character of Satan"; for Satan also is Byron's grand
exemplar, the hero of his poetry, and the model apparently of his conduct.  As in Burns's case, too,
the celestial element will not mingle with the clay
35 of earth; both poet and man of the world he must

not be; vulgar Ambition will not live kindly with
poetic Adoration; he *cannot* serve God and Mam-
mon. Byron, like Burns, is not happy; nay, he is
the most wretched of all men. His life is falsely
5 arranged; the fire that is in him is not a strong,
still, central fire, warming into beauty the products
of a world; but it is the mad fire of a volcano; and
now—we look sadly* into the ashes of a crater, which
ere long will fill itself with snow!

10   Byron and Burns were sent forth as missionaries
to their generation, to teach it a higher Doctrine, a
purer Truth; they had a message to deliver, which left
them no rest till it was accomplished; in dim throes
of pain, this divine behest lay smoldering within
15 them; for they knew not what it meant, and felt it
only in mysterious anticipation; and they had to die
without articulately uttering it. They are in the
camp of the Unconverted; yet not as high messengers
of rigorous though benignant truth, but as soft,
20 flattering singers, and in pleasant fellowship will
they live there; they are first adulated, then
persecuted; they accomplish little for others; they
find no peace for themselves, but only death and
the peace of the grave. We confess, it is not
25 without a certain mournful awe that we view the
fate of these noble souls, so richly gifted, yet ruined
to so little purpose with all their gifts. It seems to us
there is a stern moral taught in this piece of history
—*twice* told us in our own time! Surely to men of
30 like genius, if there be any such, it carries with it
a lesson of deep, impressive significance. Surely it
would become such a man, furnished for the highest
of all enterprises, that of being the Poet of his Age,
to consider well what it is that he attempts, and in
35 what spirit he attempts it. For the words of Milton*

are true in all times, and were never truer than in
this: "He who would write heroic poems must make
his whole life a heroic poem." If he cannot first so
make his life, then let him hasten from this arena;
5 for neither its lofty glories nor its fearful perils are
for him. Let him dwindle into a modish balladmonger; let him worship and besing the idols of the
time, and the time will not fail to reward him. If,
indeed, he can endure to live in that capacity! Byron
10 and Burns could not live as idol-priests, but the fire
of their own hearts consumed them; and better it
was for them that they could not. For it is not in
the favor of the great or of the small, but in a life
of truth, and in the inexpugnable citadel of his own
15 soul, that a Byron's or a Burns's strength must lie.
Let the great stand aloof from him, or know how
to reverence him. Beautiful is the union of wealth
with favor and furtherance for literature; like the
costliest flower jar enclosing the loveliest amaranth.
20 Yet let not the relation be mistaken. A true poet
is not one whom they can hire by money or flattery to
be a minister of their pleasures, their writer of occasional verses, their purveyor of table-wit. He cannot
be their menial; he cannot even be their partisan.
25 At the peril of both parties, let no such union be
attempted! Will a Courser of the Sun work softly
in the harness of a Dray-horse? His hoofs are of
fire, and his path is through the heavens, bringing
light to all lands; will he lumber on mud highways,
30 dragging ale for earthly appetites from door to door?

But we must stop short in these considerations,
which would lead us to boundless lengths. We had
something to say on the public moral character of
Burns; but this also we must forbear. We are far
35 from regarding him as guilty before the world, as

guiltier than the average; nay, from doubting that
he is less guilty than one of ten thousand. Tried
at a tribunal far more rigid than that where the
*Plebiscita** of common civic reputations are pro-
5 nounced, he has seemed to us even there less worthy
of blame than of pity and wonder. But the world
is habitually unjust in its judgments of such
men; unjust on many grounds, of which this
one may be stated as the substance: It decides,
10 like a court of law, by dead statutes; and not
positively but negatively, less on what is done right
than on what is or is not done wrong. Not the few
inches of deflection from the mathematical orbit,
which are so easily measured, but the *ratio* of these
15 to the whole diameter, constitutes the real aberration.
This orbit may be a planet's, its diameter the breadth
of the solar system; or it may be a city hippodrome;
nay, the circle of a ginhorse,* its diameter a score of
feet or paces. But the inches of deflection only are
20 measured; and it is assumed that the diameter of the
ginhorse, and that of the planet, will yield the same
ratio when compared with them! Here lies the root
of many a blind, cruel condemnation of Burnses,
Swifts, Rousseaus, which one never listens to with
25 approval. Granted the ship comes into harbor with
shrouds and tackle damaged, the pilot is blameworthy; he has not been all-wise and all-powerful;
but to know *how* blameworthy, tell us first whether
his voyage has been round the Globe, or only to
30 Ramsgate and the Isle of Dogs.*

With our readers in general, with men of right
feeling anywhere, we are not required to plead for
Burns. In pitying admiration he lies enshrined in all
our hearts, in a far nobler mausoleum than that one of
35 marble; neither will his Works, even as they are, pass

away from the memory of men.  While the Shake-
speares and Miltons roll on like mighty rivers through
the country of Thought, bearing fleets of traffickers
and assiduous pearl-fishers on their waves, this little
5 Valclusa Fountain* will also arrest our eye; for this
also is of Nature's own and most cunning workmanship, bursts from the depths of the earth, with a full-
gushing current, into the light of day; and often will
the traveler turn aside to drink of its clear waters,
10 and muse among its rocks and pines!

# NOTES

## POEMS

### POOR MAILIE'S ELEGY

Page 44. The stanza of this poem was used by Burns more than any other form of verse and has often, since his day, been called the "Burns stanza." He was by no means the originator of it, or even the first popularizer, for it was also very common in the works of his direct models, Fergusson and Ramsay, and has been found as far back as the works of the troubadours of the Middle Ages. Technically the rime-scheme is *a a a b a b*, the *a*'s being lines of four stresses, the *b*'s of two.

Page 45. Stanza VI. **Tweed.** A river that forms part of the boundary between Scotland and England. Mailie, therefore, was of English breed.

Stanza VIII. **Doon, Ayr.** Small rivers flowing into the Irish Sea; the former a few miles south of the town of Ayr, the latter at Ayr.

### EPISTLE TO DAVIE

Page 49. The intricate stanza is that of a famous old Scottish poem of 1597, "The Cherry and the Slae" (Sloe), by Alexander Montgomery. The same stanza was also used by Thomas Howell, an obscure Elizabethan English poet, in "A Dream." The rime-scheme is *a a b c c b d e d e* for the main part of each stanza, followed by four lines of which the second and fourth rime, while the first and third consist each of an internal rime, thus: "But *hanker,* and *canker.*" The *a* and *c* and *d* lines have four stresses each; the others three, except the lines with the internal rime. Each of these latter lines consists of two amphibrachs (feet consisting each of an accented syllable between two unaccented syllables); the meter of the rest of the poem is prevailingly iambic.

Stanza I. **Ben Lomond.** "Ben" in Scottish proper names means "Mount." Ben-Lomond is a famous mountain near Loch Lomond, in Scott's "Lady of the Lake" country—the southern part of the Highlands. This peak may be seen to the north from some parts of Ayrshire.

Page 50. Stanza II. Burns attributed the quoted line (line 11) to Ramsay, but these exact words have not been found in Ramsay's poems, or elsewhere, though a very similar line has been found in several places.

Page 53. Stanza VIII. **My darling Jean.** This is the earliest important reference to Jean Armour in Burns's poems; it was written early in their acquaintance.

Page 54. Stanza X. Notice that **world's,** in line 4, is metrically two syllables. We very often find in Burns's poetry that a strongly "burred" *r* gives a word an extra syllable.

Stanza XI. **The famous Nine.** The Muses. For Phœbus and Pegasus, see a dictionary of mythology.

## SECOND EPISTLE TO DAVIE

Page 55. Stanza II. Note that **bairns' bairns** consists metrically of four syllables, the *r* each time being "rolled" to syllabic value.

Page 56. Stanza IV. **On Parnassus' brink.** Absorbed in poetry; about to publish. Parnassus, a mountain ridge in Greece, was a haunt of Apollo and the Muses.

## EPISTLE TO J. LAPRAIK

Page 58. Stanza IV. **Steele.** Richard Steele, who was associated with Addison. The allusion here is to his sentimental comedies.

**Beattie.** James Beattie, a Scottish poet and philosophical writer, whose most noted poem, *The Minstrel* (in Spenserian stanzas), was published in 1771-74. Although twenty-odd years older than Burns, Beattie survived the latter several years.

**Muirkirk.** A small town on the river Ayr not far east of the "Burns country."

Stanza VI. **Inverness.** A city far up in the Highlands, the north of Scotland.

**Tiviotdale.** A poetic name for Roxburghshire, a county in the south of Scotland, through which the Teviot River flows.

Page 60. Stanza XII. **Parnassus.** The mountain of the Muses.

Stanza XIV. **Allan.** Allan Ramsay (see page 20).

## EPISTLE TO WILLIAM SIMPSON

Page 63. Stanza III. **Allan.** Allan Ramsay.

**Gilbertfield.** William Hamilton of Gilbertfield. The three earlier Scottish poets mentioned in this stanza were considered by Burns to be his chief models.

Page 64. Stanza IV. The allusion is to the neglect of Fergusson by those who might have helped him and prolonged his career (see page 20).

Stanza VII. **New Holland.** A former name for Australia.
Page 65. Stanza VIII. The proper names after the first line are those of Scottish rivers, the last four being in the "Burns country."

Stanza IX. **Ilissus** is the small river flowing through Athens.

## THE HOLY FAIR

Page 76. The stanza of "The Holy Fair" and "Halloween" is important and interesting. It consists of eight lines of four and three accents alternating, for the most part with alternate rime, plus a short final line of two accents for each stanza. This final line is a sort of infinitely varied refrain, ending with the same word throughout a poem— "day" in "The Holy Fair," "night" in "Halloween." The commonest rime-scheme for the stanza is *a b a b c d c d e;* the *a* and *c* lines having four accents, the *b* and *d* lines three; but variety is introduced by occasional substitution of rime *within the four-stress lines* for rime of one such line with another. This variation occurs most often in the second quatrain of the stanza. See, for example, stanza XXI of "The Holy Fair": the seventh line does not rime with the fifth, but both the fifth and the seventh break into halves that rime:

His piercin *words*, like Highlan' *swords*,

\*      \*      \*      \*      \*

His talk o' *Hell*, whare devils *dwell.*

It must be remembered, too, that Burns's rimes are often only assonances; he did not attempt to secure the exact correspondence of sound demanded by strict rime, as we now use the term. Thus, in stanza VI, "hame" and "time," "clad" and "side," are satisfactory rimes for him. These variations by means of internal rime or assonance, he used with the utmost freedom and with decided effectiveness in avoiding monotony.

Stanza I. **Galston.** The parish next north of Mauchline (see page 13).

Page 79. Stanza VIII. **Black-bonnet.** The elder who received the offering.

Stanza XII. The allusion is to the beginning of Chapter II of the *Book of Job.*

Page 80. Stanza XV. **Antonine.** Marcus Aurelius, author of the famous *Meditations.*

Page 81. Stanza XVI. **The Cowgate.** "A street . . . which faces the tent in Mauchline." (R.B.)

Page 82. Stanza XXI. As his reason for quoting "sauls does harrow" Burns made reference to Shakespeare's *Hamlet,* meaning, doubtless, the speech of the Ghost, I, v, 16.

Page 83.   Stanza XXIV.   The last part of the stanza alludes to the way in which one of the "auld guidmen" said grace.

## HALLOWEEN

Page 85.   Stanza I.   **Cassilis Downans.**   Certain little, romantic, rocky, green hills, in the neighborhood of the ancient seat of the Earls of Cassilis.   (R.B.)

**The Cove.**   A noted cavern near Colean House, called the Cove of Colean; which, as well as Cassilis Downans, is famed, in country story, for being a favorite haunt of fairies. (R.B.)

Stanza II.   **Carrick.**   The ancestors of Robert Bruce, the famous Scottish patriot, were earls of Carrick.   Carrick is the part of Ayrshire south of the River Doon.

Page 86.   Stanza IV.   The first ceremony of Halloween is, pulling each a "stock" or plant of kail.   They must go out, hand in hand, with eyes shut, and pull the first they meet with; its being big or little, straight or crooked, is prophetic of the size and shape of the grand object of all their spells—the husband or wife.   If any "yird," or earth, stick to the root, that is "tocher," or fortune; and the taste of the "custock," that is, the heart of the stem, is indicative of the natural temper and disposition.   Lastly, the stems, or, to give them their ordinary appellation, the "runts," are placed somewhere above the head of the door; and the Christian names of people whom chance brings into the house are, according to the priority of placing the "runts," the names in question.   (R.B.)

Page 87.   Stanza VII.   Burning the nuts is a favorite charm.   They name the lad and lass to each particular nut, as they lay them in the fire; and according as they burn quietly together, or start from beside one another, the course and issue of the courtship will be.   (R.B.)

Page 88.   Stanza X.   **The fause-house.**   When the corn [oats] is in a doubtful state, by being too green or wet, the stack-builder, by means of old timber, etc., makes a large apartment in his stack, with an opening in the side which is fairest exposed to the wind; this he calls a "fause-house." (R.B.)

Stanza XI.   **And in the blue-clue throws then.**   Whoever would, with success, try this spell, must strictly observe these directions:   Steal out, all alone, to the kiln, and, darkling, throw into the "pot" a clue of blue yarn; wind it in a new clue off the old one; and, towards the latter end, something will hold the thread: demand "Wha hauds?" i. e., who holds? and answer will be returned from the kiln-pot, by naming the Christian and surname of your future spouse.   (R.B.)

Page 89.   Stanza XIII.   **I'll eat the apple at the glass.**
Take a candle and go alone to a looking-glass; eat an apple
before it, and some traditions say you should comb your hair
all the time; the face of your conjugal companion, *to be*,
will be seen in the glass, as if peeping over your shoulder.
(R.B.)

Page 90.   Stanza XVI.   **He gat hemp-seed.**  Steal out,
unperceived, and sow a handful of hemp-seed, harrowing it
with anything you can conveniently draw after you.  Repeat,
now and then, "Hemp-seed I saw [sow] thee, Hemp-seed
I saw thee; and him (or her) that is to be my true love,
come after me and pou [pull] thee."   Look over your left
shoulder, and you will see the appearance of the person
invoked, in the attitude of pulling hemp.   Some traditions
say, "Come after me and shaw thee," that is, show thyself;
in which case it simply appears.   Others omit the harrowing and say, "Come after me and harrow thee."  (R.B.)

Page 91.   Stanza XXI.   **To winn three wechts o' naething.**
This charm must likewise be performed unperceived and
alone.   You go to the barn and open both doors, taking
them off the hinges if possible; for there is danger that the
being about to appear may shut the doors and do you some
mischief.   Then take that instrument used in winnowing
the corn [oats], which in our country dialect we call a
"wecht," and go through all the attitudes of letting down
corn against the wind.   Repeat it three times, and the third
time an apparition will pass through the barn, in at the
windy door and out at the other, having both the figure
in question and the appearance or retinue marking the
employment or station in life.   (R.B.)

Page 92.   Stanza XXIII.   **The stack he faddom't thrice.**
Take an opportunity of going (unnoticed) to a "bear-stack,"
[*bear* means barley] and fathom it three times round.   The
last fathom of the three, you will catch in your arms the appearance of your future conjugal yoke-fellow.  (R.B.)

Page 93.   Stanza XXIV.   **Whare three lairds' lands met
at a burn.**   You go out, one or more (for this is a social
spell), to a south-running spring, or rivulet, where "three
lairds' lands meet," and dip your left shirt-sleeve.   Go to
bed in sight of a fire, and hang your wet sleeve before it
to dry.   Lie awake; and, some time near midnight, an apparition having the exact figure of the grand object in question will come and turn the sleeve, as if to dry the other
side of it.   (R.B.)

Page 94.   Stanza XXVII.   **The luggies three are ranged.**
Take three dishes, put clean water in one, foul water in
another, and leave the third empty; blindfold a person, and
lead him to the hearth where the dishes are ranged; he (or

she) dips the left hand: if by chance in the clean water, the future (husband or) wife will come to the bar of matrimony a maid; if in the foul, a widow; if in the empty dish, it foretells, with equal certainty, no marriage at all. It is repeated three times, and every time the arrangement of the dishes is altered. (R.B.)

Stanza XXVIII. **Sow'ns** [sowens] were made from the liquor obtained by steeping grains of oats in water. When the liquor had soured it was boiled to the thickness of porridge and eaten, commonly with milk, but on Halloween with butter.

## THE JOLLY BEGGARS

Page 98. Recitativo. Stanza 1. **Poosie-Nansie** was a nick-name for a woman named Agnes Gibson, who kept a low tavern in Mauchline.

Page 99. Stanza II. **The heights of Abrám** (Abraham). In battle on these heights above Quebec, in 1759, the British captured that city from the French.

**The Moro.** The castle defending the harbor of Santiago de Cuba, stormed by the British in 1762.

Stanza III. **Curtis.** A British admiral who commanded at the destruction of French floating batteries at Gibraltar in 1782.

**Elliot.** Another British leader at Gibraltar.

Page 102. Stanza III. **From Tweed to Spey.** From the south to the north of Scotland.

Page 103. Stanza II. **Arioso.** Like an air or melody (as distinguished from *recitative*).

**Wee Apollo.** The fiddler was so called because Apollo was a musician and the god of music.

**Allegretto.** A moderately quick movement.

**Giga.** A jig.

Page 107. Stanza II. **Castalia.** A fountain on the slope of Mount Parnassus, one of the haunts of the Muses.

**Helicon.** Another Greek mountain that the Muses were said to frequent. On it were two fountains which were considered the sources of poetic inspiration.

Page 108. Recitativo. **Deborah** was a prophetess in Israel who sang a famous song of triumph after victory over Canaan. See *Judges* IV and V.

## THE COTTER'S SATURDAY NIGHT

Page 110. The metrical form is the Spenserian stanza, taken, however, not from Spenser, but from imitations by the English poet Shenstone (author of *The Schoolmistress*) and the Scotch poet Beattie (author of *The Minstrel*).

Page 114. Stanza XIII. The names of popular hymn-tunes are given in lines 3-5.

Stanza XIV. Burns is mentioning portions of the Old Testament, to be found by use of a Concordance. For the decree of warfare against "Amalek's progeny," see *Exodus* XVII: 16. The "royal Bard" is David.

Page 115. Stanza XV. The allusion in the last three lines is to St. John and his book of *Revelation*.

Stanza XVI. The quoted bit is slightly varied from a line in Pope's "Windsor Forest."

Page 116. Stanza XIX. The quoted line is from Pope's *Essay on Man*, Epistle IV, line 248.

Stanza XXI. The second line originally read: "That stream'd thro' great, unhappy Wallace' heart." It is said to have been changed to please Mrs. Dunlop, who was a descendant of Wallace, the Scottish patriot. Sir William Wallace (1274-1305) carried on war against the English for several years before and after 1300.

## THE AULD FARMER'S NEW-YEAR MORNING SALUTATION TO HIS AULD MARE, MAGGIE

Page 118. Stanza VI. **Kyle-Stewart.** Kyle is the central division of Ayrshire, between the Doon and the Irvine rivers, and Kyle-Stewart is the northern part of Kyle—north of Ayr; the part in which Burns's homes at Lochlea and Mossgiel were situated.

## THE TWA DOGS

Page 122. Line 2. **King Coil.** A legendary king who ruled in Kyle (see note next above). Observe that Burns evidently pronounced *Coil* as we pronounce *Kyle*, riming with *isle*.

Page 125. Lines 95 ff. In his autobiographical letter to Dr. Moore, written in 1787, Burns wrote thus of the latter part of his family's stay at Mount Oliphant: "My father's generous master died; the farm proved a ruinous bargain; and, to clench the curse, we fell into the hands of a factor, who sat for the picture I have drawn of one in my *Tale of Two Dogs*."

## ADDRESS TO THE DEIL

Page 135. Stanza XIX. **Michael.** The archangel Michael is meant. See Milton's *Paradise Lost*, Book VI, line 326.

## EPISTLE TO JAMES SMITH

Page 141. Stanza XXIII. **Dempster.** George Dempster, a Scottish member of Parliament from 1762 to 1790, especially interested in agriculture.

· **Willie Pitt.** The second William Pitt who was prominent in English politics; he was prime minister from December, 1783, to 1801. Both he and his father, the first William Pitt, Earl of Chatham, were friendly to the American colonies. Burns suggests conferring on him the famous Order of the Garter.

Page 142. Stanza XXVI. Compare this with the "Address to the Unco Guid" and the "Epistle to McMath."

Stanza XXVII. **Arioso.** In the manner of an elaborate air in song.

**Gravissimo.** Very slow and solemn.


## ADDRESS OF BEELZEBUB

Page 154. Line 13. **Hancock, Franklin.** John Hancock, first signer of the American Declaration of Independence, and Benjamin Franklin are meant. Burns sympathized with the Americans whose freedom had been so recently recognized. He wrote an "Ode for General Washington's Birthday"; and once, when a toast to the health of Pitt was proposed in his presence, he suggested "the health of George Washington, a better man."

Line 16. **Montgomery.** General Richard Montgomery, the American who captured Montreal in 1775 and was killed in an attack on Quebec.

Line 21. **North, Sackville.** Lord North, premier during the troubles with the American colonies and a staunch supporter of the coercive policies of George III. (See Burke's *Speech on Conciliation*.) Sackville, prominent in George III's government about the same time.

Line 23. **Howes and Clintons.** Viscount Howe and Sir Henry Clinton, British generals against the Americans.

Page 155. Line 44. **Drury Lane.** A street in London in which there was a famous theater. At the time Burns wrote, this street bore a rather unsavory reputation.

Line 58. **Polycrate.** Polycrates, tyrant of Samos in the sixth century, B.C.

Line 60. **Almagro and Pizarro.** Spanish soldiers concerned in the conquest of Peru. In these lines Burns is mentioning historical examples of brutal harshness to common people, resembling the harshness proposed against the Highlanders mentioned in the heading to the poem.

## EPISTLE TO MRS. SCOTT

Page 167. Stanza V. **To the nine.** Probably an allusion to the nine Muses.

## EPISTLE TO DR. BLACKLOCK

Page 173. Stanza V. Burns is humorously alluding to the classical Muses, who made use of the fountain of Castalia.

Page 174. Stanza X. Burns's greetings in this last stanza are to Dr. Blacklock's sister and his wife; but the language of a poultry farmer has been criticized as not in very good taste in view of the character of the blind poet.

## TAM O' SHANTER

Page 180. Line 28. **Kirkton Jean.** Supposed to mean one Jean Kennedy of Kirkoswald, though the tavern kept by this woman was so reputable as to be sometimes called "the ladies' house."

Page 181. Line 61. A relative pronoun is to be understood between *snow* and *falls.*

Page 186. Line 206. Burns provided the following note for this passage: "It is a well-known fact that witches, or any evil spirits, have no power to follow a poor wight any farther than the middle of the next running stream. It may be proper likewise to mention to the benighted traveller, that when he falls in with *bogles,* whatever danger may be in his going forward, there is much more hazard in turning back."

# SONGS

## MY NANIE, O

Page 189. Line 1. **Lugar.** A small stream not far from Burns's home.

## GREEN GROW THE RASHES

Page 191. Stanza IV. **Wisest man,** etc. The allusion is to King Solomon.

## FAREWELL SONG TO THE BANKS OF AYR

Page 193. Stanza IV. **Coila.** Kyle, the central district of Ayrshire, in which Burns lived.

### OF A' THE AIRTS THE WIND CAN BLAW

Page 195. Stanza I. An alternative reading of the fifth line, preferred by some editors, is, "There's wild-woods' grow, and rivers' row." In this peculiar line, *grow* and *row* are nouns equivalent to *growing* and *rolling*.

### O, WERE I ON PARNASSUS HILL

Page 196. Stanza I. **Parnassus.** The mountain of the Muses.

**Helicon.** Another mountain frequented by the Muses, but Burns seems to have reference to the fountains. See page 107.

### AULD LANG SYNE

Page 197. The last line of the first stanza and the first line of the chorus are not printed as in the best-known version, in which these lines read, respectively:

And auld lang syne
\* \* \* \* \* \* \*
For auld lang syne, my dear.

Burns, however, once declared the text adopted on page 197 to be the best.

### CARLYLE'S ESSAY ON BURNS

Page 233. Line 3. **Butler.** Samuel Butler (1612-1680), author of *Hudibras*, the noted satire on the Puritans, is supposed to have died in abject poverty, neglected by King Charles II and his court (see page 293). Carlyle's allusion is to the following epigram prompted by the erection of a monument to Butler in Westminster Abbey in 1720:

While Butler, needy Wretch, was yet alive
No Generous Patron would a Dinner give.
See him when starv'd to death and turn'd to Dust
Presented with a monumental Bust.
The Poet's Fate is here an Emblem show'n;
He asked for Bread and he receiv'd a Stone.

Line 4. **Supply and demand.** Carlyle speaks ironically of one of the fundamental maxims of the political economy of John Stuart Mill and his school.

Line 6. **The inventor,** etc. James Hargreaves, inventor of the spinning jenny, did in fact die in poverty, in 1778, though his invention was one of the most important in the history of modern manufacturing.

Line 16. **Brave mausoleum.** Carlyle means the tomb at Dumfries—a structure of Greek design, adorned with pillars and surmounted by a tin dome. Inside is a marble group representing the genius of Scotland throwing the mantle of inspiration about the figure of Burns standing beside a plow.

Line 18. **The street,** etc. Burns Street in Dumfries, which while the poet lived in it was called the Mill Vennel.

Line 22. **Sixth narrative.** It is not certain precisely what *five* biographies of Burns antedating Lockhart's (1828) Carlyle means. Lockhart at the beginning of Chapter VIII mentions "the four principal biographers of our poet, Heron, Currie, Walker, and Irving." The fifth in Carlyle's mind might possibly be Cromek (from whom Lockhart often quotes), but is probably Peterkin. In chronological order the books by these men are as follows:

Heron, Robert: *A Memoir of the Life of the Late Robert Burns.* 1797.

Currie, James: *The Works of R.B.* With an account of his life, etc. 1800; many times revised and reprinted.

Irving, David: *The Lives of the Scottish Poets.* 1804.

Cromek, R. H.: *Reliques of R.B.* 1808. (Not a formal biography, but contains much valuable biographical material.)

Walker, Josiah: *An Account of the Life and Character of R.B.* 1811. (First appeared in an edition of Burns's Poems.)

Peterkin, Alexander: *A Review of the Life of R.B.,* etc. 1815.

Line 32. **No man . . . is a hero,** etc. A proverbial saying in approximately the form used by Carlyle has been attributed to several different noted French persons—Madame de Sévigné, Madame Cornuel, Marshal Catinet, the Prince de Condé. The idea phrased differently has also been found in Montaigne and in Plutarch.

Page 234. Line 9. **Sir Thomas Lucy.** Owner of an estate near Stratford from which, according to Shakespeare's earliest biographers, he and some evil companions stole deer. The tradition says that after Shakespeare wrote a satirical ballad about the case Lucy pushed the prosecution so far that the future poet left his home and went to London.

Line 10. **John à Combe.** A wealthy wool merchant of Stratford, on whom Shakespeare is said to have written a satirical epitaph.

Line 19. **The Honorable Excise Commissioners.** Burns's superiors during the years when he was in the revenue service.

Line 20. **The Caledonian Hunt.** An organization of Scottish noblemen and gentry interested in sports, to whom Burns, by permission, dedicated the second edition of his *Poems* (Edinburgh, 1787).

Line 22. **Ayr Writers, . . . New and Old Light Clergy.** See "Holy Willie's Prayer" and "The Holy Fair" (pages 68, 76).

Page 236. Line 3. **Constable's Miscellany.** A series of standard works published at popular prices by Archibald Constable, the noted Edinburgh publisher who founded the *Edinburgh Review* and published many of Sir Walter Scott's works, and whose failure in 1826 (together with the failure of the Ballantynes) involved Scott in a tremendous financial loss.

Line 14. **Morris Birkbeck.** Author of *Notes on a Journey in America, from the Coast of Virginia to the Territory of Illinois.* London, 1818.

Page 237. Line 29. **The "nine days."** An allusion to the common phrase "a nine days' wonder"—a prodigy that rouses interest for only a short time.

Page 238. Line 7. **No eye but his,** etc. Carlyle's statements are greatly exaggerated, for Ramsay, Fergusson, and others had recognized the poetical value of the sort of material Burns used and had used forms which Burns closely imitated. In fact, Burns seldom wrote without a model before him, but luckily he usually managed to improve on his model.

Line 34. **Fergusson.** Robert Fergusson (1750-1774), in spite of his very short life, is an important poet because of Burns's frank recognition of him as a master. For the extent of Fergusson's influence, see page 20.

**Ramsay.** Allan Ramsay (1686-1758) was the most famous Scottish poet of the eighteenth century before Burns. See page 20.

Page 240. Line 4. **Sir Hudson Lowe.** The British commander of St. Helena, the island in the South Atlantic where Napoleon Bonaparte died in 1821 after six years of exile.

Line 5. **"Amid the melancholy main."** "Plac'd far amid the melancholy main" is a line from James Thomson's *Castle of Indolence,* Canto I, Stanza 30.

Line 6. **"Spectacle of pity and fear."** An allusion to the explanation of tragedy in Aristotle's *Poetics.* By moving in us fear and pity, tragedy is said to purge our minds of those emotions.

Line 20. **"Eternal Melodies."** This phrase is undoubtedly a translation from Carlyle's German readings. In a letter to Emerson (1837) he speaks of his [Emerson's] "ear for the ewigen Melodien, which pipe in the winds around us."

Page 241. Line 9. **The "Daisy."** See page 146.

Line 10. **"Wee, cowrin, tim'rous beastie."** See page 94.

Line 17. **"It raises his thoughts,"** etc. A slightly inaccurate allusion to a passage in Burns's *First Common*

*Place Book* under the date, April, 1784, in relation to his short poem called "Winter, a Dirge." He is writing of his pleasure in a winter walk and says: "It is my best season for devotion; my mind is rapt up in a kind of enthusiasm to Him who, in the pompous language of Scripture, "walks on the wings of the wind.'" The Biblical allusion is to *Psalm* CIV, 3.

Page 242. Line 12. **"Insolence of condescension."** Carlyle's use of quotation marks may be due to a vague recollection of such sentences as this from Lockhart: "There was probably no blast that pierced this haughty soul so sharply as the contumely of condescension." Elsewhere Lockhart speaks of Burns's "nervous intolerance of condescension."

Line 24. **"Quick to learn."** From line 20 of "A Bard's Epitaph"; see page 154.

Line 30. **"A soul like an Æolian harp,"** etc. This quotation may be an echo from the letter of Burns to Mrs. Dunlop which Carlyle quotes later (page 257). The figure has been used by a number of British poets.

Line 33. **The world found no fitter business.** Since the excise scheme was Burns's own, Carlyle's sarcasm here seems not entirely justified.

Page 244. Line 21. **"In homely, rustic jingle."** Apparently a slightly inaccurate allusion to line 6 of the "Epistle to Davie"; see page 49.

Line 25. **Si vis me flere.** Carlyle quotes the first few words of a passage from Horace's *Ars Poetica*, which means, "If you would have me weep, you yourself must first know sorrow."

Page 245. Line 32. **His Harolds and Giaours.** An allusion to Byron's hero, Childe Harold, who is in the main a sort of portrait of Byron himself, and to his poem, *The Giaour* ("giaour" is a Turkish name for Christian, meaning "infidel").

Page 247. Line 33. **Mrs. Dunlop.** Shortly after the publication of the Kilmarnock edition of Burns's poems in 1786, Mrs. Dunlop, a wealthy woman living about fifteen miles from Burns's home at Mossgiel, was so delighted on reading "The Cotter's Saturday Night" that she immediately sent a messenger with a note expressing her admiration for the work and ordering half a dozen copies of the *Poems*. Thus began a correspondence that lasted during the remainder of Burns's life, and which contains much important biographical material.

Page 248. Line 16. **Virgins of the Sun,** etc. Carlyle is making a general allusion to romantic and unreal fiction and poetry, dealing with remote times and peoples, such as Moore's *Lalla Rookh*, Byron's verse tales of Turkish setting (*The Giaour*, etc.), Campbell's *Gertrude of Wyoming* (for the "copper-coloured Chiefs in wampum"), and possibly such works of Scott as *The Talisman*, or Cooper's Indian tales.

**Page 249. Line 32. A vates** (Latin) was primarily a prophet, one who foretold events, but the word came to mean an inspired singer—the sense in which Carlyle uses it here.

**Line 35. Delphi.** The location of the most famous of Greek oracles, where future events were foretold.

**Page 250. Line 4. The Minerva Press.** A London press, noted for turning out sentimental and trashy novels.

**Line 21. "Travels from Dan,"** etc. An allusion to a passage in Sterne's *Sentimental Journey*: "I pity the man who can travel from Dan to Beersheba and cry, ''Tis all barren.'" The Biblical allusion is to *Judges* XX, 1.

**Line 30. Borgia.** The Borgias, Cesare and Lucrezia, of an Italian noble family of the end of the fifteenth century, have been accepted as types of wickedness and are here contrasted with Martin Luther, the leader of the Protestant Reformation in Germany.

**Line 34. Mossgiel and Tarbolton.** Early homes and haunts of Burns.

**Line 36. Crockford's.** A famous gambling club-house in London.

**The Tuileries.** A royal palace in Paris that occupied the present site of the Jardin des Tuileries. The name means tile-kilns.

**Page 251. Line 20. The "Wounded Hare."** See page 171.

**Line 23. Halloween.** See pages 85-94.

**Line 25. Theocritus.** The most famous writer of *idyls* in Greek—little pictures of real life and rustic scenes; a Syracusan of the third century B.C.

**Line 26. The "Holy Fair."** See pages 76-84.

**Line 27. Council of Trent.** Held at Trent in the Tyrol, 1545-1563; its chief work was in condemnation of the Protestant Reformation.

**Roman Jubilee.** In the Roman Catholic church a jubilee is "a year in which remission from the penal consequences of sin is granted by the church to those who repent and perform certain acts." (Century Dictionary.)

**Page 253. Line 2. Retzsch.** A German artist famous for his etchings illustrative of the works of Goethe, Schiller, Shakespeare, and others. A burin is an engraver's or etcher's tool for cutting lines in metal.

**Line 8. "Winter Night."** See page 161.

**Line 31. The "Auld Brig."** See Burns's poem, "The Brigs of Ayr," which is a discussion between the old bridge and the new bridge in process of erection. It is the *new* bridge of which the fall is prophesied.

Page 254. Line 15. **Poussin.** A French landscape artist of the seventeenth century, one of whose paintings, hanging in the Louvre in Paris, has for its subject *The Deluge.*

Line 20. **"Auld Mare."** See page 117. The passages in Homer mentioned by Carlyle occur in the *Odyssey,* Book IX, in Odysseus' account of his adventure with Polyphemos; and in the *Iliad,* Book XXIV, lines 265 ff.

Line 23. **"Burn-the-Wind."** Burnewin (a contraction of the form Carlyle uses) is a blacksmith in Burns's poem "Scotch Drink."

Line 30. **"The pale moon is setting,"** etc. This stanza is inaccurately quoted from the song "Open the Door to Me, O." It should read:

> The wan moon is setting behind the white wave,
>> And Time is setting with me, O!
> False friends, false love, farewell! for mair
>> I'll ne'er trouble them nor thee, O!

Page 255. Line 7. **Richardson and Defoe.** The eighteenth century realistic novelists, Samuel Richardson, author of *Clarissa Harlowe,* and Daniel Defoe, author of *Robinson Crusoe,* are here meant.

Line 24. **"A gentleman that derived,"** etc. See the "Elegy on Captain Matthew Henderson," page 175.

Line 27. **"Red-wat-shod."** See page 65.

Line 34. **Professor Stewart.** Dugald Stewart, professor of moral philosophy in the University of Edinburgh, 1785-1810, was one of the group of intellectual people who made much of Burns after the appearance of his first volume of poems. Professor Stewart communicated various notes regarding the poet to Dr. Currie, the first important editor of Burns's works, including what Carlyle quotes here.

Page 256. Line 9. **Such cases as that of Keats.** This passage is grossly unfair and was modified when the essay appeared in the *Edinburgh Review;* but Carlyle evidently maintained his prejudice against Keats, for in collecting his essays for separate publication he restored the sentence as printed.

Line 25. **Novum Organum.** The chief philosophical work of Francis Bacon; written in Latin, as the title indicates. The title means "a new method" and refers to Bacon's championship of the inductive method of reasoning.

Page 257. Line 10. **"The highest . . . cannot,"** etc. In Carlyle's *Reminiscences* he mentions this thought as from Goethe.

Line 20. **"We know nothing,"** etc. Carlyle quotes from a letter of Burns to Mrs. Dunlop dated "Ellisland, New-year-day Morning, 1789."

Page 258. Line 20. **"Love furthers knowledge."** This exact expression does not appear in dictionaries of quotations; but in Carlyle's essay on the death of Goethe he repeated what was evidently to him a familiar idea: "Love is ever the beginning of knowledge as fire is of light."

Line 30. **"The hoary hawthorn,"** etc. See the passage quoted on page 257.

Page 259. Line 3. **"I thought me,"** etc. Quoted from "A Winter Night"; see page 161. For the "ragged roof and chinky wall," see line 79.

Line 20. **The very Devil**, etc. See "Address to the Deil," page 130.

Line 27. **"He is the father,"** etc. The quotation is from Laurence Sterne's famous *Tristram Shandy*. "My uncle Toby"— Captain Toby Shandy—is famous for his sympathy with all creatures.

Line 32. **"Indignation makes verses."** A bit of translation from the famous Roman satirist, Juvenal (Satire I, 79)— Facit indignatio versum.

Page 260. Line 7. **Johnson said he loved a good hater.** In Mrs. Piozzi's *Anecdotes of Samuel Johnson*, the "famous lexicographer" is quoted as saying, "Dear Bathurst . . . . was a man to my very heart's content: he hated a fool, and he hated a rogue, and he hated a whig: he was a very good hater."

Line 20. **"Dweller in yon dungeon dark."** The poem to which Carlyle gives rather grotesque over-emphasis in these lines was ironically entitled "Ode, Sacred to the Memory of Mrs. Oswald of Auchencruive," and was written in 1789, after Burns and a friend had been driven out of an inn one stormy night by "the funeral pageantry of the late great Mrs. Oswald." Burns declared in a letter to Dr. Moore that the lady was detested by her tenants and servants "with the most heartfelt cordiality"; but "indignation" over being caused a little temporary discomfort on a winter night can hardly justify such a poem as this about a dead lady. To be sure, Burns's habitual dislike of the rich and the great, especially if he had the slightest reason for considering that they displayed a mean spirit, is an important element of his "indignation" in this case; nevertheless the poem savors too much of petty spite to be in any way a credit.

Line 22. **The Furies of Æschylus.** One of the important surviving plays of Æschylus, the first of the great Greek writers of tragedy, is *The Eumenides* (or Furies).

Line 24. **"Darkness visible."** See Milton's *Paradise Lost*, Book I, line 63.

Line 32. **"Scots wha hae,"** etc. See page 219.

Page 261. Line 13. **McPherson's Farewell.** See page 194.

Line 16. **Cacus.** A giant son of Vulcan who stole cattle from Hercules (see Virgil's *Aeneid,* Book VIII, lines 18 ff). McPherson was hanged for cattle-stealing.

Line 28. **Thebes.** The scene of some of the most important events treated in Greek tragedy (notably the story of Œdipus). "Pelops' line" was the family to which belonged Agamemnon and Menelaus, Greek leaders in the Trojan War. In his phrasing Carlyle alludes to lines 99, 100, of Milton's *Il Penseroso.*

Page 262. Line 17. **"Address to the Mouse,"** etc. For the three poems here mentioned see pages 94, 117, 44.

Line 33. **Tam o' Shanter.** See pages 179-187. Subsequent opinion has generally disagreed with Carlyle's comparative depreciation of this poem, which is considered one of the most effective of verse tales.

Page 263. Lines 14, 15. **Tieck, Musäus.** These two German writers of tales dealt with material from ancient folklore. The point of Carlyle's comparison lies in the fact that Tieck was considered to enter more fully into the spirit of the past; Musäus to be more artificial.

Line 30. **"Shakespearean" qualities.** Carlyle is alluding to the fact that Sir Walter Scott said, in discussion of "Tam o' Shanter," "No poet, with the exception of Shakespeare, ever possessed the power of exciting the most varied and discordant emotions with such rapid transitions." Lockhart quotes this from an article by Scott in the *Quarterly Review.*

Page 264. Line 2. **"Poems."** Quoted for distinction from Songs.

Line 5. **"The Jolly Beggars."** See pages 97-109.

Line 33. **Teniers.** A noted Flemish painter of the seventeenth century whose subjects were predominantly realistic interior scenes from the life of the people of his day.

Page 265. Line 3. **"Beggar's Opera,"** etc. *The Beggar's Opera* (1728), by John Gay, and *The Beggar's Bush* (1622), by John Fletcher and others, were comedies representing somewhat the type of life presented by Burns in "The Jolly Beggars." Burns, however, is much more realistic. Lockhart said these two works "sink into tameness in the comparison" with Burns's "cantata."

Line 24. **"By persons of quality."** It was a very common device in poetic miscellanies to print trivial songs as "by a person of quality."

Line 26. **"In the flowing and watery vein,"** etc. Carlyle quotes from Bacon's *Advancement of Learning,* Book One, IV (2). Jeronymo Osorio (1506-1580), bishop of Silves from 1567, and author of a Latin history of the reign of Emanuel I, King of Portugal, is the person mentioned.

Page 266. Line 34. **"Willie Brew'd,"** etc. See page 204.

Line 35. **"Mary in Heaven."** See page 201.

Page 267. Lines 1-3. For the songs here mentioned, see pages 197, 214, 219, respectively.

Line 10. **Our Fletcher's aphorism.** Andrew Fletcher (1655-1716), a Scottish politician and political writer. Carlyle alludes to the following passage from a letter of Fletcher's to a Scottish nobleman: "I know a very wise man that believed that if a man were permitted to make all the ballads, he need not care who should make the laws of a nation."

Page 268. Line 6. **Grays and Glovers.** It is hard to see why Thomas Gray, author of the famous "Elegy in a Country Churchyard," should here be associated with Richard Glover, an unimportant contemporary of Gray. Perhaps the association is partly because of the alliteration, but apparently Carlyle underestimated the "Elegy."

Line 12. **Rambler, Rasselas.** Dr. Johnson's *Rambler* was a publication somewhat in imitation of Addison and Steele's *Spectator,* consisting of essays on various topics of current interest, tales to illustrate points the author wished to make, etc. *Rasselas* was a brief "novel with a purpose," with its scene laid in Abyssinia.

Line 18. **Geneva.** Carlyle is here alluding to the fact that owing to the great freedom allowed in the Swiss city Geneva, a great many foreign scholars and writers lived and wrote there. The situation, however, was not parallel in Edinburgh, for there the writers were natives subject to foreign influences.

Line 22. **Boston.** Thomas (not John) Boston, a Scottish Presbyterian divine, published *Human Nature in Its Fourfold State* in 1720. *The Spectator* was several years earlier—1711-12.

Line 30. **Lord Kames.** Henry Home, Lord Kames (1696-1782), published *Essays on the Principles of Morality and Natural Religion* in 1751, and other works followed.

Line 32. **Hume, Robertson, Smith.** David Hume (1711-1776), most famous for skeptical views in philosophy, author of a *History of England* and a number of religious and philosophical works; William Robertson (1721-1793), author of a *History of Scotland* and other historical works; and Adam Smith (1723-1790), whose *Wealth of Nations* is regarded as the foundation of the science of political economy, are the authors meant here.

Line 35. **"Fervid genius."** An allusion to a phrase in Buchanan's Latin history of the Scotch attributing to this people a "perfervid genius."

Page 269. Line 16. **La Flèche.** A town in France where Hume lived for three or four years and wrote some of his earlier works.

Page 270. Line 7. **"Doctrine of Rent,"** etc. Adam Smith announced the "doctrine of rent"; Hume was the author of *Natural History of Religion.*

Line 26. **"A tide of Scottish prejudice,"** etc. From Burns's autobiographical letter to Dr. Moore, written August 2, 1787.

Page 271. Line 7. **"A wish,"** etc. Quoted from Burns's "Epistle to Mrs. Scott"; see page 165.

Page 272. Line 29. **"Rock of Independence."** In one of Burns's letters (to Miss Davies, 1791) he says, "Ascend that rock, Independence."

Page 274. Line 27. **The crossing of a brook.** An allusion to Cæsar's crossing the Rubicon.

Page 275. Line 10. **"Let us worship God."** An allusion to stanzas XII and XIV of "The Cotter's Saturday Night." See page 114.

Line 16. **A "little band of brethren."** Possibly an allusion to this line from Shakespeare's *Henry V:* "We few, we happy few, we band of brothers."

Line 33. **"In glory and in joy,"** etc. Quoted (not quite accurately) from stanza seven of Wordsworth's "Resolution and Independence."

Page 277. Line 34. **"Passions raging like demons."** Another allusion to Burns's autobiographical letter to Dr. Moore; the passage reads: "My passions, when once lighted up, raged like so many devils till they got vent in rime."

Page 278. Line 17. **"Hungry Ruin,"** etc. Quoted by Burns toward the end of the autobiographical letter to Dr. Moore.

Line 20. **The "gloomy night is gathering fast."** See page 192.

Page 279. Line 4. **A "mockery king."** Apparently an allusion to Shakespeare's *Richard II*—IV, i, 260—"a mockery king of snow."

Line 7. **Rienzi.** A Roman political reformer of the fourteenth century, who led a revolution that overthrew the aristocracy, but who subsequently alienated the people by arbitrary conduct. Bulwer Lytton has a novel on his career; Wagner an opera.

Page 280. Line 10. **Sir Walter Scott's.** Quoted by Lockhart from a letter of Scott's.

Line 13. **Virgilium vidi tantum.** I have seen Virgil to this extent.

Page 281. Line 48. **"In malam partem."** Disparagingly.

Page 283. Line 14. **Blacklock.** See page 172.

Page 284. Line 11. **Lie at the pool.** An allusion to the pool of Bethesda, *John* V:2 ff.

Line 28. **"Did not intend,"** etc. Carlyle, following Lockhart, slightly twists a passage from a letter of Burns to Bishop Geddes, dated February 3, 1789: "There is a certain stigma affixed to the character of a revenue officer; but I do not pretend to borrow honour from my profession."

Page 286. Line 1. **Convivial Mæcenases.** An allusion to the famous Roman Mæcenas, friend and patron of the poets Virgil and Horace.

Line 17. **The "Rock of Independence."** See note on page 272, line 29.

Page 289. Line 10. **"If he entered an inn,"** etc. This is quoted from Lockhart.

Line 25. **"Thoughtless follies,"** etc. Quoted from "A Bard's Epitaph"; see page 152.

Page 291. Line 27. **A close observer of manners.** Carlyle may have had in mind Dr. Johnson, whose famous letter to Lord Chesterfield is often quoted in relation to literary patronage. In calling patronage "twice cursed," Carlyle is parodying Portia's words (*Merchant of Venice*, IV, i, 186) as to "the quality of mercy"—"It is twice blessed," etc.

Page 293. Line 6. **Butler.** See page 314.

Line 7. **Cervantes.** This great Spanish novelist, author of *Don Quixote*, was very poor and was even imprisoned during the latter part of the reign of King Philip II of Spain, because of debt to the government.

Line 8. **Cut down our thorns,** etc. Thorns (hawthorn bushes or trees) are used for hedges or *fences*, and their fruit, which is useless, is *haws*.

Line 10. **"Nobility and gentry,"** etc. An allusion to the phrasing of Burns's dedication of the first Edinburgh edition of his poems "To the Noblemen and Gentlemen of the Caledonian Hunt": "A Scottish Bard, proud of the name, and whose highest ambition is to sing in his Country's service— where shall he so properly look for patronage as to the illustrious Names of his native Land?"

Page 294. Line 3. **"Love one another,"** etc. Carlyle has put together, as if one quotation, two important elements of Christ's teaching; the first from *John* XV:12, 17, the second from *Galatians* VI:2.

Line 22. **Roger Bacon.** This English philosopher of the thirteenth century (1214-1294) must not be confused with Francis Bacon, the contemporary of Shakespeare. Roger Bacon was a Franciscan monk whose advanced scientific views caused his writings to be condemned by the Church as heretical, and himself to be imprisoned.

**Galileo** (1564-1642). The noted Italian physicist and astronomer, who got into trouble with the Inquisition because of his insistence (among other heresies) that the earth moves.

Line 23. **Tasso** (1544-1595). Italian poet, author of the famous poem of the Crusades, *Jerusalem Delivered*. He was confined as insane for a number of years. Carlyle was probably influenced, in writing as he does, by the theory adopted by Goethe, in his play *Torquato Tasso,* that the confinement of the poet was not because of real insanity, but because of his aspirations to the hand of the sister of the Duke of Ferrara.

Line 24. **Camoëns** (1524-1580). A Portuguese poet, author of the *Lusiad,* an epic dealing chiefly with the exploits of Portuguese explorers (Vasco da Gama and others).

Line 25. **"Persecuted they the Prophets."** See *Matthew* V: 12.

Page 296. Line 2. **Restaurateur.** The keeper of a restaurant.

Line 34. **Locke.** John Locke (1632-1704) was a refugee in Holland from 1683 to 1689 because he was suspected, though wrongly, of being involved in the conspiracy of Shaftesbury against the succession of James II. He was not, however, literally "banished as a traitor."

Page 297. Line 1. **Was Milton rich,** etc. Carlyle alludes to Milton's blindness and to his humble and even dangerous position after the restoration of Charles II, because of the prominent position he had held as Cromwell's Latin secretary. In *Paradise Lost,* VII, 30, he speaks of himself as writing for a "fit audience, though few."

Line 6. **Did not Cervantes,** etc. The circumstances of the composition of *Don Quixote* are here meant. See note on page 293, line 7.

Line 8. **The Araucana.** A long poem by Alonso de Ercilla dealing with the Spanish conquest of a portion of Chile called Araucania. The poet took part in the expedition.

Line 27. **The "golden calf of Self-love."** An allusion to the golden calf which Aaron made for the Children of Israel; see *Exodus* XXXII.

Page 298. Line 20. **Rabelais** (1495-1553), though a monk, was a "free thinker." A familiar but unproved legend about him is that on his deathbed he said, "I am going to seek a great perhaps."

Page 299. Line 17. **Jean Paul.** Jean Paul Richter (1763-1825) was one of Carlyle's favorite authors. See pages 32 and 33.

Page 300. Line 30. **"Purchased a pocket copy,"** etc. Carlyle alludes here to a letter Burns wrote to his friend William Nicol from Mauchline, June 18, 1787. He says: "I have bought a pocket Milton, which I carry perpetually about with me, in order to study . . . that great personage, Satan."

Page 301. Line 8. **We look sadly,** etc. Byron had been dead but four years when Carlyle was writing this essay.

Line 35. **The words of Milton,** etc. Carlyle alludes to a

passage in Milton's *Apology for Smectymnuus:* "I was con-
firmed in this opinion, that he who would not be frustrate
of his purpose to write well hereafter in laudable things
ought himself to be a true poem . . . . not presuming to
sing high praises of heroic men . . . unless he have in
himself the experience and the practice of all that which is
praiseworthy."

Page 303.  Line 4.  **Plebiscita.**  Decisions by the common
people.

Line 18.  **Ginhorse.**  A horse that goes around and around
in a circle, turning a "gin"—a machine or mill of some sort.

Line 30.  **Ramsgate and the Isle of Dogs.**  Places only a
short distance from London.

Page 304.  Line 5.  **Valclusa Fountain.**  A fountain at
Vaucluse, near Avignon, in southern France.  The Italian
poet Petrarch lived at Vaucluse and celebrated the fountain
in his poems.

# APPENDIX

## HELPS TO STUDY

### THE LIFE OF BURNS

Make additions to the list of historical events during Burns's life (p. 9). With regard to English and American relations see particularly the Lake English Classics edition of Burke's *Speech on Conciliation* (by C. H. Ward, 1919).

For more detailed explanation of the literary movement summarized briefly on pages 10 and 11, see Newcomer's *English Literature* (pp. 217 ff.). For specimens illustrative of the movement and of the authors mentioned see Newcomer and Andrews's *Twelve Centuries of English Poetry and Prose* and the Lake editions of *English Poems* (edited by Vida D. Scudder), *The Golden Treasury*, and *English Popular Ballads*.

When, where, and in what condition of life was Burns born (p. 11)? What parental influences are important?

What do you find significant about Burns's education (p. 12) as preparation for his career as a poet? Examine Carlyle's statements on this matter (pp. 238, 274).

What sort of life did Burns lead during his boyhood? Collect reflections in the poems, and in all that you learn about Burns, of the influences of this manner of life.

At what age and under what inspiration did Burns first write poetry (p. 13)? Study the poem in question (p. 187) and Burns's own comments on it (pp. 165 ff.).

Where and when did Burns write most of his best poems? Identify in the selections the poems alluded to on page 14.

Who was Jean Armour (p. 14)? Examine all mention of her that you find in this volume (see the Index).

On the basis of all material you can get (pp. 15, 201, 213, and authorities mentioned in the Bibliography, pp. 38-40), what are your own conclusions as to the dispute regarding "Highland Mary"?

When and where were Burns's poems first published (p. 15)?

With what success (p. 16)? What were the principal results as to the main course of his life?

Study Carlyle's discussion of Burns in Edinburgh (pp. 278 ff.). What, on the whole, was the effect on Burns of his Edinburgh experience?

What occupations did Burns attempt to combine (pp. 16, 17)? With what success? And what final result?

Examine in connection with the brief summary as to Burns's life in Dumfries (p. 17) Carlyle's more detailed discussion and analysis (pp. 285 ff.), and try to draw your own conclusions.

What poetical work did Burns do during his last years? Study the songs on pages 208-232 for your conclusions as to the quality of this work.

When, and in what circumstances did Burns die (p. 18)?

## BURNS'S WORKS IN GENERAL

Find for yourself notable examples of the chief merits of Burns's poetry as summarized on page 18.

What was Matthew Arnold's main criticism of Burns? Specify poems that seem to you to furnish a basis for this criticism. How far do you agree with it? Find examples, also, of the good qualities that Arnold mentions (p. 19).

The bit of quotation at the end of the paragraph on Burns's democracy (p. 19) is from one of Wordsworth's poems on Burns, which may be read with interest and profit.

Find all the passages you can where "Burns the rebel" and the democrat is revealed (e.g., pp. 48, 50, 153, etc.).

Which poems in this volume are least to be characterized as "mere occasional effusions" (pp. 19, 243)? Point out some of the best qualities in poems that were "occasional effusions."

What were Burns's principal models in composition (p. 20)? Find all mention of these models in the selected poems.

Into what two main divisions are Burns's poetical works divided (p. 20)? Discuss the subordinate classification informally indicated on pages 20-23.

What is it important to remember as to the manner in which Burns composed his songs (p. 22)? After study of the selections—both poems and songs—in this volume, how far do you agree with Carlyle's comparative estimate (pp. 265-67)? Work out carefully reasons for your conclusion.

List the love songs in this book, and as to each one decide whose point of view is being presented (hints on p. 23).

Do you find the songs really singable? Have you a favorite song, or a favorite stanza, among those selected? Discuss the choice, with reasons.

## SELECTED POEMS FROM BURNS

The "Mailie" poems.—Find evidences of both humor and sympathy in the treatment of "Mailie." Make a list of the poems of Burns which you find have the stanza of "Poor Mailie's Elegy" (described on p. 305). Can you come to any conclusion as to the kind of poetry to which this stanza is best adapted? See Carlyle's estimate of the "Elegy" (p. 262).

"Man Was Made to Mourn."—Sum up the ideas most characteristic of Burns in this poem.

"Epistle to Davie."—In what other poems of Burns do you find the stanza (p. 305) of this Epistle? Pick out the most significant and characteristic ideas of Burns expressed here.

"Second Epistle to Davie."—Compare other poems in which Burns gives his views of "the bardie clan" (pp. 59, 66, 137, etc.).

"Epistle to J. Lapraik."—What are the chief personal revelations as to Burns here given?

"Epistle to William Simpson."—Sum up Burns's ideas as to the province of a patriotic poet. What aspects of nature inspired him most? Find in other poems confirmation of your conclusions.

"Holy Willie's Prayer."—What is the point of view here assumed? Is this an irreverent or sacrilegious poem? Answer with reasons.

"Epistle to the Rev. John McMath."—Sum up the attitude toward religion that you find indicated here. Take into consideration the related poems you have read and decide whether Carlyle was right in saying Burns had no religion (p. 298).

"The Holy Fair."—Note the peculiarities of the stanza of this poem and "Halloween" (p. 307). Do you know of any religious observances of recent times, or of the present, that may be compared with those here described? See Carlyle's mention of this poem (p. 251).

"Halloween."—How many of the customs here portrayed, or similar ones, have you ever encountered or read about elsewhere? Enumerate American Hallowe'en customs. This is one of the most difficult of Burns's poems to understand. Do you find it any less interesting than the others? What does Carlyle mean in calling this a "Scottish Idyl" (pp. 251, 318)?

"To a Mouse."—What attitude toward animals is indicated here? Consider this with the other poems in which a similar feeling is expressed. How is this poem given a personal application? See Carlyle's allusions (pp. 241, 262).

"The Jolly Beggars."—Examine this work carefully in connection with Carlyle's comments (pp. 264-5), trying to decide for sufficient reasons whether you agree with him, both in general and on specific points. Was Arnold inconsistent in calling this a "puissant and splendid production" (p. 97), in spite of his criticism of Burns for presenting an ugly world of "Scotch drink, Scotch religion, and Scotch manners" (p. 18)?

"The Cotter's Saturday Night."—Does this seem to you to deserve the exceptional popularity it has always had among Burns's works? Is it as a whole particularly characteristic of the poet? Does it all give the impression of perfect sincerity? What do you think of the English parts of it?

"The Auld Farmer . . . to His Auld Mare."—Where do you place this for difficulty among the poems read? Note Carlyle's allusions to it (pp. 254, 262).

"The Twa Dogs."—Why do you suppose this was placed first in the early editions of Burns? Do you see any reasons why he or his publisher should regard such an arrangement as "putting his best foot foremost"? Sum up the view of the life of common folk, and the life of the gentry, here given.

"Address to the Deil."—Do you find this mainly humorous or mainly serious? Are there notably poetic passages? Answer specifically. See Carlyle's allusion to the poem (p. 259).

"Epistle to James Smith."—What does this indicate as to Burns's purpose in poetry? How seriously do you take him on this point? What does it indicate as to his "philosophy of life"? What elements of self-defense are involved?

"To a Mountain Daisy."—Compare this with other poems of Burns as to the prominence of the note of pure poetic beauty. See Carlyle's mention on page 241.

"Epistle to a Young Friend."—In what ways does this differ from all the other verse epistles in this volume? In what parts, particularly, has Burns been accused of inconsistency? Do you find a similar note in "The Cotter's Saturday Night"?

"A Bard's Epitaph."—To what extent do you find this true self-characterization? Note Carlyle's quotations (pp. 242, 289).

"Address of Beelzebub."—What is the point of view here? Do you find it perfectly sustained? Explain in plain terms what the poem means to you.

"Address to the Unco Guid."—Sum up in a sentence or two the main idea of this poem, and consider with it other expressions by Burns of similar meaning (pp. 21, 142, etc.).

"A Winter Night."—Do you find sufficient merit here to justify Carlyle's references (pp. 253, 259)?

"Epistle to Mrs. Scott."—See Carlyle's allusion (p. 271).

"The Wounded Hare."—See Carlyle's mention (p. 251). Do you find this little poem of poetic value?

"Epistle to Dr. Blacklock."—What is the important personal revelation? The important assertion as to one's duty?

"Elegy on Captain Matthew Henderson."—See Carlyle's allusion (p. 255). Study this poem and "The Humble Petition of Bruar Water" for detailed and accurate knowledge of nature.

"Tam o' Shanter."—Discuss in detail the fairness of Carlyle's estimate (pp. 262-3, 321). What do you think of lines 59-66? Why should there be such details as those of lines 89-96, 131-142? Find examples of the qualities Scott mentioned (p. 321). Do you know of any other witch story so well told as this?

"Mary Morison."—Do you detect any way in which this poem differs from other early songs of Burns—e.g., in perfection of finish, lack of wordiness, restraint, or suggestiveness?

"McPherson's Farewell."—What reasons do you find for Carlyle's stress on this song (p. 261)?

"Auld Lang Syne."—If told that two stanzas of this poem

are finer poetically than the others, which two would you assume to be meant?

"To Mary in Heaven."—Do you think this very famous song deserves its fame from its poetic merits? How do you think it compares with "Highland Mary" (p. 213)? What does your comparison lead you to conclude on the matter of Burns's mastery of English as compared with Scottish?

"Scots Wha Hae."—Compare Burns's own statement as to the composition of this poem with the story about it that Carlyle repeats from Lockhart (p. 260).

"Contented wi' Little," etc.—Compare this as a self-revelation of Burns at the age of thirty-five with self-revelations in some of his friendly epistles of nearly ten years earlier.

"The Braw Wooer."—Who is the speaker and what is the story? Compare this with such other humorous love songs as "Tam Glen" and "Duncan Gray."

## The Scottish Dialect

How is the dialect of Burns related to literary English (pp. 23-24)? When was Scotch literature superior to English?

Which poems in this volume would you call predominantly Scottish? Which, predominantly English? Do you find any that are wholly English?

Collect for yourself examples of pure Scottish words—the most unusual and striking you can find—and of Scottish spelling of English words.

What peculiarity in Burns's rimes is to be accounted for by Scottish custom (p. 27)? Collect examples.

## Carlyle's Life

When and where was Carlyle born (p. 28)? In what ways may his life be linked with that of Burns? Note points of similarity and of contrast between Burns and Carlyle in race, parentage, station in life, early hardships, education, struggles for recognition.

What qualities of Carlyle's parents must have been influential on their son?

Where was Carlyle educated (p. 29)? What was his opinion

of his university? What occupation did he first plan to adopt? What actually was his first occupation after leaving the university? What was his first literary work?

What did Carlyle mean by the "Everlasting No" and the "Everlasting Yea" in his life (p. 30)? Note reflections in the *Essay on Burns* of the stern morality indicated by his struggle.

Whom did Carlyle marry, and what is it important to remember about his wife (pp. 30-31)? Where did the Carlyles live? When did they, respectively, die?

## CARLYLE'S WORKS

What foreign influence in English literature was due considerably to Carlyle (p. 32)?

What were the plan and the main ideas of Carlyle's most characteristic book (p. 33)? Its chief peculiarities of style?

What was Carlyle's theory of history (p. 34), and in what books did he exemplify it? Note the relation of this theory to the view of biography expressed on pages 236-7.

What was Carlyle's attitude toward democracy (p. 35)? What were his main reasons for this attitude? Can you answer his arguments?

Do you believe Carlyle's "gospel of work" is particularly needed now? Give reasons.

## THE ESSAY ON BURNS

When and where was this essay written (p. 31)? When and where first published (p. 36)?

What does the essay purport to be? What part of it is devoted to discussion of the book that suggested it?

Do you consider Carlyle particularly fitted to write about Burns (p. 37)? State fully your reasons.

In what way was Carlyle in this essay influential as a critic of literature (p. 36)? What does he say or imply concerning the function and nature of literary criticism (p. 239, etc.)?

What did Carlyle consider the requirements of the ideal biography (pp. 236-7)? Does this essay, so far as it is biographical, fulfill these requirements?

Do you agree in all respects with Carlyle's estimate of Burns's poetical disadvantages (pp. 238-9)?

What is Carlyle's opinion of the value to the world of a true poet (p. 240 and elsewhere)? Sum up his reasons for considering Burns such a poet.

What is the first "rare excellence" which Carlyle finds in Burns (p. 244)? What poet who did not usually possess this excellence does he contrast with Burns (p. 247)? When is Burns not sincere? And why?

What is the second "peculiar merit" Carlyle finds in Burns's poetry (p. 248)?

What does Carlyle say of Burns's intellectual power? Of the range of his sympathy?

What is the essence of Carlyle's comment on the influence of Burns on nationality in literature (pp. 267 ff.)?

Why does Carlyle put the interest of Burns's life above that of his poems (p. 271)? Would you agree?

Do you think a university training would have aided Burns in writing his kind of poetry (p. 274)? Take into consideration the comparative merits of his more spontaneous poems in Scottish and his more studied poems in English.

What, according to Carlyle, was the crisis in Burns's life (p. 290)? Do you agree that there were for him only the three possibilities that Carlyle mentions? What were the chief causes of Burns's failure?

Note the points of resemblance and difference which Carlyle points out between Burns and Byron (pp. 245-6, 300-302).

Note other literary references in the essay, besides those to Byron. Show the unfairness of the reference to Keats (p. 256).

What do you conclude from this essay as to Carlyle's insight into character, his attitude toward morality, his enthusiasm?

## THEME SUBJECTS

1. The historical background of Burns (hints on pp. 9-10 to be supplemented by use of histories).

2. The literary background of Burns (pp. 10, 20, and indications in the poems and notes).

3. The life of Burns (pp. 11-18).

4. The life of Carlyle (pp. 28-32).

5. A parallel and contrast between the ancestry and early life of Burns and Carlyle.

6. "Poor Mailie's" story (pp. 41-45).

7. Burns as revealed in his verse epistles.

8. A hypocrite I know. (Comparison may be made with "Holy Willie," pp. 68-71.)

9. A modern revival meeting or camp meeting (compare "The Holy Fair," pp. 76 ff.).

10. Hallowe'en customs—in Burns's time and now (pp. 85 ff., 308-10).

11. The story of "The Jolly Beggars" (pp. 97 ff.).

12. A paraphrase of the descriptive parts of "The Cotter's Saturday Night" (pp. 110 ff.).

13. A character study of the "auld farmer" on the basis of his attitude toward his "auld mare Maggie" (pp. 117 ff.).

14. The story of "The Twa Dogs" (pp. 122 ff.).

15. A paraphrase of the "Address to the Deil" (pp. 130 ff.).

16. The story of "Tam o' Shanter" (pp. 179 ff.).

17. My favorite song of Burns (or several "candidates" may be discussed).

18. An elaboration of the story suggested by "Tam Glen," or "Duncan Gray," or "The Braw Wooer" (pp. 203, 214, 229).

19. The *Essay on Burns* as a book review.

20. What a biography should be (pp. 236-7).

21. The qualities of a true poet. (Take into account both Burns's view and Carlyle's view, as indicated in many references above given.)

22. An imaginary conversation between Burns and Scott (see pp. 280-82) on some such topic as Burns's poems (or one of them) or Scott's poetical ambitions.

23. Why Burns's life was a failure. (Discuss Carlyle's view, pp. 290 ff.)

24. Burns and Byron. (Summarize Carlyle's comparisons, pp. 245-6, 300-302.)

25. An original character sketch of Burns, taking into account all that Carlyle says, the self-revelation of the poems, and all other data available (a difficult task, but profitable for the best students).

# INDEX

(This includes the words defined in footnotes, the titles of poems printed or referred to in this volume, proper names that are mentioned, and the principal topics discussed in the introduction and in Carlyle's essay. The references are to pages.)

821
B96